Antebellum

Volume 1

The Long Road to

Sumter

George E. Parris

April 2019

Preface

Over the last few years, there has been a continuing assault on Confederate iconography in southern states. The targets have included the battle flag of the Army of Northern Virginia (which was never the flag of the Confederacy) and a number of statutes representing Confederate leaders including General Robert E. Lee and President Jefferson Davis. But most personal and disturbing to me has been the assault on memorials to common Confederate soldiers, especially in my home state of North Carolina.

"In memory of boys who wore the Gray"

toppled in Durham, NC August 17, 2017

Not only have rude mobs of mostly out-of-state thugs cursed, abused, defaced, and destroyed these statutes, the governments of the cities and administrators of the schools where these events have occurred have reacted as though the actions are justified and righteous.

On the one hand, I can see that the populations (particularly the urban and university-related populations) of the South in general and North Carolina in particular have changed, as has the population of the entire United States. It would be interesting to me to know the percentage of people in, for example, the Raleigh-Durham-Chapel Hill area of North Carolina that have antebellum roots in the area or know that they have any family history tied to the War of 1861-65. I happen to know that I have wounded Confederate veterans on both sides of my parents' families and can trace family history in the South back into the 1700s. But I am in a distinct minority. Aside from my immediate family, I can identify only a very few people who know their roots in the South back to the early 1800s. And, the interesting thing is that like my ancestors, their ancestors were typically either wounded early in the war or captured and interned in Union prisons.

The table below gives some idea of the impact of the war on the population of southern States. These are just battle deaths, not deaths from sickness and delayed deaths from wounds and it does not include serious wounds such as loss of limbs or eyes.

Confederate Military Deaths by State

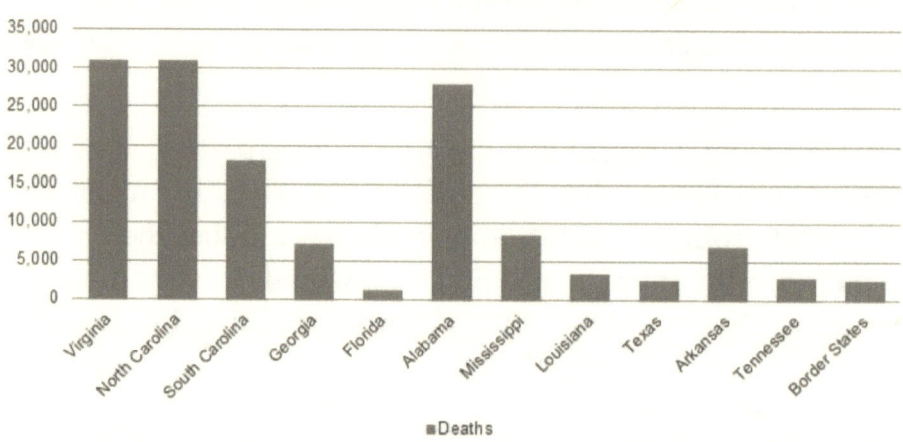

Source: American Battlefield Trust

https://www.battlefields.org/learn/articles/civil-war-casualties

The roughly 30,000 battlefield deaths of North Carolina men were out of a total white population of about 314,000 males (of all ages) or 164,000 white males between 15 and 50 in 1860. Those deaths represent about 18% of the military age white males in North Carolina in 1860. Thus, considering deaths from disease as well as combat, it is not surprising that those soldiers seriously wounded or captured in the early part of the war were the primary group to survive. The dead were typically replaced by immigration from the North or overseas during the next 150 years. So antebellum roots among today's white North Carolinians is likely a minority. Thus, it is not surprising that respect for Confederate icons is reduced particularly among college students, nearly 20% of whom are from out-of-state.

But the real question is why do people so disrespect the Confederacy and even common Confederate soldiers?

If you asked most of these people, they would say something like

> The Confederacy [unlike the North] was a racist, slave-owning society, which tortured and oppressed black African slaves. Their depravity was so great that they were traitors to the United States for the expressed purpose of maintaining and expanding slavery. They lost the war and deserve what they got.

That, however, is not how I see myself or my ancestors based on my personal experiences or "family history." My memories before 1965 were much like those of Dr. Charles T. Pace (Pace, 2015, pp. 1-12). Thus, I was motivated to examine the history of the United States and attempt to understand what led to slavery, the secession of the South and the War, which they lost.

This process began over two years ago and I very quickly realized that the history I understood (from my education[1] in the rural South) was extremely simplistic. If you had asked me in, e.g., 2000 to outline the history of the Civil War, I would have said something like this

---

[1] I am certainly not the first or only southerner to feel that the educational process is systematically failing in this area. See for example, Grady (1899) and Miller (2010) in the References.

> The South wanted slavery[2] and the North did not, so the South formed the Confederacy and started a war by attacking Fort Sumter. They lost and Lincoln freed the slaves.

Within a few days, a cursory search of general references revealed that the story was much more complicated. The "South" did not just all leave the Union at the same time and ...shockingly... Virginia, North Carolina, Tennessee and Arkansas were not in the Confederacy at the time of Fort Sumter. I will bet that most students entering college do not know that simple fact.

Focusing on "Lincoln" and "Sumter," the two key words that most people can remember, my research soon uncovered a story of deceit and intrigue regarding the political and military activities from November 1860 to April 1861. There are actually a number of very reliable eyewitness accounts and memoirs by southern and northern sources. Although this was not the answer to my larger question, the story was very illuminating and complete in itself; so, I published it under the title *Initiation of the War between the States (2017)*. Although I did not view the war as a *civil war* (I had done research on a real civil war between Patriots and Loyalist in South Carolina in what I prefer to call the American War of Independence), at the time, the events did seem to qualify as the "initiation" of the War. I now have some refined thoughts about that characterization, and I am renaming the book to reflect what it really was... a small event that was merely a pretext for war, not that actual initiation of combat or even a declaration of war. After all, in April 1861, Virginia and North Carolina were still in the Union and it was revealed that Lincoln

---

[2] With regard to slavery, Grady (1899, chapter 16, pages vary by printing) presents the false and misleading quotes found in high school text books of the late 1800s.

was trying to get Robert E. Lee to command the Union army (another poorly known fact).

Working back through history from the discover of the Americas (literally from 1492) to the events in 1860-61, was a long and difficult job. It involved may different topics involving politics, economics, technology, geography and many twists and turns. Only now, do I believe I have figured it out. Along the way, I considered many titles for this book. I think it is best to not use a title that presumes anything not in evidence, because I hope to write one or two other books in this series. I have done relatively little research on the strategy and conduct of the war and the military details have been thoroughly hashed in many books. But I would like to look at the impact of the war on the South and this may or may not warrant a separate book; but what I really want to get at and what is poorly known to me at this time is the period of reconstruction and "Jim Crow."

One of the observations I made during my research is that our modern image of the antebellum South is formed through the lens of the more recent history (1870-2000). And, I have discovered that much of what we see in the modern image of the antebellum South is based on the war-time and immediate post-war propaganda of the North screened though the filter of northern publishers.

My educational ignorance was predicted in 1864 by Confederate General Patrick R. Cleburne. Referring to what loss of the War will mean to southerners, he writes (January 2, 1864):

> ...
>
> *It* [loss of the War] *means that the history of this heroic struggle will be written by the enemy; that our youth will be trained by Northern school teachers; will learn from Northern school books their version of the war; will be impressed by all the influences of history and education to regard our gallant dead as traitors, our maimed veterans as fit objects for derision.*
>
> ...

Not only was Cleburne correct, it turns out that I was not alone in my educational ignorance. Adams (2000, p. 2) makes note of the problem:

> *Like all Northerners, I was force-fed Lincoln adoration from early school days on into university history courses. ... With time, history's final verdict will be rendered, and the sanitation brigade will have to face up to its false-hoods and errors....*

I was fascinated to read the comments of the three authors in the preface of the book *Complicity how the North promoted, prolonged and profited from slavery* (Farrow et al. 2006):

> *"We have grown up, attended schools, and worked in Northern states, from Maine to Maryland. We thought we knew our home. We thought we knew our country. We were wrong."*

In her single-author book (*The Logbooks. Connecticut's Slave Ships and Human Memory*) written nearly ten years later Farrow (2014, p. 81) writes:

> *"In the past ten years, I have often been reassured that slavery is an issue for the South to address, that the North wasn't really part of the story, and that the limited slavery that did exist in New England was too different to be regarded in the same light."*

I can appreciate their surprise[3] and would give these authors my complete sympathy, if it were not for the fact that northerners have benefited from the popular myths, while southerners (especially those with antebellum roots) have been and are being punished by these myths. I would also go so far as to argue that they have not fully shed their naivety or they are not being totally honest with themselves when they describe the North (especially the part they are familiar with, New England) as being merely "complicit" in slavery. New England, indeed, led the nation in *slavery* (particularly the brutal sugar business of the West Indies) and held the American monopoly on the more abhorrent *slave trade* (…think middle passage). It is important to recall that slaving was a venture business: The ships went to Africa, bought slaves and delivered them to the western hemisphere *on their own initiative* (they were not contracted or coerced to do it).   The northern states did an about-face when the slave trade was no longer socially acceptable, and were happy to pretend that their hands were clean…according to modern scholars, racism is attributable only to those southerners, those Confederate slave holders, those rednecks with the flag… they are solely to blame for all the ills of slavery.[4]

The recent/current wave of anti-southern/anti-Confederate violence in which monuments to common Confederate soldiers, long standing in southern cities, have been toppled, kicked, trod

---

[3] In the book *The Maritime History of Massachusetts* (Morison 1921), the author mentions the slave trade on 5 pages; and on 2 of those pages, Morison goes to pains to deny it was significant.

[4] I strongly endorse Farrow's books and when you finish them you should read mine.

upon and covered with filth was my motivation for this work. While I can appreciate that the demographics of the South is changing and in the interest of national unity perhaps Confederate monuments can be removed from the central positions they have held, it does not reflect well on the nation to tolerate this sort of abuse of southern soldiers *who shared the same racial prejudices that were common throughout the United States in their time.* Indeed, through familiarity with enslaved and free Africans, I firmly believe that southerners were more tolerant of black Africans than the average northerner in the 1860s. Industrialization and technology were going to destroy the economics of slave labor in the 1800s just as these trends had made slave labor profitable in the 1700s. And when that happened, the slaves would have (of necessity) been freed.

It was not actually slavery that bothered Abraham Lincoln and most of the abolitionists, but rather the *disposition of freed slaves* that worried them. The War was initiated by Lincoln *to maintain the neo-colonial status of the Old South* (where the freed slaves would be largely retained) not to ensure that Africans were brought into an equality with Europeans in this country.

I insist on the separation of the reasons for *secession* and the reasons for *war.* Any military analyst (and there were many West Point graduates on both sides of the conflict) knew that the North would eventually subdue the South in a war. Conversely, a peaceful and equitable allocation of the Federal (i.e., mutual/public) assets (e.g., the western territory, the Navy, public works including Washington DC) between the North and South would have proven very lucrative to the South. The South would have been free of protective tariffs that favored the North and still would have had the enormous income from the cotton trade. *The*

South had no economic motivation to go to war and Lincoln made it clear that he was not going to oppose slavery in those states where it existed. In his first Inaugural Address, he even acknowledged the proposed Corwin Amendment (of 1861) as the presumptive law of the land.

So, what was there to fight over? Lincoln called it "preservation of the Union." What is so special about the Union when a third of the States do not want to be in it?

Maybe session had to do with the fact that the South was paying all the taxes (tariffs) and the North was getting all the benefits. That would account for both *secession by the South and war by the North.*

Read this book and see what motivations for secession and war existed and who were really the racists in the antebellum period.

Conclusion and Hypothesis

I have not yet done much research on the War itself and virtually none on the post-War (Reconstruction) period. While I conclude from my current work that White Supremacy was a uniform opinion held by virtually all Europeans in the US through 1865, I see a stronger segregationist and discriminatory inclination against black Africans in the *slave-free* states than in the *slave-tolerant* states. In the antebellum South, the issue was the legal status of being a slave whereas in the North the issue had to do with the color of the skin. Science was of no real help in resolving racial issues; indeed, science was wrong and misleading at the time. The so-called Cornerstone Speech (Alexander H. Stephens in Savannah, Georgia, on March 21, 1861) was the product of a politician mislead by science, which at the time held black Africans to be inherently inferior to Europeans and probably not even human beings. The practical knowledge of southern Europeans in dealing with black Africans was not consistent with the internationally accepted science. There were many free black Africans in the South and (except for the fears of an abolitionists-led massacre of whites) southern Europeans recognized them and their rights (as non-citizens). At the risk of introducing facts that are not fully considered in this book, I am struck by the report by Lewis H. Steiner (1862) of Frederick, Maryland of the events preceding the Battle of Antietam (September 17, 1862). He estimates that of the Confederate soldiers passing through Frederick (on September 10th), approximately 5% were armed black Africans integrated into the ranks of the Confederate Army. This is consistent with the fact that throughout the War when the Confederate home-front was stripped of military-age men and black Africans undoubtedly outnumbered Europeans, there was no significant rebellion among the black African slaves, even after Lincoln's presidential proclamation on September 22, 1862 was made public. Of course, the lack of response of the Confederate states to this proclamation also underlines the disinterest of those states in the slavery issue as a cause of secession.

Thus, surveying the antagonism between Europeans and Africans in the 20th Century in the South, I am inclined to hypothesize that far and away the most of the modern racial conflict was caused by the aftermath of the War. The War (i) need never to have been fought and (ii) was not to blame on Confederate soldiers who died or their leaders during the War. I further hypothesize that slavery in the Confederacy would have ended from obsolescence and lack of economy well before 1900, if the Confederacy had been allowed to go in peace.

Sources and Citations

I assume that this book and I personally will be criticizes and categorized as racist and bigoted. This characterization, of course, is wrong. I believe the book is an objective analysis of the facts. But because of the high degree of skepticism I assume it will encounter and engender, I have reproduced many original documents in their entirety or at least reproduced their relevant parts. Most histories simply include the author's (opinionated) digest of such documents. Fortunately, most of these documents are present on the internet from reliable sources and I have tried to indicate the source and usually its URL. For general historical data with no particular political implications, I have often summarized well known information from various sources (many on the internet) without specific citations. There are a few books and documents that I thought deserved special acknowledgement and they are cited in the text (Author, date, page) with full citations at the end of this document. Most of these were purchased from internet sources.

I completely acknowledge that most of the graphics have been taken directly from the internet, most often Wikimedia Commons, but in some cases from copyrighted sources. I believe these easily fall under the doctrine of "fair use" and serve as an endorsement and advertisement for the source, which I encourage my readers to visit.

When you read this book or any other, I encourage you to be skeptical and check sources and attempt to discern biases in the way the material is edited and phrased.

Part 1.

The Slave Trade and Slavery

1.1 The New World Discovered, Exploited and Colonized

The Iberian Discovery and Conquest of the New World (1500-1600)

In the early 1500s, Europeans (primarily Portuguese and Spanish) were in ruthless competition to find the source of the valuable spices and cotton fabrics that Ottomans were importing to Europe from somewhere in the east. The problem was that the Muslims firmly blocked access to the Indian Ocean by controlling the middle east.

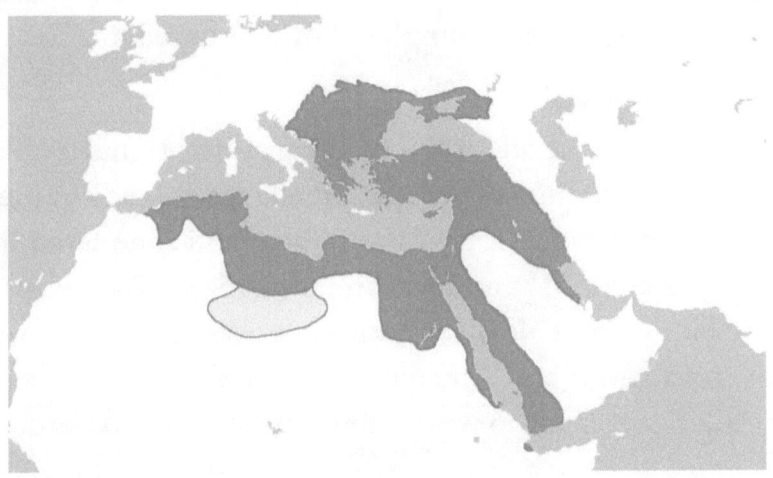

Ottoman Empire 1600

Author: Gabagool; Source: Wikimedia Commons

The Portuguese managed to circumvent the Middle East by navigating around Cape Bojador (on the west coast of Africa) and the Cape of Good Hope. They reached India where cotton was grown and spices were traded and pushed on to the Molucca Islands the source of the spices. Along the way, they became familiar with the east coast of South America (Brazil), west coast of Africa (Angola), Madagascar and India.

Seeking to circumvent both the Ottomans and the Portuguese with a novel route to the spice islands, the Spanish sent Columbus directly west (assuming the world was round and hoping that it would not be too far) where he discovered the West Indies (1492-1503, named because he thought he had reach India). But he was soon disabused of this idea when Magellan (probably using Portuguese maps) made it around South America to the Pacific Ocean (1520) and his crew completed the circumnavigation of the earth (1522).

The Spanish (with the aid of the Pope) acquired rights to most of the new world and quickly occupied the larger islands of the West Indies (e.g., Hispaniola, Cuba, Puerto Rico) and conquered the Aztecs in Mexico (1521) and Incas in Peru (1572). They were also exploring Florida and North America (De Soto, 1538-40). Along the way, the Spanish and Portuguese raided the West Indies for Native American slaves to work mines in Mexico and Peru.

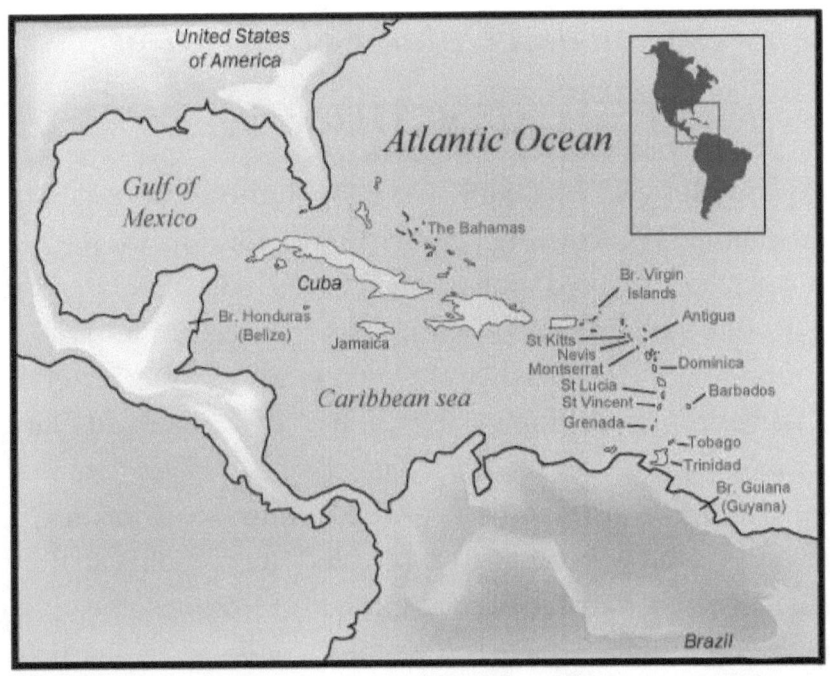

Source: http://www.abdn.ac.uk/slavery/banner6.htm

In the 1500s, their primary interest was gold and silver, which was shipped back to Spain from mainland mines worked by Native Americans enslaved from the islands and the mainland. France, Britain and the Dutch began raiding Spanish treasure fleets. France managed to acquire toeholds on western Hispaniola, some minor islands and even on the mainland of North America. But they were traders and exploiters; not colonizers. Portugal, Spain and France though primarily in terms of conquest and exploitation for the sole benefit of the home country.

British and Dutch Colonization
(1600-1700)

The British followed the Spanish and Portuguese and based most of their claims in North America on the expeditions for John Cabot (Giovanni Caboto, Italian) in 1497. Cabot sailed west from the port of Bristol, England and appears to have run into Newfoundland.[5] The British and Dutch were also motivated by financial benefit to the home country, but the British and Dutch had a more complex problem because they had become the refuge for every non-Catholic religious group in Europe. Thus, the British and Dutch were not just interested in exploitation; they were also looking to dispose of a number of troublesome, proselytizing religious groups (Puritans, Quakers, Methodists, Baptists, Presbyterians), as well as Catholics, Jews and various criminals and poor people. Colonization was seen as a way to solve domestic problems and make money at the same time. By the 1600s, the British had a toehold in the West Indies (Barbados) and mid- and north Atlantic coast of North America (Virginia, Carolina, Massachusetts). Ideally, British colonization involved the introduction of European family units fleeing oppression from mainland Europe. But the British were not above building an

---

[5] This area was already routinely visited by intrepid Portuguese fishermen from the Azores who fished on the Grand Banks. But the Portuguese government's strategic plan was focused on the circumnavigation of Africa to establish lucrative trade with India and the spice islands.

exploitive economy where large-scale colonization was not feasible (e.g., on islands of the West Indies).

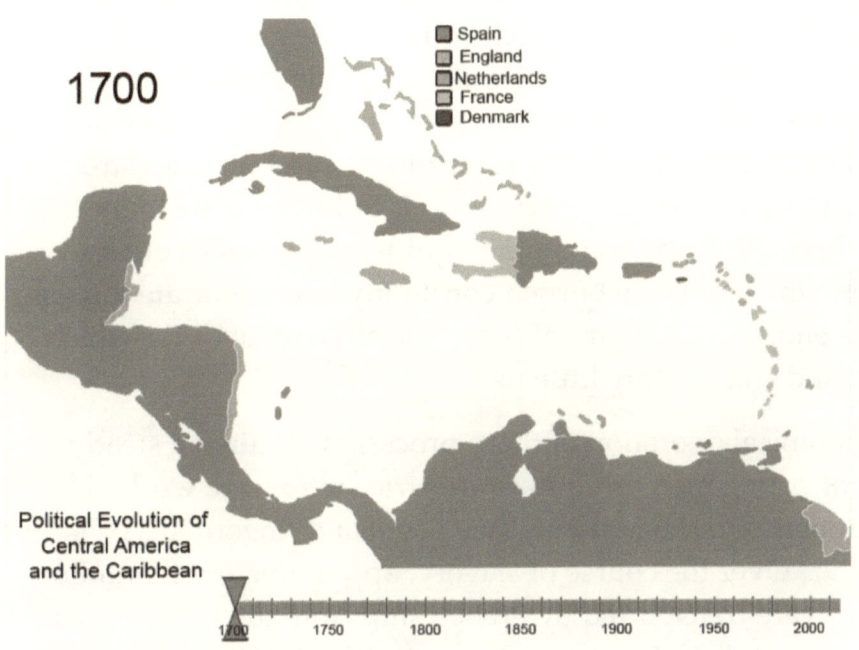

Author: Esemono; Source: Wikimedia Commons

The French & Spanish Islands

Meanwhile, the French acquired Guadeloupe and Martinique (1635-1640)[6] and Santo Domingo (Saint-Domingue, 1659). While

---

[6] During this period the French were busy crushing the native population.

the British North American colonies were being established by families, the French viewed their island colonies as pure profit centers run by soldiers/ buccaneers and businessmen. Tobacco was the initial cash crop used by the French, but by the mid-1600s, the Virginians (established 1607), Marylanders (established 1632) and Carolinians (established 1663) were dominating the tobacco market. Thus, sugar cane (which could not be grown economically on the mainland) was clearly the favored crop in the West Indies, and the islands were perfect for its cultivation and processing. Sugar cane grows continuously and requires strong men wielding machetes to harvest. It is bulky to move to the press where the sugar-containing liquids are squeezed out and the fires, which must be burned constantly to concentrate the sap, requires enormous amount of fuel. It is all hard labor for which women and children are little use.

The economical operation of these processes required a steady stream of young men brought from Africa who were worked continuously and died quickly (see Fogel and Engerman, 1974, pp. 20-29). Over the course of slavery, approximately 1.4 million Africans were transported by French ships into the West Indies. The figures cited for Saint-Domingue is 773,000 (20,000 to 40,000 per year in the 1700s). In 1790, there were only about 90,000 African slaves at work on Saint-Domingue. The rate of import and the more or less stable population size suggests that the typical African slave died within 2 to 5 years in the sugar plantation.[7] Thus, the life-cycle of slave labor *under these*

---

[7] For comparison the paid work force on the Panama Canal during the French period (1881-89) was up to 20,000 men (mainly from the West Indies) and the death rate was about 2,500 per year. Which suggested

conditions did not include the period from birth to young manhood or some period of retirement (>40 years of age) and it did not include the fact that half-of births are female for whom the sugar plantation offered very little useful work. For example, in 1803 the owner of the slave ship *Enterprise* out of Liverpool gave the following instructions to the captain (Dow, 1927/2002, p. 107-108):

> "By law this vessel is allowed to carry 400 Negros, and we request that they may all be males if possible to get them, at any rate buy as few females as in your power, because we look to a Spanish[8] market for the disposal of your cargo, where Females are a very tedious sale."

Female Africans, to the extent that they were brought into sugar plantations were typically used as "wives" for the European males who ran the plantations and thus accounted for substantial mulatto populations in French and Spanish "colonies."[9] The

---

that even then the life of a worker exposed to tropical diseases was about 8 years. Farrow (2014, p. 22) gives a figure of 1/3 in three years, which is about 9 years of service.

[8] The *Enterprise* sailed from Liverpool on July 20, 1803, bought 412 slaves (including 120 females) in Africa and sailed on Cuba where 392 slaves were sold on January 1804. 19 slaves died in passage and "...*one girl, being subject to fits, could not be disposed of.*" [Does anyone want to guess what happened to her?]).

[9] I do not really think that "colony" is the correct term for the way the French, Portuguese, Dutch and Spanish operated in the western hemisphere. They were not trying to export their culture to a new setting, they were using the opportunity of a favorable setting to generate revenue for the home country. Although the British may have

mulattos typically formed a lower rank of the local society between the Europeans and the African slaves.

The point I want to make here is that the assumption made by the British and Americans (in the 1700-1850 period) that slavery was a successful economic model was based on the experience in the (French and Spanish) West Indies and (Portuguese) Brazilian sugar plantations. The French and Portuguese model practice of slavery was (thank God) never actually implemented in British North America. Sugar plantations were established in French Louisiana (prior to the Louisiana purchase in 1804) and probably operated as close to French standards as possible. Tobacco (and later cotton plantations) in the British colonies of North America involved a substantial amount of tedious hand work (e.g., compare picking and carding cotton to cutting and pressing cane) that could be done by women, children and old men. Thus, the British colonies could and did operate with a different labor force. This model was not determined by purely economic forces; the British were trying to truly colonize, not merely exploit, North America and (in my opinion) the brutality of sugar plantations would not have been tolerated by British colonists (i.e., people living as families that were intent on building a new society), rather than a few economically-driven unmarried men seeking a fortune.

Note that the economic model used in the British colonies, thus, did not require a constant stream of new male slaves. Females and children were cheaper to buy and could do a lot of the work. Moreover, although ending the (abominable) international slave

---

intended to do the same thing, by sending European women and families to the New World they created an entirely different dynamic.

trade was not the objective, the idea of breeding slaves in America seemed like a wise economic move. Ironically, breeding slaves on the North American mainland will be shown to be the factor that drove slave labor to be uneconomical and would have caused its natural obsolescence had the War between the States not been initiated by the Lincoln Administration (1861). Although domestically-bred slavery as practiced in North America appeared to be economical at first, as soon as large numbers of children and old men and women were present on the plantation, the economics could not compete with the use of free labor. And, after a few generations, slavery *as was practiced in North America* became "break even" relative to free labor and eventually completely unprofitable (see below).

Cash Crops Introduced to the

West Indies and Subtropical America

The islands of the West Indies and equatorial South America were suitable for planting and processing sugar cane. This plant had come to the Mediterranean (e.g., Nile Valley) during the middle ages from its ancient origins in south and southeastern Asia. The Portuguese and Spanish had learned how to cultivate it in the Azores and Canaries, respectively. As early as Columbus' second voyage (1494), sugar cane was brought to Hispaniola and the first African slaves arrived in 1501. The demand for sweets in Europe was expanding rapidly and sugar cane quickly became the preferred cash crop of all Europeans wherever it could be grown.

The British originally tried to colonize the small island of
Barbados (1627), which had been overlooked by the Spanish. In
1630, the Dutch seized sugar plantations from the Portuguese in
South America and brought sugar cane and the technology of
sugar processing to the British in Barbados around 1640. They
also brought African slaves as the island's economy transitioned
from small farms to large plantations. Many of the concepts such
as slaves as "property" became established in Barbados and were
transferred to other British colonies in the West Indies and
eventually to North America (especially via New England).

Tenants and Indentured Servants

The initial settlers in the British colonies (e.g., Virginia founded in
1607 and profitable by 1618) soon discovered that they had access
to land beyond the wildest dream of people living in crowded
Europe. As soon as they figured out a way to grow profitable
crops, it was obvious that they could multiply their wealth very
quickly if they had a source of cheap labor. Initially the Virginia
Company and its individual members acquired colonists to be
tenants of the company who worked the land and shared profits
with the owners of the land. In addition, "maids" for wives and
"boys" as apprentices were supplied to the tenants and finally
"servants" were supplied to the higher-ranking colonists.

A Declaration of the Supplies intended to be sent to Virginia, in this yeare 1620. By his Majesties Counseil for Virginia. 18. Julij 1620. [10]

— page 313 —

…

First therefore we have thought fit, to make it publikely knowne, that besides the great store of particular Plantations now in providing, and like very shortly in large proportion to augment, the Company have resolved in a late generall Court, by the blessing of God, to set out this yeere at the publike charge, and to send to Virginia eight hundred choise persons, of the qualities ensuing: First, foure hundred, to be Tenants of the general land of the Company, to make up the number of those Tenants ful 500. whereof 200. to be placed at Elizabeth Citie, with the Companies Deputie: 100. at Henrico, 100. at Charles Citie: And at James Citie there are a hundred and more already. Secondly, one hundred, to be Tenants to such Officers, &c. as the Court already hath, or shall shortly appoint: viz. 10. for the Deputy of the College, 40. for the Companies Deputy: 20. for the Secretary: 10 more (besides 50. already sent) for the Ministers: and 20. for the Phisitian: their care for the ease and prosperity of the Colonie, being such and so great, as to cause them to endowe those Offices and places, (as they have formerly done others,) with faire possessions, furnished with Tenants and other fit provisions: that the people may have the benefit by them, and yet be freed from the burden. Thirdly one hundred yong Maides to make wives for these Tenants as the former 90. which have been lately sent. Fourthly, one hundred Boyes, to be apprentizes likewise to the publike Tenants. Fiftly, one hundred servants to be disposed amongst the old Planters, which they greatly desire, and have offered to defray

---

[10] "Eight hundred choise persons"; an excerpt from A Declaration of the Supplies intended to be sent to Virginia by the Virginia Company of London (1620).

their charges with very great thankes. And although by reason of the preparations already made, the difficulty may be well conceived to be in great part overcome, and the profit much more neere, and more easie to come by, yet the Companie wholly affecting the peoples prosperity, have determined to deale both as favourably in the Contracts,

— page 314 —

and as bountifully in all sorts of furniture and provisions with the Tenants which shal now goe, as they have done with those, which have beene formerly sent. Which conditions it hath beene thought fit here to reinsert and publish.

Every man transported into Virginia, with intent there to inhabit, as Tenants to the Common land of the Company , or to the publike land, shall be freely landed there at the charge of the Company: And shal be furnished with provisions of victuall for one whole yeare next after his arrivall, as also of Cattle: And with apparell, weapons, tooles and implements, both of house and labour, for his necessary use. He shall enjoy the ratable moytie of all the profits that shall be raised of the land on which he shall be Planted, as well Corne and Cattle, as other commodities whatsoever: the other halfe being due to the Owners of the Land.

He shall be tyed by Convenant, to continue upon that Land for the Terme of seaven yeares: which being expired, it shal be in his choyse, whither to continue there or to remove to any other place, at his owne will and pleasure.

Of these persons, one hundred and twenty (such as are to be Tenants) are to be slipped here for Virginia, by the midst of August now at hand: and the rest in January and February ensuing.

On the east coast, the optional sources for cheap labor were Europe and Africa. In Africa, non-Christian people who did not speak any European language and had little or no understanding about contemporary European laws, technology and customs were being sold as property (slaves) to European slave-traders and brought to the West Indies and North America involuntarily and sold as property. On the islands, this was treated as a disposable labor source. On the other hand, European labor was more accustomed to the climatic condition present north of Virginia.[11] And, of course, Europeans typically spoke languages that were understood in the British colonies, understood European laws and customs and were Christian (although these fell into at least three conflicting groups). On balance, the northern colonies were much more attractive to and mutually compatible with European labor. And, there was no contest when it came to skilled labor because many indentured servants had at least some marketable skill.

There had existed in Europe a legal system of apprenticeships since the Middle Ages. There was also a tradition of imprisoning people for debt. In Britain alone, approximately 10,000 people

[11] Most of the United States lies above 30° North latitude, which is the same latitude of North Africa. Most black African slaves were working in much cooler climates than their homelands.

entered debtors' prison each year in the 1700s and 1800s.[12] One way to escape prison or avoid this fate was to become an indentured servant. The person initially acquiring (buying) the indentured contract might be a speculator or a ships' captain/owner. The contract typically provided relief of existing debts and passage across the Atlantic to major American ports where the contract typically was sold to a local planter, business or businessman.

The Palatine German immigration to the new world took place between 1700 and 1750. The passage across the Atlantic was less lethal than the middle passage for slaves, but the north Atlantic was colder and the trips from mainland Europe (the lower Rhine) generally included several weeks just getting from European ports to British ports. The description of a passage provided by Gottlieb Mittelberger who went to Philadelphia from Germany in 1750 includes a number of interesting observations.

Gottlieb Mittelberger (1750)[13]

Both in Rotterdam and in Amsterdam the people are packed densely, like herrings so to say, in the large sea-vessels. One person receives a place of scarcely 2 feet width and 6 feet length in the bedstead, while many a ship carries four to six hundred souls; not to mention the innumerable implements, tools, provisions, water-barrels and other things which likewise occupy much space.
…

---

[12] https://en.wikipedia.org/wiki/Debtors%27_prison

[13] http://www.vlib.us/amdocs/texts/gottlieb.html

When the ships have for the last time weighed their anchors near the city of Kaupp [Cowes] in Old England, the real misery begins with the long voyage. For from there the ships, unless they have good wind, must often sail 8, 9, 10 to 12 weeks before they reach Philadelphia. But even with the best wind the voyage lasts 7 weeks.[14]

...

Add to this want of provisions, hunger, thirst, frost, heat, dampness, anxiety, want, afflictions and lamentations, together with other trouble, as . . . the lice abound so frightfully, especially on sick people, that they can be scraped off the body. The misery reaches the climax when a gale rages for 2 or 3 nights and days, so that every one believes that the ship will go to the bottom with all human beings on board.

...

Children from 1 to 7 years rarely survive the voyage. I witnessed misery in no less than 32 children in our ship, all of whom were thrown into the sea.

...

When the ships have landed at Philadelphia after their long voyage, no one is permitted to leave them except those who pay for their passage or can give good security; the others, who cannot pay, must remain on board the ships till they are purchased, and are released from the ships by their purchasers. The sick always fare the worst, for the healthy are naturally preferred and purchased first; and so the sick and wretched must often remain on board in front of the city for 2 or 3 weeks, and frequently die, whereas many a one, if he could pay his debt and were permitted to leave the ship immediately, might recover and remain alive.

---

[14] For slaves, the passage from Africa to the West Indies was typically no more than 6 weeks because of the favorable trade winds (300 km/day) and currents (several km/day). In addition, the weather was generally not stormy. But some slaves might have been aboard the slave ship for over a month before it left the African coast.

The sale of human beings in the market on board the ship is carried on thus: Every day Englishmen, Dutchmen and High-German people come from the city of Philadelphia and other places, in part from a great distance, say 20, 30, or 40 hours away, and go on board the newly arrived ship that has brought and offers for sale passengers from Europe, and select among the healthy persons such as they deem suitable for their business, and bargain with them how long they will serve for their passage money, which most of them are stffl in debt for. When they have come to an agreement, it happens that adult persons bind themselves in writing to serve 3, 4, 5 or 6 years for the amount due by them, according to their age and strength. But very young people, from 10 to 15 years, must serve till they are 21 years old.

Many parents must sell and trade away their children like so many head of cattle; for if their children take the debt upon themselves, the parents can leave the ship free and unrestrained; but as the parents often do not know where and to what people their children are going, it often happens that such parents and children, after leaving the ship, do not see each other again for many years, perhaps no more in all their lives.

It often happens that whole families, husband, wife, and children, are separated by being sold to different purchasers, especially when they have not paid any part of their passage money.

When a husband or wife has died at sea, when the ship has made more than half of her trip, the survivor must pay or serve not only for himself or herself, but also for the deceased.

When both parents have died over half-way at sea, their children, especially when they are young and have nothing to pawn or to pay, must stand for their own and their parents' passage, and serve tffi they are 21 years old. When one has served his or her term, he or she is entitled to a new suit of clothes at parting; and if it has been so stipulated, a man gets in addition a horse, a woman, a cow.

When a serf has an opportunity to marry in this country, he or she must pay for each year which he or she would have yet to serve, 5 to 6 pounds. But many a one who has thus purchased and paid for his bride, has subsequently repented his bargain, so that he would gladly have returned his exorbitantly dear ware, and lost the money besides.

If some one in this country [the British Colonies] *runs away from his master, who has treated him harshly, he cannot get far. Good provision has been made for such cases, so that a runaway is soon recovered. He who detains or returns a deserter receives a good reward.*

If such a runaway has been away from his master one day, he must serve for it as a punishment a week, for a week a month, and for a month half a year.

The experience of indentured servants once their contract was bought in America was heavily dependent on who bought their services. Mittelberger only mentions extension of contracts as compensation for running away, but in fact indentured servants were subject to "correction" by whipping. While corporal punishments were probably infrequent, some masters appear to have gravitated towards physical punishment and there are reports of lethal or crippling beatings. Obviously, educated or skilled indentures were likely to receive better terms and conditions as shown in the papers of George Mason (1725-1792) who used a standard contract to acquire a skilled carpenter to work on his home in Virginia 1755-59.

Contract and Recommendation for William Buckland (1755; 1759)
Papers of George Mason

This Indenture, Made the Fourth Day of August in the Twenty ninth Year of the Reign of our Sovereign Lord George the Second King of Great-Britain, &c, And in the Year of our Lord, One Thousand Seven Hundred and fifty five Between William Buckland of Baford Carpenter & Joiner of the one Part, and Thomson Mason of London Esq. of the other Part, Witnesseth, That the said William Buckland for the Consideration herein after-mentioned, hath, and by these Presents doth Covenant, Grant, and Agree to, and with the said Thomson Mason Executors and Assigns, That He the said William Buckland shall and will, as a faithful Covenant Servant, well and truly serve the said Thomson Mason, his Executors and assigns in the Plantation of Virginia beyond the Seas, for the Space of Four Years, next ensuing his Arrival in the said Plantation, in the Employment of a Carpenter & Joiner. And the said William Buckland doth hereby Covenant and Declare him self, now to be the Age of Twenty two Years Single and no Covenant or Contracted Servant to any other Person or Persons, And the said Thomson Mason for himself his Executors or Assigns, in Consideration thereof, doth hereby Covenant, Promise and Agree to and with the said William Buckland his Executors, and Assigns, that He the said Thomson Mason his Executors or Assigns, shall and will at his or their own proper Costs and Charges, with what convenient Speed they may, carry and convey, or cause to be carried and conveyed over unto the said Plantation, the said Wm Buckland and from henceforth, and during the said Voyage, and also during the said Term, shall and will at the like Costs and Charges, provide for and allow the said Wm Buckland all necessary Meat, Drink, Washing, Lodging, fit and convenient for Wm as Covenant Servants in such Cases are usually provided for and allowed and pay and allow the said William Buckland wages or Salary at the Rate of Twenty Pounds

The within named William Buckland came into Virginia with my brother Thomson Mason, who engaged him in London, & had a very good Character of him there; during the time he lived with me he had the entire Direction of the Carpenter's & Joiner's work of a large House, & having behaved very faithfully in my service, I can with great Justice recommend him, to any Gentleman that may have occasion [to] employ him, as an honest sober diligent man, & I think a complete Master of the Carpenter's & Joiner's Business both in Theory & practice.

G Mason

8th Novr. 1759

Source:
https://www.encyclopediavirginia.org/Contract_and_Recommendation_for_William_Buckland_1755_1759

From these descriptions, it is clear that indentured European servants shared many problems and restrictions with African slaves. Being bought and sold is not a unique feature of slavery. What was unique was that slaves were perpetually property although in practice more were obtaining freedom.

Defining Slavery

I will define *slavery* as the use of humans as domesticated animals. *Domesticated animals* are animals that voluntarily or involuntarily abandon independent actions and submit to the will of a master/owner to the limit of their ability usually without rational analysis of the consequence of the actions they are directed to undertake by their masters. Basically, domesticated animals "live in the moment" and are unable to deduce what may happen to them in the next moment of their lives. Instinct alone provokes resistance in the compliance of domesticated animals to the wishes of their masters.

Legally domestic animals are owned, used, traded, and disposed, as any inanimate property would be, by their owners. Generally, domestic animals are used for economic benefit, protection, comfort, companionship, etc. In most cases, care of domestic animals (food, shelter, rest, exercise, procreation) by the owner is inherent to maximizing the economic value (productivity) of the animal to the owner. In addition, *contemporary social norms* and personal views place a burden of "humane treatment" of domestic animals upon the owner. This usually means avoidance of unnecessary hardship or pain to the animal.

Domestic animals can generally be treated as intellectually monolithic with most variation in physical presentation and instinctual skills. In comparison, humans are much more intelligent[15] than domestic animals. But we recognize that the intelligence of humans develops over time (from childhood to adult hood); that among adults there are ranges of intellectual ability; and that the intellect/talent of adult humans takes on

---

[15] Humans that are mentally incompetent are excluded from this discussion. They are generally managed following the dictates of contemporary social norms.

many distinct forms. As a result, human culture is multifaceted and humans interact in a wide variety of ways to form an economically viable society. At various times in their development (i.e., adolescence), humans are deprived of liberties and coerced into following social patterns and learning skills and trades, ideally with the objective of producing an adult with optimized use of his/her potential.

Thus, at one time or another, we all (voluntarily or involuntarily) give up freedoms in the expectation that our sacrifice is essential to the progress of the society to which we belong[16] or that the situation we place ourselves in is a stepping stone to a better socioeconomic situation. Marriage, of course, has long been a social compact involving give and take particularly for females who, until recently, were usually in a role similar to slaves.

 In most cases, we take jobs or commit ourselves to apprenticeships in which we hope to advance. Generally, we retain the right to terminate employment with minimal notice for any cause and any binding agreements regarding the job (e.g., regarding ownership of intellectual property, secrecy, non-compete, etc.) are agreed in advance as conditions of employment. Initial salary is generally agreed along with bonuses and benefits

---

[16] In my family, we have entered the third consecutive generation of military service. My father volunteered for WWII when he believed the nation was at stake, I was involuntarily drafted during the conflict in Vietnam and my son is currently in training with the US Army as a step he sees as an introduction to a lucrative career. And my daughter plans to soon join him.

(insurance, vacation, pension); but salary is usually expected to increase. If it does not, we can always leave.

Indentured servitude has been practiced in the time period of interest to this study. It was an agreement that was a long-term contract (e.g., 7 years) in which the job requirements and the compensation were only generally defined. Of course, the *contemporary social norms* applied regarding treatment and the indentured servant had legal rights and the authority of the master did not invade the personal beliefs or behavior of the servant.

In contrast, *slavery* was an involuntary, perpetual, unlimited ownership by the master. Indeed, even the progeny of the slave was the property of the master. The legal rights of slaves might vary greatly from jurisdiction to jurisdiction and changed over time, and the *contemporary social norms* varied greatly with environment (e.g., location, jurisdiction and time). One of the problems in characterizing slavery is accounting for the *heterogeneity of the practice and circumstance*. Thus, the practice of "slavery" varied over time and in various settings, and the practice of slavery could be strongly influenced by the opinions (i.e., *accepted social norms*) of the slave owner.

The purpose of this book is to place context around the events that occurred in the United States of America in the period 1861-1865, i.e., a war in which the issue of *slavery* is widely considered to be a major cause and by which slavery was definitely ended as a legal institution. Thus, in understanding the role of slavery and the rationale of the war, I am trying to understand slavery in its many forms and as it evolved from 1492 to 1861. I find that recent and current views of this subject vary widely and depend on the impression people have of the nature of the institution of slavery. There is certainly a very wide selection of facts to pick from in drawing opinions. Slavery has been bloody, brutal, inhumane and barbarous; *but was that the normal situation in the United States in 1861 or ever?* Depending upon the motivations of educators, authors and politicians, there exist factoids and anecdotal events that can be used to support any side of the argument.

In particular, I am concerned about the relative views of the two protagonists in the War: The North and the South. In the 21st Century the history of the War (that is taught and widely accepted) places all blame for the War and for the current situation of the descendants of black African slaves (e.g., racism, discrimination and poverty) on southerners and southern institutions. In this environment, white southerners (especially those with antebellum roots) are viewed as at least "complicit in" a dark and immoral chapter of history. Thus, erasure of southern history especially anything associated with the Confederacy is considered not only justified (even if contrary to law), but also righteous.

Pre-Columbian Enslavement of Black Africans

Many cultures had taken prisoners of war as slaves from antiquity. But sub-Saharan Africa was generally isolated from the rest of the world. In the post-Roman era, the first major Mediterranean empire to be established was under the guidance of Mohammad (570 – 632) and ultimately included northern Africa, the Middle East (to India) and southern Europe. The natives of these regions were conquered by war and forced to submit to the political and religious views of the conquerors (Islam). The Islamic laws appear to have been crafted to condone the acquisition of slaves from nations at war with Islam. Because the nations that were conquered included large populations of peasants, there was little need to acquire low-skilled agricultural labor (i.e., for practical purposes the existing peasant populations had little upward mobility and were effectively slaves/surfs to begin with) in these lands.

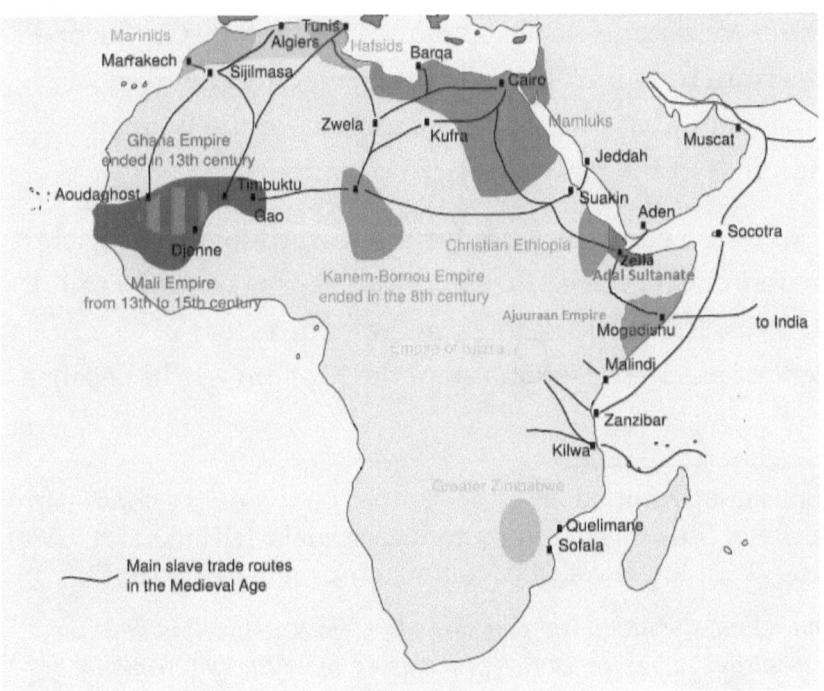

Medieval Slave Trade

Author: Aliesin; Source Wikimedia Commons

On the other hand, in the Islamic heartland including the valleys of the Nile, Tigris and Euphrates, where rice and cotton were grown, the Arabs had no interest in personally doing tedious agricultural work and this may have prompted importation of black African slaves who were familiar with rice grown in West Africa. In addition, to support the expansion of Islam, soldiers were needed and many European males (Mamluk = "property" in Arabic) were taken into a warrior cast, which endured from the 900s to the 1800s.

Because Islam encourages polygamy, rich Moslem men established harems and imported female slaves from Europe and Africa. There were large-scale slave raids in the 1100s in Europe. Male slaves from both Europe and Africa were frequently castrated to ensure that they did not compete for the women or establish families in the Arab/Moslem countries.[17]

The energies of the eunuchs were turned toward loyalty to their profession and masters (e.g., the fierce comradery of the Mamluk warriors). Thus, it is difficult to enumerate the extent of enslavement of black African males in the Muslim world because

---

[17] Castration is not permitted among Muslims, but would be consistent with the desire of Muslims to out reproduce infidels: (al-Bukhaari (4786) and Muslim (1402)) Ibn Hajar said, commenting on these hadeeths:

"The wisdom behind the prohibition on castration [of Muslims] *is that it is contrary to what the Lawgiver wants of increasing reproduction to ensure continuation of jihad against the disbelievers."*

Thus, conversion to Islam was common among subject African tribes, because enslavement and extinction was the other choice.

they have left little trace.   Nonetheless, recent evaluations suggest that although Muslim enslavement was less intense than the trans-Atlantic trafficking (mainly 1600-1800), enslavement by Muslims involved far more individuals because it continued over a much longer period (800-1900).

The struggle (800-1500), between Christian nations (northern European) organized under the Catholic church and the Muslim Empire, re-established Christian domination in western and northern Europe through a series of Crusades (1200-1400s). But the Ottoman Empire (1300-1900) persisted in holding onto North Africa and the Middle East. Thus, slaves were routinely drawn from sub-Saharan cultures (as shown in the map above) to serve in the Islamic Empire.

Tangier (across the strait from Gibraltar) became an export market for black African slaves to Christian Spain and Portugal, which retained a good deal of Moorish culture. In the 1400s, the Portuguese established themselves in the Azores and bypassed the Islamic empire in North Africa via Cape Bojador. Thus, the Portuguese established independent contacts with the sub-Saharan African tribes at the Cape Verde Islands and south of the Congo River (i.e., Angola). With the Spanish in the Canary Islands, the Portuguese began using African slave labor on these eastern Atlantic islands to grow sugar cane, cotton and other crops.

Overview of the Atlantic Slave Trade

(1492-1888)[18]

The discovery and conquest of the West Indies and central America (1492-1550) was viewed as an opportunity to enrich Spain (not necessarily to expand Spain). Thus, when the Native Americans fell to Old World diseases (small pox, malaria, etc.) it was obvious to the Spanish and Portuguese that cheap/disposable labor for the West Indies and central America was needed.[19] To avoid enslavement by Arab traders, many of the leading chiefs of sub-Saharan Africa had taken the Muslim religion. Thus, Charles V of Spain initially restricted direct importation of black Africans to the West Indies because of concerned about introducing Islam into the New World. But in 1516, to save the Native Americans, a Dominican Friar (Bartolome de Las Casas) lobbied to replace Amerindian slaves with black Africans (he eventually recognized the hypocrisy of this idea) and Charles V, issued a grant that reads in part (English translation):

> *"Our officials who reside in the city of Seville in our House of Trade of the Indies; know ye that I have given permission, and by the present* [instrument] *do give it, to Lorenzo de Gorrevod, governor of Bresa, member of my Council, whereby he, or the person or persons who may have his authority therefore, may*

---

[18] Rawley (2005) is probably the best source for objective facts quantitative data.

.

[19] On Hispaniola the native population, who the Spanish had put to work in placer gold mines and sugar plantations, dropped from about 60,000 in 1508 to only 20,000 by 1518.

proceed to take to the Indies, the islands and the mainland of the ocean sea already discovered or to be discovered, four thousand negro slaves both male and female, provided that they be Christians. ..."

Source: http://ldhi.library.cofc.edu/exhibits/show/african_laborers_for_a_new_emp/emperor_charles_v

Thus, began the Spanish practice of baptizing black Africans before exporting them from slave forts on the Guinea Coast. The first black Africans were shipped by Spain from the Portuguese Cape Verde Islands in about 1520. This Spanish monopoly was continued into the 1560s.

Black African slaves were apparently also disembarked for the New World from the Canary Islands (Dow, 1927/2002, pp. 19-23). It was here (in 1562) that John Hawkins (1532-1595, a son of British Captain William Hawkins) formed an alliance with a Spanish trader who had realized the market for cheap labor on sugar plantations in the West Indies. This idea was transmitted back to Britain[20] and the British boldly planned to challenge the Spanish in trade to the West Indies.

In the early 1600s, the Portuguese began moving Africans from territory they controlled in west Africa (i.e., Angola) to the part of South America assigned to them by the Pope (Treaty of Tordesillas 1494, i.e., Brazil). The other European countries had little access to west Africa in the 1600s, and thus relied on Muslim

[20] The Hawkins family was well established in the English court (Henry VIII-Elizabeth I).

(a.k.a., Moorish) traders to supply African slaves. Initially slaves were purchased from Morocco (Tangier); but since the slave buyers were coming by ship from North America and the West Indies, they soon redirected to the sub-Saharan coast near their sources of African slaves (Senegal). It was easier for black African chiefs to deliver the slaves taken in the interior of Africa to the coast than to march them across the desert to Tangier, which was controlled by the Arabs/Moors.

As the demand for slaves increased in the 1700s, the entire coast from Senegal to Nigeria and Cameroon became littered with trading post and slave forts established by national monopolies such as the Royal African Company (British) and West Indies Company (Dutch). The Spanish imported Africans to the West Indies (Cuba, Puerto Rico, eastern Hispaniola/Santo Domingo). The French imported slaves to western Hispaniola (Santi Domingue) and other islands. Dutch imported slaves to South America and the British initially (1600s) imported slaves to Barbados, Jamaica and Antigua. By the mid-1600s, the ship-builders and merchants of New England entered the slave trade as an extension of the close ties they had with Barbados and as a supplier to wood and food[21] to many islands in the West Indies. But, New England contribution to the overall slave trade was very minor until the late 1600s.

---

[21] The small islands were quickly deforested; and we will see that where cash crops (sugar and cotton) can be grown, it was usually more profitable to devote all efforts and resources (land) to raising these crops and importing food, fuel and building materials from areas where these crops cannot be raised.

The British and the Dutch had somewhat come to control the importation of slaves to the West Indies and North America by the late 1600s and provided monopoly status for the Royal African Company (RAC, British) and the West Indies Company (WIC, Dutch). The Dutch West Indies Company (1602-1792) was progressively displaced by the British Royal African Company (1660-1752). Freelance (illegal) slave trading was also practiced by private "interlopers" and coincidentally by pirates that took slaves from any ship they could capture.

As it turned out, virtually anyone with a ship capable of crossing the Atlantic could engage in the slave trade. But the more haphazard the operation, the less profitable the business was and the hardships of the trafficked slaves (while never much better than survivable) went from bad to completely savage. Examples of poorly executed (hence savage) slaving voyages will be given below.

After 1698, the RAC was in competition primarily with a collection of independent colonial ship owners operating from New England. There were numerous New England slaving ports especially Boston, Newport and New London in the 1600s and early 1700s. The major English trading ports moved from London to Bristol in 1720 and then to Liverpool (center of the cotton trade) in 1740 to 1807. By the late 1700s, New York became the major port for American slave traders although ownership and financial interests were still spread throughout New England. Most British and New England deliveries were made to the West Indies. New England seemed to have had about 10 to 20% of this trade in the late 1700s.

Following the conquest of Ireland (Battle of the Boyne, 1690), British also took the opportunity to transport Irish Catholics (especially from Kinsale, Ireland) to the sugar plantations on Barbados, Antigua and Jamaica. These fair-skinned people fared poorly in the tropics and have virtually gone extinct in the islands, although many likely were integrated into British families that moved to North America in the 1700s.[22]

After independence was won, New England benefited from European wars, by claiming neutrality and being able to trade while European merchants were both threatened by privateers and banned from ports of their enemies. According to Rawley (2005, p. 281), New England ships delivered about 60,000 slaves to the US mainland between 1791 and 1808. The delivered a similar number to the West Indies mainly Cuba (Spain), and Martinique and Guadeloupe (French). New England ships carried about 200,000 Africans to the West Indies and North America from 1861-1807.

In 1698, the British monopoly was restructured so that New England ships could legally participate in the African slave trade and New England shipping activity grew until 1807 when the British and Americans outlawed the international slave trade. Dow (1927/2002, pp. 14-16) provided the following dates of national abolition of the trans-Atlantic trade: Denmark 1812; Holland 1814; France 1818; Spain 1820 (the British actually gave

---

[22] They were called "redlegs" probably for the same reason that European farmers in the South are called "rednecks": The effects of sun on the legs of men with long hair and short pants versus the effect of sun on men with short hair and long pants.

Spain £ 400,000 to facilitate this; but slave trade to Puerto and Cuba was only inhibited by efforts of British and French squadrons on the African coast); Portugal 1830 also received financial support from Britain but also depended on the British and French to stop the flow to Brazil until 1888. Gradually the slave forts/factories on the Guinea Coast were destroyed (by 1847) and the trade fell to a small fraction of its earlier levels. The illegal (post-1807) slave trade continued until slavery was made illegal in the West Indies, and South America in 1888.

The busy port of New York was a good place for slaving ships (formerly operating from New England ports) to be inconspicuously prepared to participate in the illegal trade (post-1807) to the West Indies and South America into the 1860s (yes, 1860s!).

THE SLAVE-TRADE;
The Bark Cora, of New-York,
Captured on the African Coast.
SEVEN HUNDRED AFRICANS ON BOARD,
History of the Vessel and Her Movements List of Her Cargo...
New York Times December 8, 1860
[To preserve these articles as they originally appeared, *The Times* does not alter, edit or update them.]

UNITED STATES SHIP <u>CONSTELLATION</u>.
ST. PAUL DE LOANDO, Sunday, Sept. 30, 1860.

We arrived here this afternoon, after a cruise of 23 days' duration off the coast, during which we have visited all the slave ports of importance from this place as far to the northward as Loango. Nothing very remarkable occurred until the evening of the 25th, being about 80 miles from the coast and to the southward of the congo river, when a sail was discovered about five miles to windward, steering northwest. We made all sail, and after three-and-a-half hours' chase succeeded in overhauling her, firing four 32-pound shot before she hove-to. She proved to be the bark Cora, of New-York, one day out from the coast, and having on board 705 slaves. Sailing master EASTMAN, with an armed crew of fifteen men, was immediately sent on board and took charge of her as a prize. Her officers and crew, amounting to 28 persons, were transferred to this ship, and with the exception of her first, second and third mates, who were sent to the United States in her as prisoners, were brought to this port. During the chase she made every exertion to escape, showing no light and throwing overboard her boats, hatches, spare spars, and in fact clearing her spar deck of everything moveable to lighten the vessel. She had on board a Spanish and an American crew. An individual giving the name of LORRETTO RINTZ (supposed to be fictitious) was found on board, and stated that he was master of the vessel. His real name is supposed to be LATHAM, by whom the vessel was cleared at New-York.

. . .

OCT. 1...

Within the last six weeks 2,221 recaptured Africans have been sent to Monrovia, having been captured on board the following vessels by our present African squadron, viz.: The ship Erie, of New-York, captured by the steamer Mohican, Commander S.W. GODON, on the 8th of

August, with 997 slaves on board. The brig <u>Storm King</u> also captured on the 8th of August, by the steamer <u>San Jacinto</u>, Capt. T.A. DORNING, and having on board 619 slaves; and the bark <u>Cora</u>, captured by the flagship <u>Consultation</u>, Capt. JOHN S. NICHOLAS, in the vicinity of Manque Grande, with 705. ...

***The bark <u>Cora</u>, as already stated, hailed from New-York**. She was a fine vessel, of 431 tons register, built in Baltimore in 1851, from which port she was engaged in the South American trade. She was afterwards purchased by E.D. MORGAN & Co., who finally sold her to JOHN LATHAM for $14,000, and on the 4th of May, 1860, a register was issued to him from the New-York Custom house as master and owner. The <u>Cora</u> was immediately taken to Pier No. 52 East River, where important changes were made in her rig, with the evident design of increasing her spead as a sailer. Her hold was stowed with a large number of casks, which were filled with fresh water; and provisions, lumber and other articles in large quantities, such as usually constitute a slaver's cargo, were put on board. These suspicious circumstances were reported to Mr. ROOSAVELT, the United States District-Attorney, and on the 19th of May she was arrested and examined upon a charge of being about to engage in the slave-trade. The proceedings were in the United States District Court, by which appraisers were appointed, who estimated, the value of the vessel at $9, 000, and the cargo at $13,128 23 -- total, $22,128 23, and she was accordingly bonded for that amount, ROBERT GRIFFITH and CHARLES NEWMANN becoming joint sureties for the vessel.*

https://www.nytimes.com/1860/12/08/archives/the-slavetrade-the-bark-cora-of-newyork-captured-on-the-african.html

Before the War of Independence virtually all the international slave trade was pursued by British and New England ships and merchants. The expanding cotton market (after 1790) induced slave traders to shift some management operations to Charleston, SC and New Orleans, LA. In the case of Charleston, most of the slaves that entered here were actually destined to Georgia and Alabama as well as North Carolina, while slaves entering New Orleans were supplied to Mississippi, eastern Texas, Arkansas and western Tennessee (Rawley and Behrendt, 2005, pp. 352-354).

Slaves were illegally imported by sneaking them into Cuba, Haiti, and the sea isles of Georgia (Amelia Island) and other out-of-the-way places in the South. Dow (1927/2002, pp. 319-344) synopsizes a story of a wily Cuban slave trader who took advantage of an opportunity to send a large ship to Africa (nominally to repatriate slaves freed by a Louisiana planter in 1859) under American ownership. But once the freed slaves were deposited in Liberia, the Spanish captain (traveling as a passenger) took charge of the ship and played a complex game of cat-and-mouse with the American, British and Portuguese ships that were patrolling the Guinea Coast to prevent the transport of slaves. The captain managed to pick up over a thousand slaves that had been gathered as part of the complex plan and sneak them into Cuba.

1.2 Elements of the Atlantic Slave Trade

It is important to separate and analyze the Atlantic slave trade in its three elements: (i) **slavers/slave hunters**-those who capture slaves; (ii) **slave traders**-those who traffic in slaves and (iii) **slave holders** (slave owners) those who end up owning the slaves and use their labor. These activities rarely involve the same people.[23] Moreover, each element evolved over the period of interest.

It is not clear to what extent, the Muslims had organized the enslavement, and trafficking of black African slaves (1700-1500). But the traditions of tribes in equatorial Africa were influenced by Islam. To immunize themselves from being enslaved, leading chiefs and their families had adopted Islam and some spoke and wrote Arabic. It seems likely that before the 1600s, the process of enslavement was fairly informal. The local king/chief would send out emissaries to collect criminals, social outcast, debtors

---

[23] The first two groups can be compared to drug manufacturers and drug dealers (drug pushers); they are typically ruthless and can become fabulously rich and may walk away without a care in the world. The third group are comparable to drug addicts who have been fooled into believing that what they are doing is good for them and end up "holding the bag" (i.e., suffering the social, physical and economic ruination of the business). Steppenwolf (1969) got it right:
Well, now if I were the president of this land
You know, I'd declare total war on The Pusher man
I'd cut him if he stands, and I'd shoot him if he'd run
Yes I'd kill him with my Bible and my razor and my gun
God damn The Pusher
Gad damn The Pusher
I said God damn, God damn The Pusher man

and their children and prisoners of tribal wars and deliver them to
him to be paid as tribute to the North African slave markets. This
system, of course, was subject to abuses including extortion and
kidnapping. But we will assume that it was a minor element of
African life. It appears that most of these slaves were females
(Manning, 1990, p.82) who went into domestic servant activities
and had duties in households, except for the Mamelukes.

Slave Forts/Factories

With the opening of commercial agriculture for export (especially
the sugar plantations on the islands of the West Indies), a new
demand for slaves was created. And with that demand, a crude
infrastructure was created by the more organized and
sophisticated tribes (most of whom were led by kings/chiefs that
had already risen to power through contact with the Muslims).
These leaders assembled "fairs" hundreds of miles in the interior
of West Africa where slaves were brought and bartered. There
was no legal process involved. Stronger persons brought weaker
persons or people who were otherwise compelled to submit to
enslavement as described by Falconbridge[24] (1788). Once
collected into groups, the slaves had the potential to rebel and
were thus typically bound and guarded. From this point on, they

---

[24] Alexander Falconbridge was writing as an abolitionist without
personal knowledge and was likely summarizing what he had heard
from slaves brought to the slave factory on the coast where he worked
or was extrapolating from what he saw. He is quoted in many sources;
see for example Dow (1927/2002, pp. 133-154).

were subject to substantial abuse because they were a financial burden to their new owner who had no social ties to them. They were then, moved to the coast where, overtime, most European countries (Britain, Spain, Portugal, Dutch) established slave forts (a.k.a., slave factories) as trading post.

The slave factories were usually small walled-forts with a few European troops armed with a few cannons and arms. The forts were intended to be large enough to defend against pirates and the local natives. For easy access to the transportation routes (inland rivers and the ocean), forts were typically located on islands or headlands at the mouth of rivers. These turned out to be typically very poor choices for health because the water was brackish and the surrounding swamps were ideal for disease carrying mosquitoes. The tidal waters also were poor for removing waste from the forts (e.g., cholera and typhoid were common). The European soldiers that were posted there were lucky to live more than a couple of years. The government representative (a job held by Falconbridge) might have his wife with him, but generally native women (and later mulatto women) were readily available as concubines. The local king/chief would typically have a village nearby. The trading was generally done between the European ship captains that arrived at the forts at random times and African traders who came down the rivers or who received slaves transported down the rivers. The European and native traders were sanction by the native king/chief who typically demanded a commission and various gifts. Since the gathering of slaves was generally a gradual process, a European or American ship might be docked at a fort for months and often cruised along the coast shopping for slaves and looking for a market where the trade goods brought from Europe or America were most valuable.

The principal trading objects brought by Europeans and Americans changed over the years. But they included iron bars, which could be locally forged into tools and weapons, large knives, pewter and brass bowls (that were often cut up for decoration), cloth, coral and cowrie shells (*Cypraea moneta*, note that cowrie is frequently written as cowpie) used as coins (Dow, 1927/2002, p. 51, p. 63, p. 80). The Muslims apparently introduced cowrie shells into trade in west Africa. Subsequently, the Portuguese who controlled the Maldive Islands, where the shells are plentiful, then used them extensively for trade in the early slave trade. By the time the Americans were deeply involved in trade, rum was an important trading item. Indeed, New England rum was so popular in Africa that British ships were sailing to American to buy rum for the African trade. However, it should be noted that most (~90%) rum distilled in New England was consumed in New England (Rawley, 2005, pp. 297-98).

Slave Hunts

The enslavement of Africans occurred in Africa and was generally barbarically brutal. I will not go into extensive detail here because at least two excellent books are available. I refer you to *Slave Ships and Slaving* (Dow, 1927) and *The Slave Ship* (Rediker, 2007). As I read these first-person accounts from various periods of between 1600 and 1860, I was struck by the enormous callousness and

waste of life involved in every step of the process. It is tempered
only by the knowledge that European immigrants suffered some
of the same harrows. Let me briefly summarize my understanding
of these documents. I should first say that while there is little
documentary evidence of the facts in the various stories, (i) the
settings described in the stories have been corroborated by other
observations and the stories from various sources are generally
consistent; and (ii) except for commentary by abolitionists (e.g.,
Falconbridge) in the late 1700s, when the stories were written,
there was no obvious motivation to slant the facts for political,
religious or economic benefit. Thus, within the usual limits of the
ability of people to remember the events of their lives, I believe
these stories can be taken as fact.

As indicated above, "slave hunting" (i.e., slaving) had long been
practiced in Africa. It went hand-in-hand with tribal warfare,
which was probably rare, but merciless. Such behavior was not
unique to Africa. The Aztecs, Vikings, Huns and Persians
followed similar patterns on other continents. When the
Moslems introduced the element of economic benefit to African
tribal warfare, the frequency of these slaving raids likely
increased and the scope was likely enlarged. By the late 1600s,
large, well-planned and coordinated slave hunting *armies* were
assembled, marched into the territories of the weaker tribe and
ambushed villages. Whereas the original wars were likely fought
over territorial rights and for religious sacrifice, the slave hunts
were specifically designed to ensnare entire villages (hundreds to
thousands of people) who were then brutally culled on the spot,
i.e., a large percentage of weak individuals (young, old and
infirm) were immediately slaughtered without the least concern.

In addition to those who died trying to defend the village, the death toll from the initial encounter likely approached 50%.

The remaining people were enslaved (probably more than half males), shackled (using various expedient techniques) and marched back to the invaders' villages. For the benefit for the tribal "king," there were typically brutal celebratory sacrifices of weak, injured or troublesome individuals. At this point only about 40% of the original population of the victims were alive. A relatively small number of unique individuals were kept as local slaves (based on beauty or prowess) and the rest were destined for sale to Muslims and Europeans.

The details of this process were specifically recalled by Richard/Phillip Drake (born about 1790) who was initially sent as a pauper from England to Boston about 1803 and was introduced to the slave trade by his uncle on the ship *Coralline* in 1805 (Dow, 1927, 189-209). Ironically, he was on a slave hunt when he was captured by a different group of Africans. Because of his race and youth, he was spared and was a slave that was forced to marry the King's daughter (which he actually was very happy to do). But again, with irony, after about two years, he was captured while on another slave hunt and eventually bought by the British. His story is full of twist and turns and is either an accurate summary of his adventures or an amazingly imaginative novel. His story is more detailed than others, but is consistent with independent descriptions of the internal working of African slave hunting provided by others (e.g., Ayuba Suleiman Diallo) elsewhere in Dow's book.

Once the slaves arrived at a European slave fort (factory) on the coast, they were temporarily fairly safe. They were probably sold to the first of several middlemen for a profit.

The Middle Passage

The commercial slave ships of all nationalities (British, French, Dutch, Spanish, American and Portuguese) generally were crewed by men that were essentially acquired because of their poverty. Except for the owners and captains this was not a lucrative job. Most ships had a physician of some sort in an effort to keep the slaves and crew alive. The crew was subject to short rations and cruel punishments while almost continuously at sea and their life expectancy was not long (e.g., they were particularly susceptible to scurvy). The ships faced the threat of pirates and the guns of other nation's slavers as they typically had to loiter on the coast for more than a month to pick up slaves from several locations. Thus, the earliest slaves acquired might also spend more than a month on the ships in sight of land.

Depending on the size of the ship, from as few as a dozen to over a thousand slaves might be acquired and they were packed into the ships as tightly as possible. The depravation of being constantly in contact with naked bodies around you was undoubtedly as bad as it seems. The slaves might be shackled most of the time and sat or lay in their mutual sweat, vomit, blood and excrement. They were typically rotated on deck in shifts during the day, weather permitting, to exercise and allow for some cleaning of their spaces. But the stench of slave ships was universally reported.

The slaves must have been extraordinarily cheap in Africa because the typical ship was packed absurdly tight. Perhaps it was understood that no amount of kindness (and there was none) or personal space could get the slaves across the Atlantic with no losses; and it was assumed that the living quarters would become much less crowded within a few weeks. The real problem here was disease and, of course, no one knew what disease was or how it was transmitted. Not only were small pox, dysentery and cholera likely to break out and spread throughout the ship (regardless of how the slaves might be quarantined), many of the slaves and crew had chronic malaria and other African fevers or venereal diseases. One of the most interesting diseases that affected both the slaves and the crew was ophthalmia[25], which frequently broke out and could literally blind everyone at least temporarily (it seems that a cycle would be about 10-14 days) and the victims might or might not recover partial sight in one or both eyes. There are stories about the entire ship's company being simultaneously blind and simply drifting. Overall, it was not unusual to lose more than half of the slaves and part of the crew

---

[25] Curry J. 1812. History of a case of remitting Ophthalmia, and its successful treatment by Opium. *Med Chir Trans*. 3:348-71. The descriptions of the disease on slaving ships is not readily identified with any single cause. I would hypothesize that trachoma produces a chronic scaring of the cornea that set the victim up for an infection by *Pseudomonas aeruginosa* associated with the unsanitary conditions on slave ships. River blindness and syphilis would not be synchronized like this.

in a trip that took about 40 to 50 days to the West Indies. Once in the West Indies, the remaining slaves were cleaned and fed to improve their health to obtain the best price for them. The crew generally descended into drunkenness and debauchery.

Loss of slaves to violence was also an issue but generally paled in comparison to disease. Pirate encounters and attacks by ships of other nations were also likely to cause loss of life. Slaves that did not obey were of course painfully beaten. Slave revolts broke out periodically and usually resulted in loss of a few percentage of the slaves and often a few of the crew. In the event of revolts, the ring leaders were generally killed before the other slaves in the most brutal ways. It is said that sharks routinely followed slave ships to feast off the dead and dying slaves that were thrown overboard. As horrible as these shipboard punishments were, it is likely that the slaves had seen and endured similar atrocities in Africa. Moreover, in the European and American navies, sailors routinely were punished by flogging (usually in multiples of twelve lashes, averaging about 15 lashes, for such offenses as neglect, disobedience or fighting).[26]

Reading these blood-drenched descriptions of wonton murder and abuse, it is easy to view the whole business of slavery with disgust. However, some of the participants rationalized the practice. Captain Snelgrave wrote a book in 1734, which was quoted by Dow (1927, pp. xix-xx). I will not quote it here (nor do I think the arguments are particularly compelling), but they include the argument that by offering to buy slaves, the Europeans were

---

[26] https://www.cnrs-scrn.org/northern_mariner/vol09/nm_9_1_53to66.pdf

providing an alternative to genocide for captives taken in tribal wars. The problem I see with this argument is that on the scale that the Europeans bought slaves, the fact that there was a market demand actually was the motivation for most of the slave hunts among the African tribes. Snelgrave also argued that slavery for debt was common among the Africans. Again, that might be true, but as we see above, becoming a slave in your own village was not the same as the Atlantic slave trade, where if you survived, you were certain to never see your people ever again.

The only plausible alibi I have found for the slave traders is the rationale that once a slave reached a plantation, he/she had better prospects than had they remained in Africa. But this rationale is also flawed in the case of (West Indies) sugar plantations run for profit off the labor of a cheap and expendable resource of African slaves. On the other hand, given the living conditions in central Africa, life on a mainland tobacco or cotton plantation in the South or a small farm in New England was generally much better. At the very least, the constant pressure of malaria, sleeping sickness, river blindness and a dozen other afflictions was avoided or mitigated.

The Plantation

The purpose of slave hunting and slave trafficking was to economically meet labor needs in plantations. While that is true for West Indies sugar plantations, it is not so obvious as generally accepted that the use of slaves provided economical labor to mainland British plantations, but it was able to provide labor quicker than Europe could. I can hear your guffaws from here. You have all been told that rich southern planters worked their slaves mercilessly and that was the only way they made a living or got rich. In a subsequent chapter, I will address the economics of slave trafficking and slave holding in some detail. For now, I will merely point out two things: (1) there were two distinct economic models of slave ownership and labor and (2) the model applied in the American South was completely destroyed (along with the social and infrastructure base) between 1861 and 1865; nonetheless, by 1870, cotton production in the American South had virtually completely recovered…without slaves. Think about that…if slave labor was essential to productive agriculture in the South, how did that agriculture ever recover (much less quickly recover) in the face of enhanced international competition fostered by the war and destruction of southern infrastructure (railroads and shipping) during the war? Slavery was instituted in the mainland British colonies because the *British* (prior to 1783) though slave-labor was economical and because black Africans were more readily available than Europeans in the critical period 1760-1840.

I call the two plantation models: ***exploitation agriculture*** and ***colonization agriculture***. These models are closely tied to the type of cash crops being grown (i.e., sugar cane versus tobacco/cotton), which I will introduce below. For the moment, we only need to look at the effect on the population of black Africans to prepare for this comparison: Farrow (2014, p. 123-4) notes that in spite of the British importing approximately 3-million black Africans to the West Indies (sugar plantations) over a period of 200 years (roughly 1607-1807), there were only about

700,000 African slaves in 1834 (when the British emancipated their colonial slaves). In comparison, only about 400,000 slaves were imported into the mainland British colonies and southern states (mostly between 1775 and 1807 with the cotton boom), but by 1865 the population of African slaves in the South was about 4-million with over 500,000 *free African-Americans* (i.e., American-born) living in the United States, over half of them in the South where slavery was legal.

It is relevant to compare the dramatic growth of the black African population as slaves in the North American South just mentioned from (e.g., 1700 to 1850) to the population changes in Arica, where the slaves were being drawn from. The total population of Africa stood at about 150-million from 1700 to the late 1800s (growth rate less than 0.5% per year). In central and western Africa, the population actually declined (est. 2%/year), in part due to the trans-Atlantic slave trade and Middle eastern slave trade and in part by immigration to other areas:

"1790 – 1890. The shifts in enslavement in the nineteenth century were immense, and clearly contributed to overall African population change. … in the period from 1790 to 1820, the volume of the Atlantic slave trade peaked after a long expansion, then declined modestly. But in the same period the volume of slave exports to the north and east of sub-Saharan Africa increased by a factor of four, so that the total drain of export slave trade from sub-Saharan Africa nearly doubled over three decades. From 1820 to 1860 the volume of captive exports to the north

and east declined only slightly, while exports from West and Central Africa declined precipitously."[27] Patrick Manning. 2013.

Comparing the stagnant or declining population of Africans in Africa to the rapidly expanding population of Africans in the southern mainland British colonies/states is arguably support for the argument that Africans were better off (as slaves) in North America than in Africa. After 1870, population growth began in all regions of Africa (probably because of establishment of European colonies) in spite of continued enslavement into the middle east and Brazil (e.g., rubber plantations).

African Population by Region 1700-1850[28] (In millions)			
Area/Year	1700	1790	1850
Central	21.0	18.5	16.2
West	52.7	47.9	46.5
All Africa[29]	150	150	150

---

[27] The quote is taken from African Population, 1650 – 1950: Methods for New Estimates by Region. African Economic History Conference Vancouver, BC, April 2013. The graphs can be found there or in (Manning, 1990, p. 83).

[28] This table is derived from Figure 1 and Table 1 of the paper by Patrick Manning. But, the graph does not seem to match the Figure in all aspects.

Patrick Manning. 2013. African Population, 1650 – 1950: Methods for New Estimates by Region. African Economic History Conference Vancouver, BC, April 2013
https://www.mortenjerven.com/wp-content/uploads/2013/04/AfricanPopulation.Methods.pdf

1.3 Comparison of Plantation Operations and Economics

Sugar Plantations

Sugar cane is a tall grass and grows continuously in warm wet climates. The mature stalks (2 inches diameter x (6 to 12) feet tall) are cut near the ground with a machete and bundled to the processing house. Until modern times, teams of oxen were used to crush the cane and release the crude sugar sap. The islands of the West Indies also use windmills to crush the cane. The watery sap was further pressed out of the woody pulp with a screw press. The expressed liquids were then boiled down in several stages. The woody part of the cane stalks provided most of the fuel for these fires, but the islands were progressive deforested to

---

[29] Other sources indicate a fairly stable total African population between 90 and 95 million in the period 1800-1850. Regardless, the population of Africa in general and west and central Africa was not growing in the early 1800s.

provide timber and fire wood. In the process of concentrating the sugar from the sap, lime was added to the first evaporation stage to remove acids and alcohol impurities. The liquid was decanted from the lime and solids into a second boiler; then to a third boiler, which brings the liquid to a supersaturated and partially caramelized syrup that is poured into a cooling trough where it deposits sugar crystals. The residual syrup is decanted from the sugar as molasses. Because, the growing season is continuous and the harvest season is long, there is never an "off season;" heavy work is continuous.

Caribbean Sugar Plantation (Antigua, 1823)

Source: http://spartacus-educational.com/USASsugar.htm

A slave's life on a sugar plantation was typically brutal (thanks to heavy, non-stop work) and short (thanks to malaria, yellow fever, cholera, malnutrition and abuse). Thus, sugar plantations were characterized by a constant input of slave labor, which turned over every few years. The slaves were used and treated like animals…total dehumanization.

This form of agriculture began in the 1500s and early 1600s; no question was even considered regarding the morality of such an enterprise. The slaves were viewed as expendable animal labor with a relatively short working life. No slaves really lived long enough to contemplate retirement. Moreover, females were not well suited for most of the heavy labor of cutting and transporting cane; thus, most of the slaves were male (Manning, 1990, pp. 60-90). The female Africans that arrived in the sugar plantations were often taken by Europeans as concubines; and together they produced a large number of mixed-race children (mulattos) who often held comfortable positions of management and trade separating the Europeans from the black African men doing the heavy labor.

The system required cheap replacement slaves. In Africa, the slaves were relatively cheap because (at that time 1600s-early 1700s) the demand was relatively small. Thus, the slaves on sugar plantations were merely an expendable commodity. In the sugar plantation model of slavery, the slaves never really moved from a status of commodity to a status of individualism (e.g., establishing personal skills). But we will see other types of labor in which slaves were not viewed as disposable commodities and had a much better life.

Tobacco and Naval Stores Plantations of

Virginia and Carolina

The colonies of Virginia (1607) and Carolina (1663) were clearly begun as business ventures. But they were not suitable for growing sugar. A variety of industries were attempted with the objective of creating a viable export market for the Lords who owned the colonies. It appears that concurrent with the British defeat of the Spanish Armada (1588), seafaring friends of the Virginia colonists managed to steal a superior tobacco seed (Orinoco Gold) from a Spanish settlement on the Orinoco River. These seeds were delivered to Jamestown, Virginia just in time to save it from economic failure (1612). Tobacco was discovered to be a viable cash crop by about 1615. The first African slaves[30] arrived in 1619.

Virginia and the Carolinas provided an excellent environment for growing tobacco and when the tenable land exceeded the colonists' abilities to work it, African slaves were imported in moderate numbers usually from plantations in the West Indies. The slaves frequently brought knowledge and seeds to support the establishment of agriculture especially in the southern colonies (e.g., rice and cotton in South Carolina, and Georgia; tobacco in Virginia, Maryland and Delaware; rice, tobacco, cotton

---

[30] The slaves were brought by a Dutch ship that had taken them from a Spanish slave ship. The British who were familiar with indentured servants treated these first black Africans as indentured servants.

and naval stores in North Carolina). Rice cultivation required low-land and warm areas and was soon abandoned as suitable land was limited.

A slave's life on a tobacco plantation was completely different from the situation in the sugar plantations. Tobacco has a very discrete growing and harvesting cycle. Indeed, nothing much happens most of the autumn and winter. There are perhaps four hard months of backbreaking work in the summer and early fall to get in the crop and harvest it. However, even this work has to be spaced out because the tobacco leaves ripen progressively: You only harvest about three leaves per plant each week. Tropical diseases were much less of a concern on the mainland and the cold winter months required that slaves be provided with clothing and heated shelter. In addition, much of the work is relatively light (e.g., breaking off tobacco leaves and stringing them onto sticks to dry) and can be done by women. Thus, female slaves as well as male slaves were highly employable.

The author has actually worked on a tobacco farm in North Carolina owned by my aunt and uncle. I was assigned to "prime" tobacco (remove the leaves from the stalk) and assist a group of black women (descendants of former slaves) at the tobacco barn. The women were stringing the green tobacco onto sticks, see photo. My job was to lift the loaded sticks (about 20 lbs), take them into the tobacco barn and hanging the sticks between the lowest tiers (rafters). Later the sticks were handed up about ten feet over a series of tiers to the top of the barn. The barn was ultimately filled from the top down. Typically, a small oil heater was used to warm the barn and warm air circulated up through the almost solid mass of leaves hanging from the sticks (i.e., flue-cured). The worst nightmare for the farmer was for a stick to break and drop dry leaves on the heater, which would soon burn the entire barn of tobacco. Tobacco tar is nasty especially when you come into contact with the fine sandy soil of the coastal plain. You are covered with black tar, grit and sweat. When the dry leaves are taken from the barn, sand rains down as it is shaken off the leaves. The work day (in August in 1960, began about 0600 and ran until noon. There was then a break for lunch and rest (including swimming) in the heat of the day until about 1500 (3 PM), then work continued until 2000 (8 PM) for five days a week. The pay for me in 1960 was $3.00 per day, my cousins were not paid directly; they inherited the property. This was typical farm life in North Carolina.

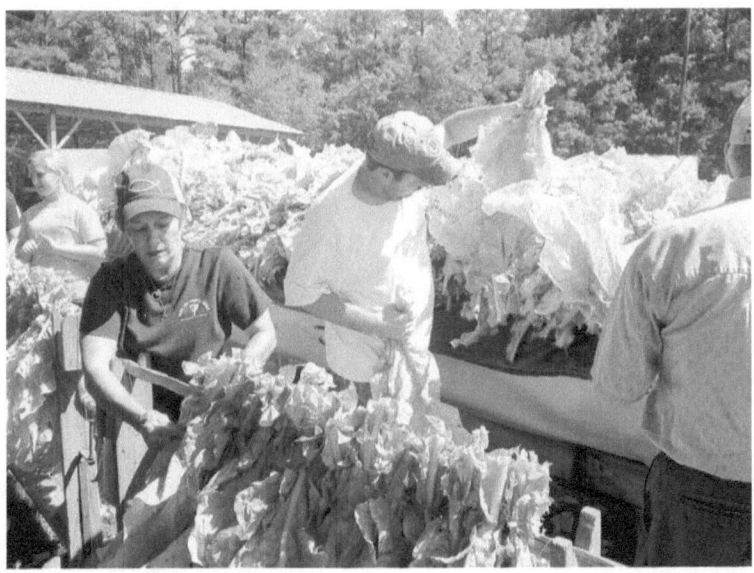

Stringing tobacco leaves on a tobacco stick for curing in a tobacco barn
Source: https://blogthefair.files.wordpress.com/2013/09/fairphoto.jpg

Tobacco[31] made Virginia and North Carolina successful colonies, but its nature required the plantations and general economy to diversify. A wide variety of crops were grown. Farm animals included cattle, pigs, horses, chickens; and, of course, dogs and cats were found everywhere. Winter months included hunting (rabbits, turkey, deer, bear).

The longleaf pine forest of the Virginia-Carolina coastal plain were excellent sources of tar, pitch and turpentine (a.k.a., naval stores) that are essential for a wooden maritime fleet. Pine sap could be obtained directly from live trees or by pyrolysis of dead wood. The crude liquids were farther refined by distillation of turpentine. Several of my ancestors were turpentine distillers in the 1800s.

---

[31] It is worth noting that to this day, the tobacco grown in Virginia and Carolina farms is renown worldwide and the technology developed to process the tobacco into cigarettes has always kept the states in the economic game. Regrettably, the product is physically addictive and has a wide variety of adverse health effects and dangers. The sooner it is phased out, the better.

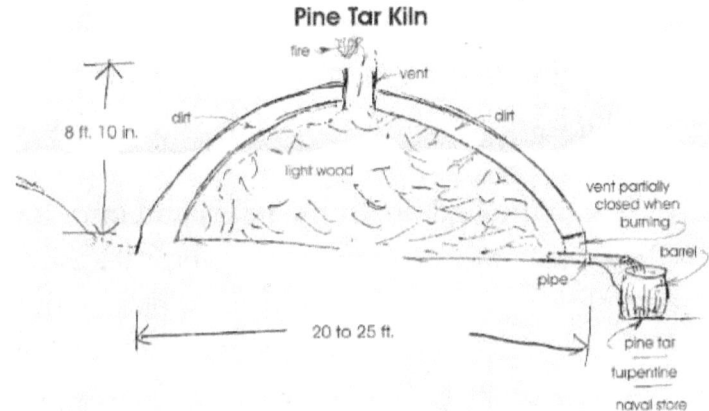

Source: http://pammack.sites.clemson.edu/lec392/earley6.html

North Carolina Turpentine Still[32]
Source: Agricultural Extension and Research Services
(UA023.007),
Special Collections Research Center at NCSU Libraries

---

[32] Both of my great grandfathers on my mother's side (eastern North
and South Carolina) were turpentine distillers in the period after the
War.

/

Thus, slaves in Virginia and Carolina had to be multi-talented and when they developed skills, they became more valuable. With longer lives and families they became part of the plantation "community." Many moved out of the fields and into domestic positions as they aged and it was not unusual for black women to care for white children or for white children to play with black children.

In an age when "rape" and "seduction" sometimes had overlapping meanings, many children born to back mothers in Virginia and Carolina had white fathers. Thomas Jefferson is, of course, the leading historical example. Fictional books by Mark Twain (1835-1910) and William Faulkner (1897-1962) are probably indicative of the interaction of black and white persons in the antebellum South. In South Carolina and Georgia, the warmer climate and the domination of the tobacco economy by Virginia and North Carolina led land owners to attempt grow rice and indigo. Neither of these crops proved to be very important. However, late in the 1700s and 1800s cotton would dominate the deep South.

1.4 The Economics of Slave-Trading and Slavery[33]

Slave-Trading Economics

The real money in the slave business was in **slave-trading**. There is limited data on the profitability of slave trading, but it was obviously very lucrative considering the personal risk that were taken by ship owners, masters and crews to venture to West Africa and risk death from tropical diseases, ocean storms, slave mutinies, and pirates or foreign competitors (privateers). The capital expense to finance a slave trading expedition was also very large. Nonetheless, the trade was never wanting participants even when it was made illegal (1807) and the participants generally had a very large return on investment.

Dow (1927/2002, pp. 107-108) provides some very interesting data: The *Enterprise* sailed from Liverpool on July 20, 1803; arrived at Bonny (west Africa) September 23rd; bought 412 slaves and sailed from Africa on December 6th. The ship presumably stopped in Barbados for instructions as had been ordered by the owner and proceeded to Havana, Cuba where 392 slaves were sold on January 9, 1804. The ship loaded sugar in Havana and returned to Liverpool on April 26, 1804. The net profit on the voyage (including sugar imported from Cuba to England) was

---

[33] One of the more readable sources is (Fogle and Engerman, 1974),

£24,430 on an investment of £17,045 (143% return on investment in about 9 months). Dow (p. 108) provides the following quote:

> "...during the eleven years from 1783 to 1793, 878 slavers [i.e., slave ships] owned in Liverpool, imported to the West Indies, 303,737 slaves whose estimated value amounted to the total of £15,186,850 – a brilliantly successful traffic that brought great wealth to the principal adventurers and an unhappy reputation to the busy port of Liverpool."

After the slave trade was made illegal, it was still profitable. Dow (1927/2002, pp.189-254) related the story of Captain Richard Drake. In that story (pp. 247), Drake summarizes a voyage in about 1835. Drake calculates that a cargo of 350 slaves bought at an average cost of $16/each in Africa and delivered in Cuba were sold at $360/each. With a cost of $20,000 for the ship and crew for the voyage producing a profit of about $100,000 for the trip. Another example of illegal trading in 1859 was similarly profitable. Because this voyage was illegal, it was much more complex and dangerous (Dow, 1927/2002, pp. 327, 330, 342). The slaves were bought for the equivalent of $8/each in Africa and sold for $350/each in Cuba. The crew is estimated to have been paid around $20,000 and there were expenses associated with circumventing the law (estimated at $20,000) and the cost of buying and outfitting an old Baltimore clipper that was destroyed to conceal the event must be included (est. $100,000). The trip involved about 1,500 slaves with losses of only about 100 (that was a cost of only $800). With these figures, I calculate a net profit of about \$178,000 on an investment of \$152,000 for a return on investment of 117% in a period of about one year.[34, 35]

One brutal fact that must be considered is that the cost of the slaves is the least important item. Of the 1,500 embarked, the venture would have turned a profit as long as 444 of 1,500 Africans survived the middle passage.[36, 37] Even if half of the

---

[34] This is consistent with an 1858 prospectus that Dow (1927/2002, p.17) mentions to send a steamer to Africa at a cost of \$300,000 and bring back a cargo of slaves that could be sold for a net profit of \$480,000 (i.e., 160% return on investment).

[35] Note that in the triangle trade, profit was also earned by bringing sugar from the West Indies or cotton from the US southern colonies/states, to the home ports of the shave ships (England or New England).

[36] In some cases, slaves were insured. This was bad news for the slaves that became injured during the trip and were not likely to bring a fair price at auction. Dow (1927/2002, p. xxxv) recounts a case in 1819 when a group of slaves became blind and 39 were cast overboard to recover the insurance money. Morison (1921, pp. 33-34) mentions a policy of \$200/slave who might be killed in insurrection underwritten in 1803 by a number of leading merchants from Boston. Rawley (2005, pp. 301) discusses the Boston insurance business and this case.

[37] Dow (1927/2002, p.68) describes an expedition in 1693-94 in which 14 crewmen and 320 of 700 slaves died of "flux" during middle passage of 2 months and 11 day to Barbados. In Barbados, the surviving slaves were sold for £19 each and they had been bought for about £5 each. This voyage appears to have been a loss.

slave died in route, the profits would be attractive;[38] and, in the case described here, the ship was sacrificed. If the ship had been sold or reused, the profit margins would have been much greater.

On a smaller scale, slave trading was less profitable. Dow (1927/2002, p. 260) indicates a much lower sale price for slaves in 1773 (£35 to £39 per slave in Granada) with a profit of £400, which he reckoned at 23% profit. As we will see below, the profit to be made in using slave labor was not nearly as much and took much longer to realize. From the stand point of those who financed the slave trade voyages (mainly wealthy people from New York and New England), the slave trade had the advantages of never having to see the salves and having no residual financial commitment. When "your ship came in," you were independently wealthy.

The Plantation Economic Models

Sugar plantations of the West Indies represent the economic model of **Exploitation Slavery.** This model of slavery was economically effective and inhumanely brutal. The slaves were viewed and treated as an expendable resource. Young men were

---

[38] An overall average mortality of slaves in the middle passage can be estimated from data provided by Dow (1927/2002, 90):

> "From 1680 to 1688 the African Company sent out 249 vessels and shipped 60,783 slaves, losing 14,387 lives…." [24% mortality]

captured in Africa, transported to the plantations of the West
Indies and forced to work cutting cane and related dangerous
tasks with the expectation that they would die on the job from
accident or more likely tropical diseases (malaria, yellow fever,
dysentery, cholera) or the bites of poisonous insects or reptiles.
The slaves, thus, had no "life" and would (of course) attempt to
escape, commit suicide or otherwise revolt at any opportunity. I
have not found any one who has tried to analyze this model. It
was clearly *profitable* and *sustainable* (i.e., the profitability
continued over several hundred years) because it only ended
when laws were passed against it in the late 1800s. The key here
is that the labor costs were very low… the total cost of three-years
of labor was probably not much more than the purchase price of
the healthy young slave. A large fraction of their energy was
likely provided by otherwise wasted sugar and molasses (i.e., the
slaves on a sugar plantation were probably malnourished, but not
hungry).

It is worth noting here that the profitability and sustainability of
the **exploitation model** likely inspired the idea that **slavery** *per se*
would be *profitable and sustainable* in all other environment. This is
a fallacy, which as far as I can tell has never been clearly analyzed.

Robert Evans, Jr. (Evans, 1962), who draws upon earlier work,
created a model that is supposed to represent the situation in the
American South, but it does not. According to Evans (1962, p.
214) *"The rates of return earned by slave capital are calculated by
considering the rates of return received by owners who buy 1,000 male
slaves at age twenty and hold them for periods of twenty or thirty years
and sell them."* The only difference between the calculation by

Evans and the exploitation model applied on sugar plantations is
that the workers in the exploitations die in two or three years and
are replaced (an expense) and not sold (for profit). Thus, Evans's
model is like the exploitation model in that it avoids and ignores
any of the indirect cost of labor, which include (i) child rearing of
slaves, (ii) retirement of salves, (iii) health concern of slaves
including reduced productivity due to pregnancy, illness or
injury, (iv) training or education of slaves, (v) down time
associated with seasonal crops (tobacco and cotton) and (vi) the
lost time associated with social and religious practices in a
continuing and expanding slave population. As summarized
below, at best Evan's calculations look like hypothetical *upper
limits* on profitability of southern plantations:

Rates of Return on Capitol 1830-1860 (Percent)				
	Short Term Money Lending	Railroads	Slaves	
			Upper South (Tobacco)	Lower South (Cotton)
1830-35	8.4-9.2		10.5	12.0
1836-40	12.5-13.0		9.5	
1841-45	6.1-6.1		14.3	18.5
1846-50	12.2-12.4	4.9-6.7	12.6	17.0
1851-55	9.1-9.6	4.6-8.6	13.8	12.0
1856-60	8.1-8.5	5.8-9.8	11.3	10.3

Thus, the sugar plantations should be more profitable than Evans calculates.[39] These results are similar to the analysis by Fogel and Engerman (1974, pp. 149-157) who calculated *"on average, 12 percent of the value of the income produced by slaves was expropriated by their masters"* [as profit].

Looking at the situation on the mainland tobacco and cotton plantations in comparison to the West Indies sugar plantations in more detail, it is apparent why slavery *initially appeared* to be an attractive economic model but it soon evolved into a major liability. The reputation of profitability in the West Indies led the British government and the initial colonists to believe that slave labor was virtually free and efficient. They would begin with young, healthy slaves and for the first generation, the situation on the Mainland (colonization model) looked much like the situation on the Islands (exploitation model), in fact it might even seem better because (i) the slaves did not die out and require replacement, (ii) cheaper female slaves could do many of the jobs and (iii) the slaves were breeding new slaves (naively considered to be "bonus" slaves). Also, in the early days, the cost of expanding onto new lands was relatively small; but when plantations were firmly established, they had a defined area...being hemmed in by other plantations. By 1763 there were no unclaimed lands as the British government limited westward

---

[39] He looks at a number of variables and attempts to selected the most reasonable from a statistical standpoint. Although this is objective and the results seem reasonable, he does not translate his results into what we know about the industries in which the slaves were working or the trends in technology in those industries.

expansion, which was one of the reasons for the War of Independence (1775-1783).

But after the first generation, slavery *as practiced in the American South* (tobacco and cotton plantations) started to make slave-labor more expensive (less economical) as there were now unproductive children (that required care from adult slaves) and there were slaves that could not work because of age or infirmary. Referring to sugar plantations, Farrow (2014, p. 23) comes to the same conclusion: "*...slaves were worked to death and then replaced because it cost less to import a life from Africa than to raise a child to slavery in the Caribbean.*" Also see Farrow (2014, p. 121) for a virtually identical quote. As the demographics of the slave population in the American South evolved to mirror the demographics of the free population, the cost of slave labor approached and then exceeded the cost of free labor.

Why would slave-labor be more expensive than free-labor? Because a slave owner took responsibility for *all the slaves all the time* (cradle to grave). The slave owner...owned the slaves, whereas free-labor is effectively only rented *when it is needed/productive.*

In Evans's model (table above), there is never any children or retired slaves to worry about. [40] For example, Evans's model is naïve because selling a slave that has been worked hard for thirty years is not realistic (i.e., the market for "worn out" slaves with no

---

[40] Based on several sources, the working life span of a male slave was regarded as 10 to 55 years of age.

skills is soon saturated, if it ever exists). Moreover, if you have worked daily with a slave for 30 years, there is some social attachment. It was difficult for European families to "turn out" (e.g., "free") aged slaves. The slave system was a socialist system, in fact it is probably a good model for what happens overtime in a country that attempts to implement socialism (e.g., the Soviet Union).

Based on Evans's calculations and the reality of the plantations systems (sugar cane *versus* tobacco/cotton), I come to the following conclusions:

(i)   Trans-Atlantic slavery was only sustainable in the sugar plantation/exploitation model; and it persisted from 1550 to about 1888 when it was ended by being outlawed (rather than lack of profitability[41]).

(ii)   The fabulous profitability of the slave trade, which primarily benefited government-run enterprises (e.g., RAC, WIC) and royal patrons, caused slavery to be

---

[41] Although African slavery was officially ended in Brazil in 1888, the "rubber boom" (1879 and 1912) resulted in peasants and Amerindians being enslaved under a system as bad, and possibly worse, than the sugar plantations. Concurrent with decline in slavery in Brazil, rubber plantations were established in the East Indies where labor was very cheap. When Japan captured these plantations in the 1940s, the US developed a petroleum-bases synthetic rubber. The subdivision of Africa by European powers also led to virtual slavery for many Africans on plantations especially in the Congo River Basin largely controlled by Belgium via Leopoldville (Kinshasa).

forced onto the British colonies in North America in lieu of importation of more free European labor. The fact that both practical (climate, geography) and social differences would not allow slavery to be practiced in the mainland colonies the way it was practiced in the West Indies was not anticipated.

(iii)   Although the colonization model initially looks like the exploitation model (i.e., the first generation of slaves begin as healthy young adults), within a few generations (e.g., 100 to 150 years), the number of children and retired slaves build up in the mainland colonies and greatly increase the cost of slave-ownership as practiced in the American South. As the slave demographics started including children and retirees; the labor cost would necessarily approach (and then exceed) the cost of indentured servants. The only economic relief would be to free the retired slaves (manumission), more bluntly known as "turning the slaves out" to fend for themselves. [42]

---

[42] Slavery as practiced in the South included an implied responsibility to care for slaves throughout their lives. I'm not aware that shaves were actually starved or worked to death in the South. Nor were they routinely turned out and certainly not killed when too old to work. Thus, if you look at the life-cycle of slave ownership, there was a fairly narrow margin for profitability, which was being reduced as the slaves brought from Africa in the 1700s were beginning to retire in numbers in the 1830s. The only way to make the system economical was to split up families and sell excess young slaves into expanding markets (e.g.,

(iv)   The steady state assumed in Evan's model is only achieved with a slave population that does not reproduce or which can expand over the land without inhibition. But the problem of a plantation owner is that the plantations stays the same size while the population of slaves grows without limit. The result is an oversupply of labor, which means that the owner is supporting slaves that are unemployed or unemployable. The temporary solution for that problem is to rent out the slaves that have skills that can be used by others. But skilled and educated people are ultimately not going to tolerate lack of freedom of choice.

The Effect of Union Propaganda

Now, more than 150 years after the War between the States, our image of slavery is blurred thouth the telescope of time. In particular, during the War, and immediately after the War, Union propaganda was strongly influenced by the need to have a cause worth the emense expense and loss of blood that the War was demanding. The initial reason Lincoln decided to oppose secession was not slavery, indeed, most northerners were white

---

cotton plantations not contiguous with the existing tobacco plantation). This was practiced in Virginia from 1830 to 1860 but was destined to stop as the cotton acreage was now saturated and by 1870 there would be no market for excess slaves anywhere in the US. The system was soon to end.

supremacists and had no desire to have black Africans freely moving about the United States. While slavery was seen as morally wrong, the preferred cure was to deport black Africans out of the United States. The politics of secession will be discussed fully below, but I think it is important to make this point here. One of Lincoln's assumptions (1861) upon enterning the War was that the defeat of the South would be quick and relativly bloodless and financially unimportant. When this proved to be wrong, his problem became a way to motivate northerners to continue the fight. To do this, he needed a moral issue like ending slavery and he had to make slavery in the South seem as cruel and inhumane as possible. And, to a large extent, he succeeded.

The presidential proclamation of September 22, 1862 (i.e., the so-called "emancipation proclamation") was a successful propaganda effort by Lincoln that morphed the political rationale for the war from naked economic domination of the South by the North into a righteous crusade by the North to end slavery and preserve "the Union" (under northern political and economic domination.).

To do this, slavery had to be made to seem as horrible and unjust as possible. Thus, we have the famous photograph of "Gordon" a beaten slave taken in March 1863 by William D. McPherson at a Union military encampment near Baton Rouge, LA. The beatings apparently occurred in the fall of 1862. The only facts that seem certain is that Gordon must have been on a plantation west of Baton Rouge in south western Louisiana. This was almost certainly a sugar plantation where conditions were typically much harsher than cotton plantations or tobacco plantations.

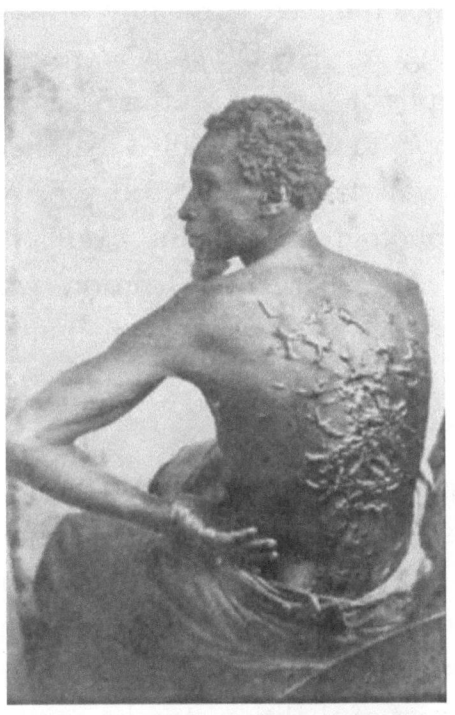

According to Frank H. Goodyear, III (assistant curator of photographs at the National Portrait Gallery, Smithsonian Photography Initiative): *"While the plantation owner discharged the overseer who had carried out this vicious attack, for the next two months as Gordon recuperated in bed, he decided to escape."* The reason for the beating is unknown (presumably some sort of punishment was justified)[43], but at least its intensity must have exceeded the

---

[43] It is relevant that flogging was widely practiced in the U.S. Navy until 1850. Unintentional accidents could bring a man a dozen or more lashes.

policy of the plantation owner as the overseer was fired. Nonetheless this unique[44] photograph was widely circulated in the North including a full page in the July 4, 1863 *Harper's Weekly* depicting the photograph as "*A Typical Negro.*" I have searched for other photographs of "beaten southern slaves" on the internet and cannot find any. It must be recalled that there were thousands of runaway slaves in the North where abolitionists could easily have photographed them...*but this is the only photograph of a beaten slave.* Clearly, "Gordon" was *not typical*; he was merely the perfect case upon which to build wartime propaganda. Unfortunately, today, he represents slavery to most American school children.

The abolitionists movement began among the children and grandchildren of slave-trading Quakers and other New Englanders and was largely presented in dramatic and emotional religious terms, which turned to deeds of their ancestors into the guilt of southern slave holders. We will deal with this later, but there was also a series of abolitionists who appear to have projected their white-supremacist views onto the institution of slavery and propagated the idea that black African (slave) labor was inferior to white European (free) labor. For example, Fogel

---

[44] I have not seen any other photographs of badly (actually any) beaten slaves from the antebellum South (before 1865). Most depictions of whip-wielding overseers come from drawings from the West Indies. There have been some recent photographs from Namibia (with German captions) that show much worse damage than suffered by Gordon. I believe that if there had been the widespread abuse claimed by various movies, blogs and history books, the abolitionists would have provided us with much more photographic evidence during and after the War.

and Engerman (1974, pp. 178-79) explain, *"racism runs through the words of…[these economic arguments]…like a red line."*

Starting with this assumption, men like Cassius Marcellus Clay, Rowan Helper and Frederick Law Olmsted (1822-1903) built (what to people with similar biases seem objective) economic analyses of slavery that purported to show that slave labor was less efficient than *"the commonest, stupidest Irish…drudges at the North"* (see Fogel and Engerman, 1974, at p. 174). These men were not economists, and in retrospect their arguments drip of anti-black African bias. Fogel and Engerman (1974, pp. 158-190) easily point out the misunderstanding and mathematical errors that these men made in coming to the conclusion that black African labor was not as efficient as white European labor (even Irish!). One factor that Fogel and Engerman do not mention in critiquing the comparison of the northern economy to southern economy by Clay/Helper/Olmsted[45] was the impact of the protective tariffs, which favored the North at the expense of the South. In the end, the white supremacy of Olmsted led to ridiculous conclusions that Fogel and Engerman (1974, p. 177) characterize as follows: *"If as Olmsted also argued…slaves were exploiting slaveowners rather than slaveowners exploiting slaves."* Clay/Helper/Olmsted extended their arguments to the southern white population as discouraged workers and lackadaisical managers. From these

---

[45] In 1865, "The Nation" magazine that is considered to be a continuation of "The Liberator" was established with the aid of F.L. Olmsted who is today most remembered as a landscape architect.

characterizations come the (still popular) popular notion that white southerners are lazy and stupid as well as racist.

Punishment and Reward of Slaves in the South

Motivation of slaves in the south was far from the image of northern propaganda. Probably the best discussion is provided by Fogel and Engerman (1974, 144-157). They point out that in the system where the owner is continually responsible for the laborer, discipline that prevents the slave from working or which induces the slave to rebel or runaway is absolutely the last thing that the owner wishes. In the extreme, capital punishment is almost unheard of because it represents a loss of the potential value of the slave's labor and was typically only associated with punishment for armed rebellion or murder. The more effective maximum punishment was to sell the slave to the West Indies, which produced some value for the owner and was a virtual death sentence for the slave.

While it is very had to obtain data regarding the ages of whipped slaves or the intensity of the whippings, Fogel and Engerman (1974, pp. 144-46) report data for one Louisiana plantation (1841-42). The data seem to be bimodal (i.e., zero whippings per hand and 4 whippings per hand). I will speculate that the juveniles were receiving more and less-intense whippings. It is worth noting that of the 200 slaves on the plantation only about 120 were actually in the work force.[46] Many of these people not-in-the-

---

[46] While 40% of the slaves were non-productive, this is actually substantially better than most free labor markets.

work-force were, of course, children; and it is likely that they received the majority of the corporal punishment.

Fogel and Engerman (1974, 148-57) go on to describe relatively enlightened positive incentives used by planters to both increase the esprit and morale of slaves and motivate them. Not only were privileges including personal property and time-off provided, there were cash bonuses and even-profit sharing schemes. Slaves were encouraged to identify with and pride themselves in the plantations to which they belonged. This pride can account for the extensive use of "slave names" among African Americans of antebellum origin. Far from the negative image engendered by the civil rights movement in the mid-1900s, slaves took the names of their owners because they were proud of their accomplishments and, of course, it was obvious that some slaves were actually related to the plantation family by blood.

While slaves were not "free" they were not necessarily in abject poverty. Indeed, some were highly motivated, earned and saved money and even loaned money and sold products of their private labor to the plantation that owned them. These situations, while not universal, suggest a level of respect and common understanding among Europeans and black Africans in the South; and it is consistent with the fact that there were many free black Africans and even successful black African planters and artesian in the South in the antebellum period. Thus, to an extent not understood in the North, in the South slavery was about *property*, not about *racism* in 1860.

The Obsolesce of Slavery

The economic viability of slavery was in constant flux after 1700 especially in the mainland British colonies and the successor American States. Above, I have summarized the bogus arguments for the immediate abolition of slavery propagated by Clay/Helper/Olmsted and ultimately the Republican Party who embraced Halper's rhetoric in 1860. Ironically, I also embrace the notion that slavery would become obsolete in the American South, but not when they said it was obsolete (and not for the reasons they said it was obsolete).

Fogel and Engerman (1974) do an excellent job of demolishing the white-supremacy attitude (held especially in the North) that black Africans were inherently inferior to Europeans and thus their work was inefficient.

> *"What bitter irony it is that the false stereotype of black labor, a stereotype which still plagues blacks today, was fashioned not primarily by the oppressors who strove to keep their chattel wrapped in the chains of bondage, but by the most ardent opponents of slavery, by those who worked most diligently to destroy the chains of bondage."*

(Fogel and Ebgerman, 1874, p. 215)

Here I want to point out that the features that made black African labor superior to free labor (up to 1860) were dependent upon (i) the constant expansion of southern plantation agriculture, which became saturated in the late 1850s and (ii) the absence of technologies (steam power/coal, railroads, kerosene/petroleum and electricity) that were brought on line between 1850 and 1900.

When these technologies became available (after 1860), the advantages of slave-labor disappear and the economy must shift to free-labor. Thus, I project that slavery would have ended in the South before 1900.

Free Blacks by State 1860 (source: 1860 census)		
State	Free Black Population	Total Black Population and (Percent Free)
Maryland	83,942	87,189 (49.%)
Delaware[47]	19,829	21,627 (91.%)
Virginia	58,042	548,907 (11.%)
North Carolina	30,463	361,522 (8.4%)
Louisiana[48]	18,647	350,373 (5.3%)
Kentucky	10,684	236,167 (4.5%)
South Carolina	9,914	412,320 (2.4%)
Tennessee	7,300	283019 (2.6%)
Missouri	3,572	118,503 (3.0%)
Georgia	3,500	465,698 (0.8%)
Alabama	2,690	437,770 (0.6%)
Florida	932	62,677 (1.5%)
Mississippi	773	437,404 (0.2%)
Texas	355	182,921 (0.2%)
Arkansas	144	11,259 (0.1%)

---

[47] Delaware was the end of the underground railroad and received numerous escaped slaves from Maryland and Virginia.

[48] The population of free blacks probably includes creoles from French and Spanish settlement of New Orleans.

Total Population (Percent Free Blacks)	
Maryland	687,049 (12.%)
Delaware	112,216 (18.%)
Virginia	1,596,318 (3.6%)
North Carolina	992,622 (3.1%)
Louisiana	708,002 (2.6%)
Kentucky	1,155,684 (0.9%)
South Carolina	703,708 (1.4%)
Tennessee	1,109,801 (0.7%)
Missouri	1,182,012 (0.3%)
Georgia	1,057,286 (0.3%)
Alabama	964,201 (0.3%)
Florida	140,424 (0.7%)
Mississippi	791,305 (0.1%)
Texas	604,215 (0.1%)
Arkansas	435,450 (0.0%)

Ultimately, slavery as practiced in the American South, was not sustainable in the face of agricultural saturation and technological development; and we see strong evidence of that in the patterns of manumissions. By as early as the 1830s, slavery was becoming uneconomical relative to free labor (i.e., socialism was giving way to capitalism) in the tobacco states although the expansion of new soil (associated with expulsion of the Native Americans) created a temporary demand for slave labor in Georgia, Alabama, Mississippi, North Florida, along the Mississippi River and its tributaries (east Texas, Louisiana, Arkansas and western Tennessee).

As shown in the Table above, slavery was already becoming obsolete (non-competitive relative to free labor) in the "upper South" (e.g., Maryland, Virginia, North Carolina, Kentucky, and even South Carolina) resulting in a growing number of manumissions and growing population of *free* African Americans. I will go so far as to suggest that this table is an indication of the natural transition of enslaved Africans into free US citizens *and it is exactly what the slave-free states feared the most…* where there were slaves, free black Africans would follow. Northern and western states were not opposed to slavery (e.g., the US never declared war on any nation because they supported slavery) northerners and westerners were opposed to the introduction of free black Africans. Lincoln opposed secession, because he opposed losing the slaves that powered his (1860) economy and release free black Africans into all the states.

The model of slavery used in the West Indies sugar plantations was viable and profitable because the cost of young black men (e.g., 10 to 30 years old) bought in Africa was very low and they were treated as disposable…most dying within 5 years due to disease. It was also convenient that they could be fed with the waste (molasses) from sugar production (in comparison you cannot eat cotton or tobacco) and the warm climate minimized needs for clothing and shelter. They worked more or less continuously as the cane literally grew like grass (i.e., sugar cane *is* a tall perennial grass).

The conditions on the mainland British colonies were quite different and different regions favored different crops. Rice was limited to the southern-most river flood zones which limited its spread. Conditions for sugar cane only existed in the southern most parts of Louisiana. Both of these crops were readily eclipsed by tobacco (Maryland/Virginia/North Carolina/Kentucky) and cotton (South Carolina/Georgia/North Florida/Alabama/Mississippi/North Louisiana/ East Texas/ Western Tennessee). The weather on these regions reaches freezing every year and these crops have a definite area-wide annual planting/growing/harvesting cycle. Thus, the labor needs are constantly changing and are very varied. Much useful work can be done by women, children and old men.

Thus, while the initial slave demographic in the mainland British colonies was likely similar to the West Indies (young African male), it soon included young African women (cheaper to buy). And over the period 1760-1860, the demographics of the slave population evolved. As the demographics evolved, that very high work force participation rate (initially ~100%) decreased because of the inclusion for children and elderly as well as infirm people. Examples given by Fogel and Engerman (1974) suggest that by the 1850s the potential work force of slaves was about 60% of the slave population and where there was a shortage of labor (the Cotton States) virtually all of these potential workers were actively employed. This is one of the secrets to the very high productivity of southern black labor compared to northern white labor. While the demographics of white Europeans might be similar to the demographics of the slave population in the South, in the North many of the white children were in school until they

were 16 or even longer and many women were limited to
domestic housekeeping (sweeping the floor and washing the
dishes at home do not generally contribute to the GDP whereas
stringing tobacco, picking and ginning cotton do contribute to
GDP).

But, in the tobacco states, the slave population was expanding
beyond that useful in routine agriculture and more were being
diverted into trades (blacksmith, carpenters, mechanics). Still the
limitation of the availability of land and the decline of
productivity of land (which is unavoidable due to farming and
which was being countered with artificial fertilization) created an
excess of agricultural (slave) labor. This faced slave owners with
the morally distasteful option of splitting up families by selling
the young/fit slaves into the newly opened cotton belt (after
1835). This option continued into the 1850s, but the cotton belt
was also susceptible to saturation with low-skilled slave labor.
And it was reaching that point in 1860.

The point I am making here is that just as the general institution
of slavery was in saturation throughout the South, the War
interrupted what would have been the economic decline of slave-
labor relative to free-labor in the South. In 1860:

> The South had saturated both the international tobacco and
> the cotton markets.

> All the well-watered, warm, agricultural lands in the US
> were already in use. Large scale agriculture was not
> possible in the arid south west.

> There were more slaves than agricultural jobs.

These features worked against agriculture where low-skilled labor could be highly organized[49] and phenomenally productive. The transition to a slave-free economy would be completed with the following changes that were just beginning to take place in the South:

> Railroads were beginning to supplement river traffic and make manufacturing feasible at inland sites by providing importation of coal.

> Steam-powered manufacturing would *for the first time* give the South an opportunity to compete with the water-power of New England. The cotton spinning and weaving industry would necessarily move south. For example, the first cotton mill came to Charlotte, NC in 1880 with 6,240 active spindles. In 1900, there were sixteen mills with "a combined total of 94,392 spindles and 1,456 looms."[50] These

---

[49] Black Africans (i.e., drivers) that organized gangs of field hands invented the assembly line (not Henry Ford). *"On a majority of the large plantations the top nonowner management* [overseers and drivers] *was black."* (Fogel and Engerman, 1974, p. 212)

[50] Thomas W. Hanchett and Dr. William H. Huffman, "Mecklenburg Mill," Charlotte-Mecklenburg Historic Properties Commission, http://www.cmhpf.org/S&Rs%20Alphabetical%20Order/surveys&rmeckmill.htm
"In 1903 James B. Duke was just becoming interested in the hydro-electric potential of the Charlotte area, an interest that would lead to the creation of Duke Power, and it may be that the nephew's textile investment and the uncle's electrical explorations were in some way connected."

Sterling per Annum Payable Quarterly And for the true Performance of the Premisses, the said Parties, the these Presents bind themselves, their Executors and Administrators, the either to the other, in the Penal Sum of Forty Pounds Sterling, firmly by these Presents. In witness whereof, they have hereunto interchanged by set their Hands and Seals, the Day and Year above-written.

Sealed and Delivered

in the Presence of

Tho Hayes

Wm Buckland

W Kidd

These are to certify, That the above-named Wm Buckland came before Me Gyles Sone Deputy to the Patentee at London the Day and Year above-written, and declared him self to be a Single Person no Covenant or Contracted Servant to any Person, or Persons; to be of the Age of Twenty two Years; and to be desirous to serve the above-named Thomson Mason or his Assigns Four Years, according to the Tenor of the Indenture above-written. All which is Registered in the Office for that Purpose, appointed by Letters Patents. In witness whereof, I have hereunto affixed the Common Seal of the said Office.

Gyles Sone DL

...

— page 2 —

mills were steam powered and located on the Southern Railway, not on a major river.

Southern ports (Norfolk, Wilmington, Charleston, Savannah, Pensacola, Mobile, New Orleans, Galveston) would become favorable for shipbuilding and shipping.

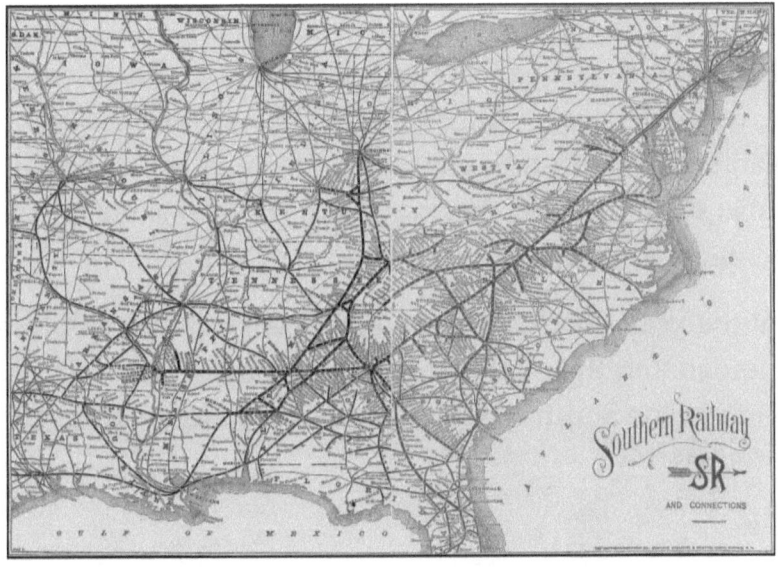

1895 Southern Railroad

https://railga.com/sr95map.html

The southern states seceded (primarily to escape the tariffs, see below) and the reduction in tariffs would have provided income needed to build a southern transcontinental rail road (linking Charleston with San Diego) and likely building a trans-isthmus canal (through Niangua) before 1900.

In this environment of southern industrial development and international trade, the favorable economics of slavery as practiced in the American South would have been further eroded. More training of slaves would have been required to take these jobs and slave-labor's advantages of (i) higher work force participation, (ii) economy of scale and (iii) production-line efficiency of work gangs (see discussions of Fogel and Engerman, 1974, pp. 153-155 and 191-209) would have been removed. Without these structural advantages, slave labor would not offer any advantages over free labor and would have been dismantled because of the general moral dislike of slavery (especially in the South) and obvious disadvantages of a socialist system relative to a capitalist system where the individual is responsible for the management of "human capital."

Without the War, the entire period of reconstruction would have been avoided and the relation for former-slaves/black Africans to Europeans in the South would have evolved along entirely different lines.

1.5 Slavery and Racism

The Psychology of Racism

In the 1700s and 1800s, people on the North American mainland (British Colonies) and in Britain began to question the *morality* and *legality* of slavery and the slave trade. I want to consider why this occurred and how it led to a rejection of the slave trade and slavery in Britain and North America. Slavery had not been tied to race before the enslavement of large numbers of black Africans. Unfortunately, scientific understanding of biology was not in a position to objectively understand the biological relationships between white Europeans and black Africans. Instead, the contemporary analysis tended to be driven by religious reasoning based on deeply held interpretations of the *Bible* heavily influenced by natural human ego (self-esteem) and suspicion of the unknown (caution). High self-esteem was manifest in a widely held view among northern Europeans (in Europe and in the colonies) that northern Europeans were superior to *all other peoples* in every way. While a high self-esteem is generally regarded as psychologically healthy, this led naturally to a general presumption of "white supremacy" relative to black Africans. As long as this pride in one's group is expressed in positive ways (e.g., like national pride, school pride, religious pride, family pride, home-town pride, or fans of a sports team), it is a useful motivator (i.e., individuals strive to live up to a presumed standard). Unfortunately, among individuals identifiable as part of the "white group" who actually have *low personal self-esteem*, the fear of failure or inability to compete among their presumed peers, gives rise to a *racist* attitude towards the presumed lower groups (southern Europeans, Asians, and Africans) which lends itself toward discrediting and actively blocking advancement of other groups. Clearly, failure in competition with a presumed inferior (e.g., African) would be a great humiliation to a person who belongs to a group that is nominally assumed to be superior (e.g., European). The stories of Jessie Owens (1913-1980) and Jackie Robinson (1919-1972) come to mind; and (of course) the Tuskegee Airmen.

The Enlightenment

The 1700s and 1800s were a time of great changes in European culture because of revolutions in science, technology and philosophy. The 1700s began with the physics and mathematics of Newton, Bernoulli, Leibnitz and others. At the end of the 1700s, Lavoisier, Priestley, Dalton, Davy, Volta and Young (to name a few) put chemistry, electricity and light on the road to modern understanding. Moreover, Black, Watt and Carnot were beginning the industrial revolution by capturing the energy of fire and turning it into mechanical work. In contrast, biology and medicine were largely empirical sciences until the 2000s when the chemical programs that underlie biological systems (i.e., the genome) came partially into focus.[51]

Until the mid-1700s, no one much considered the *morality* of slavery in Britain and the North American colonies, and the subordinate role of black Africans relative to white Europeans (i.e., white supremacy) was unquestioned. Black Africans in European society were judged not only by their personal contributions, but also by the relative socioeconomic conditions in Europe and central Africa. If there is no difference among the races, why are there differences among the intellectual achievements and economic progress of the territories dominated by these races? I will attempt to address this obvious question in a section below.

---

[51] This is considered in much more detail in the following section.

Nonetheless by the late 1700s, the scale of the slave trade had become significant and widely known in the North American British colonies and a fair number of black Africans had been present in the colonies long enough for British colonists to begin to wonder how they were to fit into their society. In particular, were the children of black Africans born in the British colonies still the property of the parent's owner? Although the parents (from Africa) might have been condemned and ostracized by their own people, British common law did not hold children guilty for the crimes of their parents and the mood in the colonies had always been towards shedding the prejudices and restrictions imposed by the highly ordered and stratified society of Europe. Moreover, when given a chance, black Africans were found to achieve intellectually and socially far beyond the status observed in their native territories.

The issue of elderly slaves that had served their masters for years (and their children who, without fault or crime, had also done so) opened up a philosophical "can of worms." These issues had not been contemplated in the 1600s and had been almost entirely avoided in the sugar plantations of the West Indies. Very few Europeans viewed black Africans equal to whites in the subjective areas of morality, intellect, or nobility/beauty. Even regarding physical strength (which could be objectively evaluated), Europeans had little doubt of their overall superiority (being physically inferior to a horse did not make the horse into the master).

Thus, the choices open to Europeans who questioned the morality of slavery seemed to be (i) to fully integrate black Africans into colonial society or (ii) to find rationales for maintaining them as slaves and/or free second-class human beings. Essentially, this was the beginning of racism against Africans in North America.

Contemporary Social Values 1600-1800

When looking at the behavior of people, we need to have some ability to understand what they understood to be the normal social values of their times (not ours). One of the great weaknesses of historical studies is that we are inclined to assign morality and reasonableness of historical decision making based on our current understanding of the universe. One of the issues is whether we should judge a historical figure's immorality and intellect based on his/her actions then or how we would judge the same actions and decisions now. Although I am not trying to resolve this debate in this book, I do want to reader to at least understand the situation in the past, and in particular consider the actions of the historical antagonist and protagonists in the same light.

Beginning in the 1600s, the western civilizations (Europe and middle-East) were driven by the Judeo-Christian-Muslim tradition in which monotheism had generally overgrown the previous existing pagan (polytheistic) beliefs. I use the term "overgrown" because the monotheisms had not fully displaced or destroyed paganism. I see the analogy of a garden plot first covered by various weeds, which is now in the process of being overgrown by a cultivated crop that still has weedy intrusions and even cross pollination with the more desirable plants. The tool being used to assert the new theology was the Judeo-history (i.e., Old Testament) as filtered through the Greek and Roman Empires with more recent inclusions by Christians and Muslims.

The people of these time periods (pre-Columbian) all seemed to recognize one another as one species descended from Adam and Eve and the family of Noah. The anatomical differences were not particularly large and while conflicts were brutally contested, the main frictions had to do with religion. In modern terms, we would recognize that these people all shared a genetic ancestry that dated back about 100,000 years when the most recent group of modern humans spilled out of northeastern Africa (via the Nile Valley) and over grew the earlier cultures of Neanderthals and Denisovans, who had exited Africa as much as 250,000 years ago. These were *all groups of the same interbreeding biological species* (although they had evolved in isolation, they were <u>not</u> different species).[52] By the middle ages, it was recognized that there were different phenotypical groups that could be catalogued among the inhabitants of Eur-Asia. And the Columbian discovery (1490s) of Amerindians did not fall far outside the expectations of anatomical variation or social organization and achievement expected by the Eur-Asians. The world (including north Africa) appeared to be populated by a family of similar human beings.

There were religious differences and the competition was primarily among religious groups. This competition existed

---

[52] For reasons I have discussed elsewhere, *speciation events* appear to happen about ever million years on average. Since these groups were known to interbreed, they were in the same species with today's humans, i.e., modern humans.

largely, because the Judeo-tradition felt that their survival was dependent upon belief and faith in their orthodoxy. The successful spread of their religion proved its superiority and ensured the blessings on earth and even beyond death that the religion promised. Thus, the Bible (the history of which few people understood) was presented to even the upper ranks of the religious leaders and all subordinate ranks as *unquestionable and infallible*.

And what did *The Bible* say about human beings and their relationships to one another?

Why Was Enslavement of black Africans Considered Acceptable by Europeans?

It is clear that what I call *contemporary social norms* are different in different places and evolve over time. In the 1500s and early 1600s, European saw Africa and the New World as exotic, strange and far-away places. Violence, oppression, poverty, serfdom and slavery were certainly well known and tolerated in Europe at this time. I call your attention to some European *social norms* of the 1600: During the reign of Mary Tudor in England (1553–1558), nearly 300 leading Protestant leaders were burnt at the stake for their religious beliefs. In the early 1600s (e.g., Pequot War of 1636), New Englanders fought savage wars with local Native American tribes and sent captured natives to the West Indies as slaves. In 1685, Louis XIV of France rescinded the Edict of Nantes, which protected Protestants in this Catholic country; the result was a level of violence and torture that prompted around 400,000 French Protestants to flee to Britain, Germany and the Netherlands for their lives (the Huguenots). After the British defeated the Irish at the Battle of the Boyne (1690), Irish Catholics were rounded up and deported effectively as slaves to the West Indies.

Colonial era punishments: The whip, the pillory, the stocks, the ducking stool

http://thosewhocansee.blogspot.com/2013/11/afros-and-transport-today-and-yesterday.html

Punishment for a wide variety of "crimes" involving Biblical prohibitions (e.g., homosexual activity) and failure to attend religious function; serious crimes threatening the safety of a colony (e.g., stealing food); generally being annoying (e.g., gossip); etc. routinely involved what we would consider cruel punishment (whipping, starting, the stocks, pillory, dunking, hanging and being shot to death) in the 1600s and 1700s.[53] Of course, women had virtually no rights independent of their husbands until the 1900s. In the 1830s, self-governing Native American tribes in the south east of the United States (including the Cherokee who had a written language and argued their case in the US Supreme Court) were forced to relocate to lands west of the Mississippi River.

With these facts in mind, it is not surprising that when European traders became aware that African tribes sold captives of war and other social outcast as slaves, there was no discernable second-thoughts about buying black Africans sold by coastal tribes as condemned prisoners for labor in the West Indies and Americas. At this point, there was no quibbling about the relations of black Africans to white Europeans (intellectually, physically or spiritually) …the Africans were condemned and sold by their own people and if they could do some useful work before they died, then that labor had a price. I am particularly struck by a recollection attributed to Alexander Falconbridge (c. 1760–1792):

---

[53] Cox, James A. Bilboes, Brands, and Branks: Colonial Crimes and Punishments. *Colonial Williamsburg Journal* Spring 2003.

"When the negroes whom the black traders have to dispose of are shown to the European purchasers, they first examine them relative to age. They then minutely inspect their persons, and inquire into their state of health; if they are afflicted with any infirmity, or are deformed, or have bad eyes or teeth; if they are lame, or weak in the joints, or distorted in the back, or of a slender make, or are narrow in the chest; in short, if they have been afflicted in any manner so as to render them incapable of such labour they are rejected. The [African] traders frequently beat those negroes which are objected to by the captains. Instances have happened that the traders, when any of their negroes have been objected to have instantly beheaded them in the sight of the captain."

Falconbridge's experience with the slave trade was between 1780-1787 as a ship's surgeon and he became an abolitionist. Although his words were intended to influence European public opinion against the slave trade, his observation in this instance reinforced the idea that the slaves were "dead men walking." This view was taught to (and accepted by) at least some black Africans in New England including Phillis Wheatley (Phyllis Wheatly) (c. 1753 – 1784) who described removal of blacks to America as an act of "mercy" in her poetry.

Other first-person descriptions of brutality among Africans are also documented. In some cases, genocidal murder appears to be completely independent of European influence. For example, Dow (1927/2002, pp. 114-117) describes events associated with an inter-tribal war in which approximately 400 captives were slaughtered in front of a British captain (Snelgrave in 1727) who was standing by ready to buy slaves. It is hard to blame the Europeans for that war or the deaths of the captives. In other cases (e.g., Richard Drake in 1805), the European market for slaves (i.e., not tribal war) was clearly the motivation for the "slave hunts" as described above (Dow, 1927, 189-209). The difference in the time (1727 versus 1805) of these two events is important, in my opinion, because although they are only anecdotal, they suggest that between 1727 and 1805 the European demand for slaves had shifted the motivations of the African tribes. In the early days (e.g., 1600-1750), slaves were likely a byproduct of intertribal conflict and assorted antisocial behavior; but by the late 1700s, the African tribes had adopted slave raiding as a self-justifying activity that actually provoked additional conflict in retaliation.

According to a black history website[54] upwards of 18-million Africans were enslaved by other Africans for the Atlantic slave trade. On the order of 16-million (90%) actually made it to European slave factories on the coast and about 12-million (67%) actually made it to the New World. About one-third of these went to Brazil, two-thirds went to the West Indies, and less than a million (5%)[55] actually made it to the North American mainland.

---

[54] http://blackhistory.com/content/61583/the-transatlantic-slave-trade

[55] Rawley (2995, p. 6) summarizes:

> "By the middle of the twentieth century the United States held about one-third of the Afro-American population of the Americas, although it had imported about 4 percent of the total."

The time of these events can be estimated from this statement:

> *"Only slightly more than three percent of the slaves exported were traded between 1450 and 1600, 16 percent in the 17th century. More than half of them were exported in the 18th century, the remaining 28.5 percent in the 19th century."*

This analysis implies all exports from Africa as follows:

1450-1600: (0.03 x 16 million)/150 years = 3,200/year

1600-1700: (0.16 x 16 million)/100 years = 25,000/year

1700-1800: (0.50 x 16 million)/100 years = 80,000/year

1800-1860: (0.285 x 16 million)/60 years = 76,000/year

Of this, mainland North America only received about 5% of the total (e.g., 5,000/year 1700-1800). I will guess that the demand during the peak years actually was in the range of 100,000/year, and I will farther assume that most of this was European demand-driven (i.e., not the product of normal tribal warfare). Unfortunately, the difference is one of degree as in both cases the *contemporary social norms* practiced within the African tribes were brutal.

Thus, while Europeans may have initially rationalized that they were saving the imported slaves from a brutal condemnation, that argument was not true after 1750. The *slave traders* likely realized the changes they were causing in the slave market by high demand in the late 1700s (i.e., changes in the time required to acquire slaves on the Guinea Coast, the quality of the slaves, and the price required to buy the slaves).[56]   Nonetheless, related rationales (e.g., that slavery was good for the Africans) were also used to supplement the basic idea that the slaves were condemned by their own people. In particular, exposing them to Christianity was considered a blessing to them by the most religious Europeans. Recall that in the 1500s and 1600s, Protestants and Catholics were burning one another at the stake (viewed as an act of mercy!) to save the blasphemers' souls from eternal hell. More generally, exposing Africans to European culture was also considered to be an advantage to the slaves.

It is relevant that in the 1700s central African had no "countries;" it was purely tribal (see map below). Notice the large unorganized areas in central Africa. Also notice, the areas in western Africa where tribal empires overlapped and produced ongoing warfare and slaves. The organized "countries" of Africa were created and imposed by Europeans as possessions largely in the 1800s (see maps below). It is relevant that once, European states took control of various territories, they frequently treated the black Africans as slaves in their own territory[57] or tried to dispossess them from their lands. This same pattern was

---

[56] The mix of slaves coming into the US Southern States likely included many more women and older men. Indeed, the 5% that the US received could easily be made up from the cast offs (unsold/unmarketable) in the West Indies.

[57] In some cases (e.g., the Congo), the horrors of this internal enslavement of Africans by Europeans in the late 1800s (well after the American War between the States) far exceeds the horrors of slavery in North America or even the brutality of sugar plantations in the West Indies. I do not have time here to go into African history, but we are still seeing it played out today.

followed by the US government in dealing with the Native American tribes, especially in the late 1800s in creating the western states.

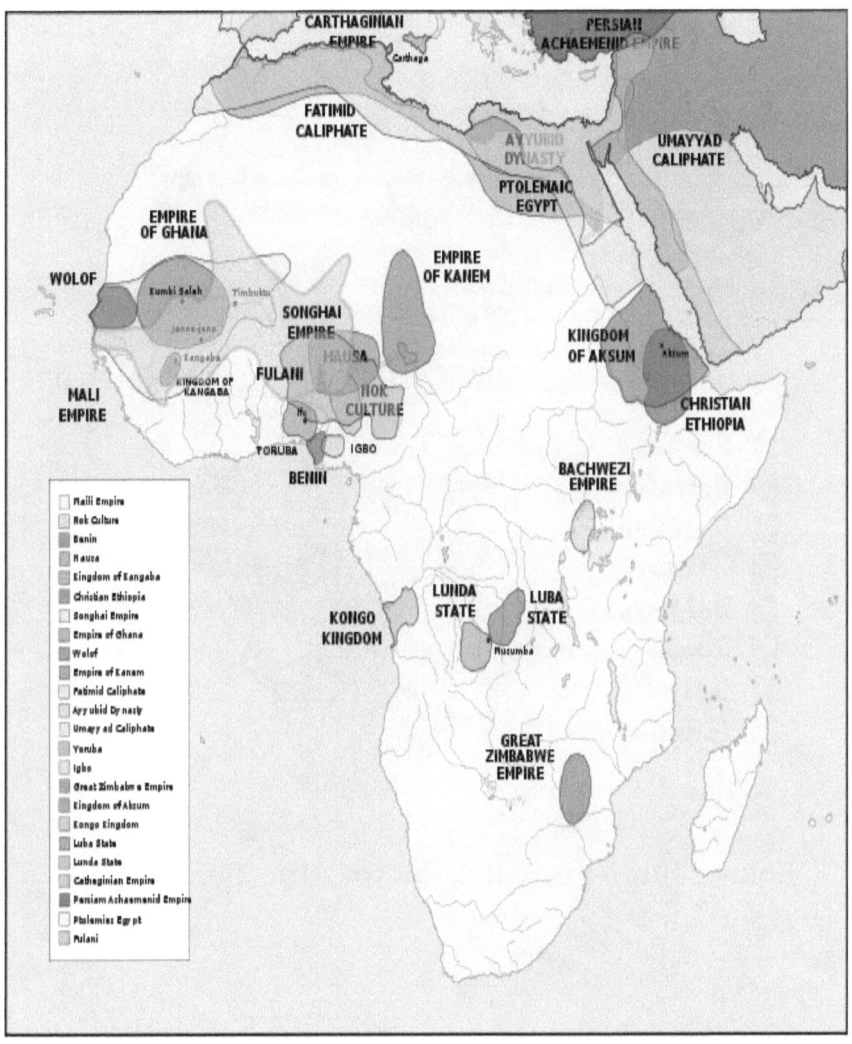

Source: http://mycontinent.co/AfricaBorders.php

France
Britain
Portugal
Germany
Belgium
Spain
Italy
Independent

Source: http://mycontinent.co/AfricaBorders.php

But there were some issues regarding black Africans that related to European understanding of "race" and "species" that began to be important in the mid-1700s. This is worth some discussion.

1.6 Scientific Understanding of Species and Race (1700-1860)[58]

The Bible and the Earth

The Biblical history of *Genesis* and *Exodus* was not merely the only guidance available; it was considered the literal word of God.

If *Genesis* is read as a hypothesis of great antiquity, it can be viewed as a logical and insightful analysis and starting point for examination of the world. But as the literal revelation of God, *Genesis* stifled investigation and understanding. The major point here is that all of humanity was believed to have been descended from Adam and Eve, i.e., all humans were ultimately in the same family. This family had at one time expanded over the earth, but betrayed God's plan. As the story goes, God had then identified and selected a specific family (two generations) that was righteous

---

[58] Note: There is a very relevant book *The Leopard's Spots Scientific Attitudes Towards Race in America 1815-59,* by William Stanton (1960), which gives much more detail than provided here. My approach is different from Stanton's approach.

(i.e., the families of Noah and his sons). Through God's guidance, that family saved itself and breeding-pairs of all the animals onto a large boat. Then all other (land) animals and humans were destroyed in a worldwide flood. That righteous family and those animals then spread out and repopulated the earth. It is relevant that in the Biblical account, the children of Ham (one of Noah's sons) were apparently condemned to be servants and to live in a region roughly identifiable as central Africa west of the Nile.

Implicit in this story is the idea of *species*, i.e., different kinds of animals. Until recently, species were defined by *appearance, environment (i.e., range) and behavior* of the organism. Although it was understood that within a species the offspring are mutually fertile,[59] it was not clear that mutual fertility was the *essential element defining a species* until Ernst Mayr, Theodosius Dobzhansky, and George Gaylord Simpson developed the idea of the "biological species" in the 1940s.

Today, it may be difficult to understand that, in the 1800s, most Europeans still had an absolute faith in the Biblical account of history and cosmology. It was viewed as **the authority** and, thus, *science* was only true to the extent that it was not in conflict with the *Bible*. This view did not have much impact on chemistry, physics, mathematics or engineering, but it directly impacted geology and biology. There were several major issues that persisted into the 1900s. In particular, the creation and age of the

---

[59] Any exceptions to mutual fertility among individuals that had descended from members of the species were regarded as some sort of disease or malfunction of individuals *within* the species.

earth were fixed by Biblical texts. The creation story was taken literally to mean that the earth was created in 7 days. Moreover, there are genealogies in the *Bible* that can be interpreted to mean that the earth is only a few thousand years old and that at one point it was completely and uniquely destroyed by a sudden cataclysmic flood.

It is worth noting that the age issue was hard to dispel even in scientific circles because the core of the earth was apparently molten (i.e., volcanoes and hot springs were known). One of the preeminent scientists of the 1800s was Lord Kelvin (William Thomson, 1st Baron Kelvin, 1824-1907) who did pioneer work in heat transfer. He correctly calculated that (*assuming no other source of energy*) in order for the earth to still be hot on the inside, it could only be a few thousand years old. He was very well respected and no one could explain the paradox. Even Ernest Rutherford (1871-1937) was intimidated by Kelvin. Regarding a 1904 speech at the Royal Institution on radiation, Rutherford stated:

> "*I* [Rutherford] *came into the room, which was half dark, and presently spotted Lord Kelvin in the audience and realised that I was in for trouble at the last part of my speech dealing with the age of the earth, where my views conflicted with his. To my relief, Kelvin fell fast asleep, but as I came to the important point, I saw the old bird sit up, open an eye and cock a baleful glance at me! Then a sudden inspiration came, and I said 'Lord Kelvin had limited the age of the earth, provided no new source (of energy) was discovered.' That prophetic utterance refers to what we are now considering tonight, radium! Behold! the old boy beamed upon me.*"

Obviously, Kelvin's views (being consistent with the literal Biblical interpretation) maintained doubt in even the most scientific mind until it was realized that Einstein's *equivalency* of mass and energy ($E = mC^2$) was also applicable to an *interconversion* of mass and energy (in nuclear fission or fusion). Long-lived ($t_{1/2} \sim 10^9$ years) radioisotopes (of U, Th, K) in the core of the earth literally have kept the core hot and molten since its consolidation (4.5 billion years ago).[60]

Within this context, the geologists (James Hutton (1726-1797); William Smith (1769-1839) and Charles Lyell (1797-1875)) who studied the mineral deposits of the earth, especially layers of sedimentary rock, were attempting to rationalize what they saw. What they saw was a slow process of erosion and deposition in which layer was laid upon layer in chronological order (i.e., geologic superposition). Although Noah's great Biblical flood, could account for sedimentary rock in concept; it could not readily account for the multi-layered progression in detail. In particular, coal became economically important in the 1600s and its relationship to other strata became a topic if great interest. Close examination of coal and sedimentary rocks revealed fossils of plants and animals that did not currently exist in that location or in any known location.

------

[60] Moreover, volcanoes are not a manifestation of the core. The earth's mantle is warmed and set into motion by fluidity of the core, but the surface eruptions appear to be energized by both radioactive heating and frictional heating as tectonic plates grind together.

The Bible and Humans

Europeans knew that there were geographically identifiable populations of mutually fertile humans that had homogeneously different appearance (e.g., skin color), and different cultures. [61] Various European authors classified these populations as *races* of humans. All of these human races recognized by 1500, had built complex societies and advanced technology. Their differences seemed only dependent on their geography and the associated climate. In general, the human races had only slightly different shades of skin color, while hair and facial characteristics were pleasant to European eyes. Indeed, within the European population, red hair and freckles (e.g., among the Irish) and blond hair (among the Scandinavians and Germans) were probably bigger variations than seen between Europeans and Asians or

---

[61] Our understanding of human evolution and biology are still incomplete and indeed we still labor under Darwinism, which dates from the 1850s. Darwinism is defended strongly in the academic community because it is right regarding *evolution* and Darwin is still attacked by fundamental Christians who continue to wield social power. Darwin's main contribution was the legitimizing of the scientific view to the upper classes of Britain. Unfortunately, I believe he got the idea of *speciation* wrong and the uncritical defense of Darwin in academia has undermined a real understanding of speciation. Of course, I have written books on the topic: *Asymmetric Division, Stem Cells and the Immortal Strand Hypothesis* (2014), *The Hopeful Monster Finds a Mate & Application to Speciation in Hominidae* (2014), *Evolution-Development and the Master Development Program Hypothesis* (2016), and *Chimps Descended from Humans* (2013) all available on amazon/kindle and related papers available on the internet. I think it will be another hundred years before these issues are sorted out among academics, and more time will be required for the ideas to sink into the general public.

North Africans (Egyptians, Moors) or Amerindians. Moreover, there were no even-vaguely similar humanoid species co-located with any of these obviously *human* races who were known to be mutually fertile with Europeans.

The idea that, in creation, God produced all species of plants and animals in their *final* form and that they did not change in time was introduced. In Europe, Georges-Louis Leclerc, Comte de Buffon (1707-1788, generally known as "Buffon") proposed that all humans had arisen from Adam and Eve and had adapted (very quickly) into a variety of (generally degenerate) groups under the influence of their environment.[62] Johann Friedrich Blumenbach (1752–1840) studied human anatomy and published his thesis (1775) *On the Natural Varieties of Mankind*, which concluded that there were five major groups of humans that were all part of the same species. But, recognizing that the observed morphology changes in humans did not take place as rapidly as required by these theories to be consistent with the Biblical story of creation, their ideas were replaced by a theory that had some experimental support. However, if the entire human population evolved from Biblical Adam and Eve, it was difficult to explain the varieties of humans that were turning up as the European explorers fanned out around the earth in the 1500s and 1600s. The Biblical story required a single human species descending from Adam and Eve.

---

[62] His ideas were not widely known and even Darwin only belatedly read his hypotheses.

The Bible and Human Relations

Slavery is clearly a prominent feature in Biblical society (*Genesis 30* provides one interesting example):

> **Genesis 30:9** *"Meanwhile, Leah realized that she was not getting pregnant anymore, so she took her servant, Zilpah and gave her to Jacob as a wife."*

Genesis 30:32-43 is a little too long to quote, but provides a look into the level of understanding of genetics that was present thousands of years earlier and still venerated in the 1800s. The situation of being a slave was not related to any particular race.

The Bible clearly assumed male domination over females, polygamy, and recognized slavery; while prohibiting homosexuality.

Consideration of the Sub-Saharan Africans

The explorations of the Portuguese along the west coast of Africa (1500s) in an attempt to circumvent the Muslims (who had a monopoly on cotton products and spices being imported into Europe) produced an unexpected discovery. The Muslims had already penetrated deep into Africa. The occasional black African that arrived in Iberia, Italy, Greece or Egypt had been viewed as rare and unique individuals. The Portuguese discovered that these individuals were merely representatives of large populations of Africans who were mostly out of sight of Europeans, south of the Sahara Desert.

These black African populations were particularly mysterious because there were commingled with a variety of other primates: monkeys, baboons, chimpanzees, and gorilla. Suddenly, the organization of life on earth was very complicated. I believe that this complexity of quasi-bipedal and bipedal species similar to recognized humans (but not within the envelop of the recognized limits of human races) is one of the things that challenged the Biblical view of creation and got the ball rolling on the concept of evolution.[63]

This would have all remained an interesting academic debate, except for one thing. The Muslims had demonstrated that black Africans could be usefully enslaved and were tolerant of tropical climates.

---

[63] At this point, I want to jump forward and interject some modern understanding into this situation. We now know that black Africans are fully members of the species *Homo sapiens*. The genetic make-up of native Africans is much more diverse that non-Africans because the modern human species has been evolving in Africa for about a million years; while there have only been two or three waves of migration from Africa that have merely sampled sub-groups of the African genetic diversity. Thus, the African phenotypes show ranges of variation greater than the non-African population spread over five continents. These various phenotypes appear as different races of Africans, some of which (i.e., Mediterranean Africans) are very similar to the waves of Africans that established non-African races, which Europeans have been familiar with since antiquity. We also know that the resistance to malaria (the most devastating tropical disease) shown in some Africans is real and related to adverse mutations that help infants survive to puberty (around 12 years of age).

As we have seen in earlier discussion of the Atlantic slave trade, when Europeans discovered and determined to exploit and/or colonize the New World, they soon found that Native Americans were not effective slaves because they were ravaged by Old World diseases including malaria, which the Europeans brought with them.[64] Thus, the idea of importing black Africans (sold by black Africans who had been converted to Islam to avoid enslavement themselves by Muslims) to the New World was introduced. As discussed above, the black Africans were regarded as animal labor…they did not fall within the phenotypic envelop of the *recognized human races of 1600*; thus, there was no (and could not be any) moral question. Humans had dominion over all the animals of the earth and were to use them to their best advantage.

But, as soon as black Africans were introduced into any sort of domestic European situation, Europeans began having suspicions that black Africans, (while perhaps not truly human in European eyes in 1700) were not mere animals. By 1800, the debate had shifted to the question of are black Africans any less human than Europeans. And the shift in this thinking is what spawned the abolitionist movement.

---

[64] Guerra F. 1993. The European-American exchange. *Hist Philos Life Sci.* 15(3):313-27.

Rodrigues PT et al. 2018. Human migration and the spread of malaria parasites to the New World. *Sci Rep.* 8(1):1993.

Thomas Jefferson was one of the first to speculate about the moral
situation evolving from our scientific understanding of the
biological status of black Africans. He was one of the most
scientifically knowledgeable and analytical men of the early
American period. His views were not (in my opinion) typical
because he was an exceptional scholar, politician and human
being. Thus, it is very interesting to see what he thought about
slavery and slaves. In general, it is well known that Jefferson and
his mentor George Wythe worked towards the freeing of slaves
(we see it in his efforts of the North West Territories and the *Notes
on the State of Virginia* (1784)).

***Thomas Jefferson,
Notes on the State of Virginia,
Query 14 137--43
1784***

[This is a discussion related to a bill he placed before the
Virginia Legislature]

*To emancipate all slaves born after passing the act. The bill reported
by the revisors does not itself contain this proposition; but an
amendment containing it was prepared, to be offered to the legislature
whenever the bill should be taken up, and further directing, that they
should continue with their parents to a certain age, then be brought
up, at the public expence, to tillage, arts or sciences, according to their
geniusses, till the females should be eighteen, and the males twenty-
one years of age, when they should be colonized to such place as the
circumstances of the time should render most proper, sending them*

---

out with arms, implements of houshold and of the handicraft arts, seeds, pairs of the useful domestic animals, &c. to declare them a free and independant people, and extend to them our alliance and protection, till they shall have acquired strength; and to send vessels at the same time to other parts of the world for an equal number of white inhabitants; to induce whom to migrate hither, proper encouragements were to be proposed.

[It is evident that he is advocating for gradual emancipation by breaking the chain of generational slavery. But like many others, he sees separation of the races as the proper solution. And, he explains why below with a rather pessimistic view.]

It will probably be asked, Why not retain and incorporate the blacks into the state, and thus save the expence of supplying, by importation of white settlers, the vacancies they will leave? Deep rooted prejudices entertained by the whites; ten thousand recollections, by the blacks, of the injuries they have sustained; new provocations; the real distinctions which nature has made; and many other circumstances, will divide us into parties, and produce convulsions which will probably never end but in the extermination of the one or the other race.

--To these objections, which are political, may be added others, which are physical and moral.

[Jefferson first enumerates physical differences based on his observations and the science available to him in his day. He begins with beauty and then discusses behaviors.]

The first difference which strikes us is that of colour. Whether the black of the negro resides in the reticular membrane between the skin and scarf-skin, or in the scarfskin itself; whether it proceeds from the colour of the blood, the colour of the bile, or from that of some other secretion, the difference is fixed in nature, and is as real as if its seat and cause were better known to us. And is this difference of no importance? Is it not the foundation of a greater or less share of beauty in the two races? Are not the fine mixtures of red and white, the expressions of every passion by greater or less suffusions of colour in the one [blushing typical of Europeans]*, preferable to that eternal monotony, which reigns in the countenances, that immoveable veil of black which covers all the emotions of the other race? Add to these, flowing hair, a more elegant symmetry of form, their own judgment in favour of the whites, declared by their preference of them* [he says black men prefer white women]*, as uniformly as is the preference of the Oran-ootan* [orangutan] *for the black women over those of his own species.*

[Taken out of context this could be very insulting, but Jefferson is stating what he believes to be scientific fact.]

 The circumstance of superior beauty, is thought worthy attention in the propagation of our horses, dogs, and other domestic animals; why not in that of man?

[There are many dog breeds and there were bred for function…healthy efficient animals are beautiful.]

Besides those of colour, figure, and hair, there are other physical distinctions proving a difference of race. They [Africans] have less hair on the face and body. They secrete less by the kidnies, and more by the glands of the skin, which gives them a very strong and disagreeable odour. This greater degree of transpiration renders them more tolerant of heat, and less so of cold, than the whites. Perhaps too a difference of structure in the pulmonary apparatus, which a late ingenious experimentalist has discovered to be the principal regulator of animal heat, may have disabled them from extricating, in the act of inspiration, so much of that fluid from the outer air, or obliged them in expiration, to part with more of it.

[Jefferson appears to be familiar with very recent (1783) experiments on heat generation by animals during respiration by Lavoisier[65] in France using an ice calorimeter. That is an impressive knowledge of contemporary science.]

They seem to require less sleep. A black, after hard labour through the day, will be induced by the slightest amusements to sit up till midnight, or later, though knowing he must be out with the first dawn of the morning.

They are at least as brave, and more adventuresome. But this may perhaps proceed from a want of forethought, which prevents their seeing a danger till it be present. When present, they do not go through it with more coolness or steadiness than the whites.

---

[65] Memoir on heat. Read to the Royal Academy of Sciences, 28 June 1783.

They are more ardent after their female: but love seems with them to be more an eager desire, than a tender delicate mixture of sentiment and sensation.

Their griefs are transient. Those numberless afflictions, which render it doubtful whether heaven has given life to us in mercy or in wrath, are less felt, and sooner forgotten with them. In general, their existence appears to participate more of sensation than reflection. To this must be ascribed their disposition to sleep when abstracted from their diversions, and unemployed in labour. An animal whose body is at rest, and who does not reflect, must be disposed to sleep of course.

[Jefferson now moves to the very touchy subject of intellect.]

Comparing them by their faculties of memory, reason, and imagination, it appears to me, that in memory they are equal to the whites; in reason much inferior, as I think one could scarcely be found capable of tracing and comprehending the investigations of Euclid; and that in imagination they are dull, tasteless, and anomalous.

[This is a rather harsh assessment made by a man with very high intellectual standards. But he modifies it below explaining that it is speculation and requires more study.]

It would be unfair to follow them to Africa for this investigation. We will consider them here, on the same stage with the whites, and where the facts are not apocryphal on which a judgment is to be formed. It will be right to make great allowances for the difference of condition, of education, of conversation, of the sphere in which they move. Many millions of them have been brought to, and born in America. Most of them indeed have been confined to tillage, to their own homes, and their own society: yet many have been so situated, that they might have availed themselves of the conversation of their masters; many have been brought up to the handicraft arts, and from that circumstance have always been associated with the whites. Some have been liberally educated, and all have lived in countries where the arts and sciences are cultivated to a considerable degree, and have had before their eyes samples of the best works from abroad.

[Here he compares Africans to Native Americans.]

The Indians, with no advantages of this kind, will often carve figures on their pipes not destitute of design and merit. They will crayon out an animal, a plant, or a country, so as to prove the existence of a germ in their minds which only wants cultivation. They astonish you with strokes of the most sublime oratory; such as prove their reason and sentiment strong, their imagination glowing and elevated. But never yet could I find that a black had uttered a thought above the level of plain narration; never see even an elementary trait of painting or sculpture. In music they are more generally gifted than the whites with accurate ears for tune and time, and they have been found capable of imagining a small catch. [catch = rhyme, think rap music] *Whether they will be equal to the composition of a more extensive run of melody, or of complicated harmony, is yet to be proved.*

Misery is often the parent of the most affecting touches in poetry.-- Among the blacks is misery enough, God knows, but no poetry. Love is the peculiar oestrum of the poet. Their love is ardent, but it kindles the senses only, not the imagination. Religion indeed has produced a Phyllis Whately [Phillis Wheatley]; *but it could not produce a poet.*

> *The compositions published under her name are below the dignity of criticism.*
>
> [Some believe that Phyllis Wheatley is a superior poet. However, Jefferson seems to be skeptical of her authorship and derogatory in this criticism perhaps because her poetry appears to support the slave-trader's view that removing her from Africa was an act of mercy. [66]]
>
> *The heroes of the Dunciad are to her, as Hercules to the author of that poem. Ignatius Sancho has approached nearer to merit in composition; yet his letters do more honour to the heart than the head. They breathe the purest effusions of friendship and general philanthropy, and shew how great a degree of the latter may be compounded with strong religious zeal. He is often happy in the turn of his compliments, and his stile is easy and familiar, except when he affects a Shandean fabrication of words. But his imagination is wild and extravagant, escapes incessantly from every restraint of reason and taste, and, in the course of its vagaries, leaves a tract of thought as incoherent and eccentric, as is the course of a meteor through the sky. His subjects should often have led him to a process of sober reasoning: yet we find*

[66] You may judge Phyllis Wheatley's poetry for yourself:

> *Twas mercy brought me from my Pagan land,*
> *Taught my benighted soul to understand*
> *That there's a God, that there's a Saviour too:*
> *Once I redemption neither sought nor knew.*
> *Some view our sable race with scornful eye,*
> *"Their colour is a diabolic dye."*
> *Remember, Christians, Negroes, black as Cain,*
> *May be refin'd, and join th' angelic train.*

him always substituting sentiment for demonstration. Upon the whole, though we admit him to the first place among those of his own colour who have presented themselves to the public judgment, yet when we compare him with the writers of the race among whom he lived, and particularly with the epistolary class, in which he has taken his own stand, we are compelled to enroll him at the bottom of the column. This criticism supposes the letters published under his name to be genuine, and to have received amendment from no other hand; points which would not be of easy investigation.

[Nature or Nurture]

The improvement of the blacks in body and mind, in the first instance of their mixture with the whites, has been observed by every one, and proves that their inferiority is not the effect merely of their condition of life. We know that among the Romans, about the Augustan age especially, the condition of their slaves was much more deplorable than that of the blacks on the continent of America. The two sexes were confined in separate apartments, because to raise a child cost the master more than to buy one. Cato, for a very restricted indulgence to his slaves in this particular, took from them a certain price. But in this country [the US] the slaves multiply as fast as the free inhabitants. Their situation and manners place the commerce between the two sexes almost without restraint.

--The same Cato, on a principle of oeconomy, always sold his sick and superannuated slaves. He gives it as a standing precept to a master visiting his farm, to sell his old oxen, old waggons, old tools, old and diseased servants, and every thing else [that] become useless. "Vendat boves vetulos, plaustrum vetus, ferramenta, vetera, servum senem,

servum morbosum, & si quid aliud supersit vendat." The American slaves cannot enumerate this among the injuries and insults they receive.

It was the common practice to expose in the island of Aesculapius, in the Tyber, diseased slaves, whose cure was like to become tedious. The Emperor Claudius, by an edict, gave freedom to such of them as should recover, and first declared, that if any person chose to kill rather than to expose them, it should be deemed homicide. The exposing them [slaves in the US] is a crime of which no instance has existed with us; and were it to be followed by death, it would be punished capitally.

We are told of a certain Vedius Pollio, who, in the presence of Augustus, would have given a slave as food to his fish, for having broken a glass.

With the Romans, the regular method of taking the evidence of their slaves was under torture. Here [in the US] it has been thought better never to resort to their evidence.

When a master was murdered [in Rome], all his slaves, in the same house, or within hearing, were condemned to death. Here [in the US] punishment falls on the guilty only, and as precise proof is required against him as against a freeman.

Yet notwithstanding these and other discouraging circumstances among the Romans, their slaves were often their rarest artists. They excelled too in science, insomuch as to be usually employed as tutors to their master's children. Epictetus, Diogenes, Phaedon, Terence, and

Phaedrus, were slaves. But they were of the race of whites. It is not their condition then, but nature, which has produced the distinction.

--Whether further observation will or will not verify the conjecture, that nature has been less bountiful to them [Africans] in the endowments of the head, I believe that in those of the heart she will be found to have done them justice. That disposition to theft with which they [African slaves] have been branded, must be ascribed to their situation, and not to any depravity of the moral sense. The man, in whose favour no laws of property exist, probably feels himself less bound to respect those made in favour of others. When arguing for ourselves, we lay it down as a fundamental, that laws, to be just, must give a reciprocation of right: that, without this, they are mere arbitrary rules of conduct, founded in force, and not in conscience: and it is a problem which I give to the master to solve, whether the religious precepts against the violation of property were not framed for him as well as his slave? And whether the slave may not as justifiably take a little from one, who has taken all from him, as he may slay one who would slay him? That a change in the relations in which a man is placed should change his ideas of moral right and wrong, is neither new, nor peculiar to the colour of the blacks.

Homer tells us it was so 2600 years ago.
(Od. 17. 323.)
Jove fix'd it certain, that whatever day
Makes man a slave, takes half his worth away.

But the slaves of which Homer speaks were whites. Notwithstanding these considerations which must weaken their respect for the laws of property, we find among them [African slaves] numerous instances of the most rigid integrity, and as many as among their better instructed masters, of benevolence, gratitude, and unshaken fidelity.

[Here Jefferson qualifies his assessments and acknowledges that his data are anecdotal.]

--The opinion, that they [African slaves] *are inferior in the faculties of reason and imagination, must be hazarded with great diffidence. To justify a general conclusion, requires many observations, even where the subject may be submitted to the Anatomical knife, to Optical glasses, to analysis by fire, or by solvents. How much more then where it is a faculty, not a substance, we are examining; where it eludes the research of all the senses; where the conditions of its existence are various and variously combined; where the effects of those which are present or absent bid defiance to calculation; let me add too, as a circumstance of great tenderness, where our conclusion would degrade a whole race of men from the rank in the scale of beings which their Creator may perhaps have given them. To our reproach it must be said, that though for a century and a half we have had under our eyes the races of black and of red men, they have never yet been viewed by us as subjects of natural history. I advance it therefore as a suspicion only, that the blacks, whether originally a distinct race, or made distinct by time and circumstances, are inferior to the whites in the endowments both of body and mind. It is not against experience to suppose, that different species of the same genus, or varieties of the same species, may possess different qualifications. Will not a lover of natural history then, one who views the gradations in all the races of animals with the eye of philosophy, excuse an effort to keep those in the department of man as distinct as nature has formed them? This unfortunate difference of colour, and perhaps of faculty, is a powerful*

> *obstacle to the emancipation of these people. Many of their advocates,*
> *while they wish to vindicate the liberty of human nature, are anxious*
> *also to preserve its dignity and beauty. Some of these, embarrassed by*
> *the question "What further is to be done with them?" join themselves*
> *in opposition with those who are actuated by sordid avarice only.*
> *Among the Romans emancipation required but one effort. The slave,*
> *when made free, might mix with, without staining the blood of his*
> *master. But with us a second is necessary, unknown to history. When*
> *freed, he is to be removed beyond the reach of mixture.*

Thus, after setting out anecdotal evidence as he saw it, Jefferson cautioned:

> *I advance it therefore as a suspicion only, that the blacks, whether*
> *originally a distinct race, or made distinct by time and*
> *circumstances, are inferior to the whites in the endowments both*
> *of body and mind. It is not against experience to suppose, that*
> *different species of the same genus, or varieties of the same*
> *species, may possess different qualifications.*

He goes on to point out that the concern of mixing races is the ultimate barrier to emancipation:

> *Among the Romans emancipation required but one effort. The*
> *slave, when made free, might mix with, without staining the*
> *blood of his master. But with us a second is necessary, unknown*
> *to history. When freed, he is to be removed beyond the reach of*
> *mixture.*

Human Race or Separate Species

To a large extent the scientific debate between 1783 and 1861 regarding the place of black Africans was boiled down first to the question of whether black Africans were an entirely different species or merely a separate race of humans.

The Biblical story required a single human species descending from Adam and Eve. That position was expressed in America by Reverend Doctor Samuel Stanhope Smith (1751 – 1819) of the College of New Jersey (now Princeton). Thus, Smith's problem was to explain the differences (skin color, hair texture, head shape, etc.) on the basis of factors that did not cross the line from one species to another. This was going to be tricky especially because Europeans had become aware of human-like primates co-existing in central Africa with the black Africans. Chimpanzees and Gorilla were found in exactly the same geographical regions as black Africans. Orangutans were found co-locates with other "lower" humans. It was a legitimate question to ask what the relationships were between Europeans, black Africans, Chimpanzees and Gorillas. Remember evolution was not an accepted concept to Jefferson and speciation is still poorly understood (Darwin not withstanding).

To an extent, this question had already been raised with respect to other non-Europeans that were clearly humans. Moreover, the fact that Europeans were the group that was travelling and finding these other groups made it easy for Europeans to believe themselves to be superior to the all the other groups. The issue of religion came into play here also since Europeans were Christian and any culture that was unfamiliar with the Judeo-Christian history must not have been favored by God. God had delegated the task of passing his religion to these groups (e.g., the Amerindians, and Chinese) to the Europeans. To do this, any pagan religion was to be stamped out. When the various codices of the Aztecs and Mayans were discovered by Spanish, they were initially not understood and might have survived as historical documents after the Spanish conquest (1521). Unfortunately, in 1562 a Spanish priest (Bishop Diego de Landa) began the systematic destruction of thousands of these documents because he saw them as elements of a pagan religion that was in the way of Christianity.

Presumably to counter these issues, Samuel Stanhope Smith published *Essay on the Causes and Varieties of Complexion and Figure in the Human Species* (1787) with the purpose of *"establishing the unity of the human species."* His principal rationale (and as it turns out the only one that really matters) was that members of the same species are known to interbreed and produce viable and mutually fertile offspring. In contrast, sexual encounters between different species do not produce viable individuals except in the cases of very close relationships (e.g., horse and donkey); and even then, the resulting offspring (mules and hennies) are not fertile with one another or either of the parent species.

The only problem with this argument (*circa* 1800) was that people defined species based on physical appearance. The idea that physical appearance determine species has died hard (if it has died at all). [67] With appearance as the critical criteria, the fact that (for example) dogs and wolves can produce fertile offspring while certain animals that looked very much the same cannot produce fertile offspring caused a muddying of the waters (i.e., mutual fertility was not recognized as the unique criterion for determining speciation). Thus, Stanhope Smith fell back to a different argument namely that the climate (e.g., latitude) could affect substantial changes in just a few generations. Although there had been enough black Africans living in New England long enough to cast doubt on climate as the immediate explanation for the differences in physical appearance, the idea had a certain appeal. Namely, by claiming the change in climate as a reason why black Africans in New England were starting to lighter skin tones, the many European men who had fathered mulatto children with their house slaves could both appease their wives and their preachers. Ironically, there was a black African (Henry Moss) who became famous about this time because, for reasons that are not understood, he began to lose his skin pigment and advertised himself as a black man who was turning white under the influences of his new environment.

Benjamin Rush (1746 – 1813), a Philadelphia physician and scientist, was a friend of Jefferson. Rush was also a well-established opponent of slavery, although he owned a slave

---

[67] I refer you to my books and papers on the subject of speciation, especially The *Hopeful Monster Finds a Mate & Application to Speciation in Hominidae* Kindle Edition (2014) and The Hopeful Monster Finds a Mate and Founds a New Species. *Hypotheses in the Life Sciences* Vol 1, No 2 (2011) (http://www.hy-ls.org/index.php/hyls/article/view/53/0.html).

(perhaps for the sake of scientific observation). Rush argued that there was no difference in the intellect of Africans and Europeans. In 1792, Rush offered up a hopeful hypothesis that black Africans were suffering from a form of leprosy that accounted for their appearance and which might one day be cured.

Philadelphia 4th Feby: 1797.

DEAR SIR

Your <u>Communication</u> upon the Subject of the large Claws, and bones of the <u>Lyon kind Animal</u>, will arrive time en'o to have a place in the Volume of the transactions of the philosophical Society which is now in the press. I have Often been struck with the Analogy of things in the natural, moral and political world. The Animals whose stupendous remains we now and then pick up in our Country, were Once probably the tyrants of our forests, and have perhaps been extirpated by a Confederacy, and insurrection of beasts of less force individually than themselves. In like manner, may We not hope that kings will be extirpated from the face of the earth by a general insurrection of the reason and Virtue of man, and that the exhibition of crowns, Sceptres and maces, like the claws and bones of extinct Animals, shall be necessary to prove to posterity, that such canibals ever existed upon our globe?

Your Philadelphia friends will rejoice in taking you by the hand After the 3rd: of March. Dr. Priestley who will be in town at that time, longs for the pleasure of your Acquaintance. You will be Charmed with his extensive information, and amiable Simplicity of manners. I will give you a Specimen of his republicanism. "The time (said he to me) will I hope one day come, when laws shall govern so completely, that a man shall be a month in America without knowing who is President of the United States."

I am now preparing a <u>paper</u> for our Society in which I have Attempted to prove, that the black Color (as it is called) of the Negroes is the effect of a disease in the Skin of the Leprous kind. The inferences

---

> *from it will be in favor of treating them with humanity, and justice, and of keeping up the existing prejudices against matrimonial connextions with them.*
>
>   *Adieu. From Dr Sir your Sincere, and Affectionate friend*
>   BENJN: RUSH

The inclination towards invoking a disease to explain the appearance of black Africans was particularly attractive because it (i) maintained the Biblical unity of the *immutable* human species descending from Adam and Eve, (ii) it was potentially curable, (iii) it suggested that from a moral and political position black Africans should be treated as equals, (iv) but it maintained the bias against intermarriage.[68] Even among European men who ventured to have sex with black or mulatto women, there was a nagging fear that even if the initial progeny appeared normal, some adverse disease would present itself in a future generation.[69]

---

[68] Note that the idea of commutable diseases (i.e., the germ theory) was not presented until 1860-64 by work done by Louis Pasteur. Had the germ theory of disease been accepted at the time in the early 1700s, it would have also supported segregation, ended the slave trade, and perhaps encouraged the repatriation of blacks to Africa. There is a difference between being *cautious* and being *prejudiced.*

[69] Based on the information available at the time, this was a rational fear and has some factual basis in genetic diseases (e.g., sickle cell). The work of Gregor Mendel (1822-1884) on inheritance (done 1856-63) was not widely known until it was rediscovered about 1900 by Hugo de Vries (1848-1935), Carl Correns (1864-1935), and Erik Tschermak (1871-1962).

Nonetheless, compared to the *recognized races of the human species*, black Africans' skin was much darker even jet black, their hair was a completely different texture, they lived in a tribal stone-age culture (without major structures[70] and without a written language[71]) and the small vestiges of civilization they displayed seemed to have been impressed on them by the North African Muslims.

Perhaps more important and confusing to Europeans, black Africans were co-located with primate species that were clearly not human (i.e., chimpanzees and gorilla). Samuel Thomas von Sömmerring (1755 – 1830) a widely respected German anatomist conducted autopsy dissections of black Africans and (according to

---

[70] The most impressive structures were adobe buildings primarily on the fringes of the desert which suggested Muslim influences.

[71] There are a few scripts used in sub-Saharan Africa such as Nsibidi (between Nigeria and Cameroon) but they were not widely used or universally understood even locally. In contrast, the Aztecs (representing Amerindians) had a sophisticated written language and recorded history, as well as advanced stone structures and central government. The Incas were similar. The North American tribes used symbols and quickly adopted the horse when it was made available. There were highly organized "mound builders" in the mid-west and south east. The Cherokee engaged in sophisticated negotiations, treaties and trade with the Europeans as early as the 1750s. Upon realizing the value of written language, the Cherokee invented a written language and within a generation had broad enough literacy to warrant publishing a bilingual newspaper in 1828. They argued the issue of removal in the US Supreme Court in the 1830. And the Cherokee owned black African slaves.

Stanton, 1960, p. 10) published *"that the negro was anatomically much closer to the ape than was the white."* French naturalist/physician Julien-Joseph Virey (1775-1846) wrote a *History of Mankind* from which was extracted and translated into English a document known as *Natural History of the Negro Race* (1837).[72] Virey concludes that sub-Saharan Africans constitute a separate species, which has many black African races:

> *"Every thing serves to prove that the negroes form, not only a race, but undoubtedly a distinct species, from the beginning of the world,[73] as we see other species among other living beings."*

Virey quotes von Sömmerring at length; and von Sömmerring makes a number of affirmative comparisons between black Africans and "apes." I take it to mean that when the black Africans and the *recognized human races* (i.e., every group except the sub-Saharan populations) were compared to the (less similar) apes, the black Africans were judged to have more anatomy in common with the apes than the *recognized human races* of the 1800s.[74] This interpretation by Virey et al. is remarkable (i.e., unexpected) because von Sömmerring was a supporter of the idea that black Africans were merely another race of humans (not a whole different species).

---

[72] Please see my review in the references. This document incorporated a large volume of anecdotal comments and influenced thought in the United States.

[73] Biblical creationism, pre-Darwin.

[74] I am not an anatomist and cannot judge von Sömmerring's work.

Ironically, the fact that black Africans were mutually fertile with Europeans and Arabs was not considered conclusive evidence of belonging to the human species. Indeed, it raised fears. Ultimately, the question for people in the mid-1800s became whether or not a *species* or *racial* distinction was justified by objective (scientific) differences. This distinction, however, was actually no more than an academic quibble. In either event, black Africans could be interpreted as subordinate to all (other) humans.

The notion of evolution of species was at the time frustrated by the Biblical short history of the earth and no apparent mechanism to create new species or for species to evolve. For example, Louis Agassiz (1807 – 1873) was born is Switzerland and became world famous for his classifications of fish and fossil fish. But his religious beliefs led him to the idea that God had created each species so as to be efficient in the environment that it was found (i.e., polygenism). He could not accept the idea that animals migrated and adapted to new environments because of his belief that the earth was only a few thousand years old. Nonetheless, there were notable people that suspected that evolution (i.e., change in *morphology* and *physiology* and *intellect*) accounted for differences in humans and the differences among species.

Meanwhile, various scientists were embarking on observational analysis of racial differences among humans. Samuel G. Morton (1799 – 1851) was born a Quaker in Philadelphia, and attended the University of Pennsylvania (1820). After study at the University of Edinburgh in Scotland, Morton began a medical practice in Philadelphia in 1824. Morton was also operating under the belief that the earth was only a few thousand years old. In 1830, he prepared a document entitled *The Different Forms of the Skull as Exhibited in the Five Races of Men*. Nonetheless, he apparently concluded that (given the Biblical parameters) what he originally called "races" should be classified as separately created "species," i.e., the result of polygenism. He then proceeded to solicit scientific colleagues and their acquaintances from around the world to send him human skulls for study. His chief method of comparison was by measuring the volume of the brain case. In 1839, he published *Crania Americana, An Inquiry into the Distinctive Characteristics of the Aboriginal Race of America*, which contained the most widespread data on skull volume: Caucasians 1,426 cc, Native Americans 1,344 cc and black Africans 1,278 cc. He discussed this data in terms of the contemporary prejudices regarding intellect and it was taken as a firm rationale for not only dividing humans into different species but also ranking them relative to one another.

The father of George Robbins Gliddon (1809 – 1857) was US consul to Egypt and brought his son to Alexandria at an early age. George Gliddon was raised almost entirely in Egypt and became a vice consul himself. Interestingly, he wrote *Memoir on the Cotton of Egypt* (1841) and became a source of skulls for Samuel George Morton's second book *Crania Aegyptiaca* (1844). In 1843, Gliddon made a tour of South Carolina with a draft of Morton's book. The motivation for this trip is unclear; it is possible he was invited by James H. Hammond, who may have met him during his grand tour of Europe (1836-37). Hammond had just been elected governor of South Carolina (1842). But more likely Gliddon correctly viewed South Carolina as a likely market for Morton's book. Hammond may have referred Gliddon to John C. Calhoun, whom he met in Washington, D.C. Calhoun got Morton involved with an ongoing controversy regarding the 1840 census. Namely, the incidence of insanity reported among Africans appeared to increase from south to north.

Meanwhile another physician entered the picture. Josiah C. Nott (1804 - 1873) of South Carolina obtained a medical degree from the University of Pennsylvania in 1828 (shortly after Morton) and set up practice in Mobile, Alabama in 1833. Apparently, he had patients of all races and developed some anecdotal opinions about mixed-race women, which he published in 1844.[75] I have been unable to find the original article(s) but the title "The Mulatto a Hybrid — Probable Extermination of the Two Races if the Whites and Blacks Are Allowed to Intermarry" suggests to me that his original concern was that given the fact that he states

> "I have found it impossible, nevertheless, to collect such statistics as would be satisfactory to others on this point; and the difficulty arises solely from the want of chastity among mulatto women, which is so notorious as to be proverbial." (Excerpts/Quotes on 2013-08-02 04:25Z by Steven)

would lead me to surmise that his concern would be that the entre populations would soon be mulatto. However, other

---

[75] Josiah Nott. 1843. The Mulatto a Hybrid — Probable Extermination of the Two Races if the Whites and Blacks Are Allowed to Intermarry, *American Journal of the Medical Sciences.* 255: 56.

interpretations seem to imply that mulattos are not as viable as either "pure" race. This idea was circulating at least until 1892.[76]

In any event, Morton read this article and sent Nott an encouraging note. Thus, Nott quickly absorbed Morton's views and befriended Gliddon.[77]

These provincial deductions from anecdotes framed by a Biblical time table received a major endorsement when the imminent natural historian Louis Agassiz (mentioned above) came to America to lecture at Harvard and visited Morton in Philadelphia in 1846. Ironically, this was the first time that Agassiz had ever seen a black African at close range and his initial reaction was revulsion. Thus, he was immediately interested in Morton's apparent experimental confirmation of their mutually held "separate species" (polygenism) theory. Agassiz received a permanent position at Harvard in 1847 and was greatly influential in scientific policy regarding Africans during and after the War between the States. In 1847, he clearly endorsed the idea that Europeans and Africans are separate species (not merely related

---

[76] Alleged Extinction of Mulatto. Howe JL. *Science*. 1892 Dec 30;20(517):375.

[77] It is interesting that Nott gave a number of public lectures on his views and frequently invoked the power of science bringing up the names of luminaries including Galileo. In what has become known as the "corner stone speech" by Alexander H. Stephens (in Savannah, Georgia, March 21, 1861, see below), Stephens proudly states that the new confederacy is founded on the scientific understanding of the proper relation of white and black people, he also mentions Galileo. This suggests to me that Stephens' political position were derived from Nott's flawed "scientific" analysis.

races). Farrow *et al.* (2005, p. 188) make an important point: in rationalizing the Biblical Garden of Eden, Morton was taking the position that "God did make the Garden of Eden—for whites only."   Gliddon and Nott then collaborated to write the authoritative work on race in *Types of Mankind* published first in 1854. This book confirmed for everyone, including Abraham Lincoln, that black Africans were inferior to white Europeans.

The idea of evolution was neither unique nor original with Charles Darwin (1809-1882). What was limiting public acceptance of the idea of evolution was proof of a *convincing mechanism* of evolution. Jean-Baptiste Lamarck (1744-1829) had produced a "use-driven" mechanism of evolution that required a mysterious intergenerational feedback mechanism where the labors of one generation would be reflected in the anatomy of the next.[78] While

---

[78] In the 20th Century, Trofim Denisovich Lysenko (1898–1976) argued on purely political grounds that experiences in one generation could mold the next. In the context of Stalin's Soviet Union, this theory caused great hardship. However, vernalization does seem to involve mechanisms that do not directly involve genes. Friedrich T, Faivre L, Bäurle I, Schubert D. 2018. Chromatin-based mechanisms of temperature memory in plants. *Plant Cell Environ*. Abstract ahead of print. He Y, Li Z. 2018. Epigenetic Environmental Memories in Plants: Establishment, Maintenance, and Reprogramming. *Trends Genet.* 34(11):856-866.

his supporters could cite rationales for the mechanisms, no one was able to point at experimental evidence for it.

Over a period of years in observing the breeding of pigeons, rabbits, dogs and horses, and reading the work of Thomas Malthus (1766–1834), Charles Darwin (1809-1882) concluded that *natural selection* was the necessary mechanism of evolution. But being an upper-class social leader, he realized that his ideas were contrary to the Biblical doctrine; and he knew that if he came forward with the idea, he would be at the center of a social firestorm. Thus, he only confided his ideas among friends and actually planned to have his hypothesis published after his death. However, a brash young man (Alfred Russel Wallace, 1823-1913) from the lower-classes, who made his meager living collecting exotic insects from around the world and had no anxiety about social criticism, reached the same conclusion and actually sent Darwin a proposed publication from his current field trip in the Malay Archipelago. Darwin described the paper as an accurate abstract of his idea and found himself in an ethical conflict. In consultation with his friends, it was clear that Darwin had provided them a sketch of his idea much earlier and they arranged for his earlier private work to be read *immediately before* reading the paper by Wallace at a scientific gathering: *"On the Tendency of Species to Form Varieties; and on the Perpetuation of Varieties and Species by Natural Means of Selection"* was published with both names in the *Proceedings of the Linnean Society* in 1858. This presentation, indeed, gathered public attention. But the real fireworks started when Darwin hurriedly published the data he had gathered over the previous decades.

It is my view that Darwin wanted to make an *unshared and completely original* scientific contribution to biology. Wallace had diluted (if not usurped) his claim to *evolution*. Thus, I believe, that Darwin felt he had to go farther and address the issue of *speciation*. Specifically, Darwin claimed that *evolution* <u>*causes*</u> *speciation*. And I believe we have continued to live with that mistake to this day.

 In fact, species were not clearly defined at the time that Darwin wrote; and, as noted above, the phenotype was the most obvious basis for defining a species. In the modern view, distinct *biological species* are groups that *cannot* interbreed…hybrids that may be formed between different species must be sterile.[79] If they are not fertile, the "hybrid presumed species" will not persist independently. However, it is now clear that a true species may encompass a wide range of morphologies (influenced by local environments) but the morphologies are not fixed; they are fluid and crosses among the different morphologies (i.e., races, of e.g., Africans and Europeans) of a biological species (e.g., *Homo sapiens*) are fertile.

Darwin entitled his book (short form) *Origin of the Species by Natural Selection*. The book was published in England in 1859, which followed the reading of the original papers on natural selection (1 July 1858). His information shook the British scientific establishment and was instantly popular with the general public. In Darwin's hypothesis (which was widely known in Europe and

---

[79] Or at least not viable more than a few generations as Morton, Nott, Gliddon and Agassiz argued.

the US by 1860), humans and other species shared common
ancestors and had evolved from lower life forms. This idea, of
course, was a complete break from the Biblical view. But
interestingly, it could still be interpreted in a way that endorsed
European (white) supremacy over all other races. It was a very
easy for well-informed Euro-Americans (in 1860) to believe that
the primates of central Africa (i.e., gorilla, chimpanzee, and black-
Africans) represented a "natural" progression of evolution of the
human species culminating in white-Europeans.

© © The Print Collector/Corbis

The White Supremacists' View of Evolution

http://i.dailymail.co.uk/i/pix/2016/03/25/14/328CA577000005
78-3509434-image-a-58_1458915048203.jpg

Indeed, exactly this fallacy was incorporated into a classical
debate between Thomas Henry Huxley (Darwin's major

advocate) and Bishop Samuel Wilberforce[80] (June 30, 1860 at Oxford University). Wilberforce representing the Biblical (Creationist) viewpoint challenged Huxley as follows by asking hypothetically if *"he* [Huxley] *considered himself descended from an ape through his grandmother or grandfather"* (paraphrased at http://darwinday.org/educate/oxforddebate/). To which Huxley responded that he would rather be descended from an ape than be a religious bigot. The image of humans descending from apes was, thus, indelibly inked in all European minds (to this day)!

Although it was certainly clear to intelligent men/women that Europeans and Africans could interbreed, the implications of interbreeding presumably created (less evolved/degenerate mulatto) animals. In short, Darwin's widely-read book (which still dominates our view of evolution) provided an apparently-scientific explanation for the state of civilization in Europe and a convenient rationalization of white-supremacy (i.e., Africans were perceived as "less evolved" humans).

To my critics, and anyone who will consider that Darwin may have erred, please note that I have specifically argued against the model introduced by Darwin, which is still popular today.

---

[80] Samuel (1805-1873) was the third son of William Wilberforce (1759-1833) who had championed abolition of slavery in Britain. Ironically, Samuel's question spawned a public perception that would prolong the idea of genetic white supremacy.

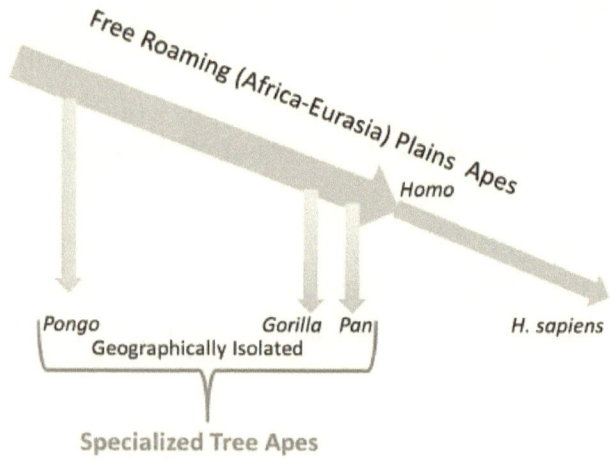

Basically, I argue that modern humans did NOT evolve from chimp-like animals (see chart above). In my view, the other primate genera (*Pongo*, *Gorilla* and *Pan*) actually are (highly evolved) *specializations* from the *Homo* line. In my view, *Pongo*, *Gorilla* and *Pan* evolved (*after speciation events*) to take advantage of the ready supply of vitamin C in tropical fruits that are available only in forest.[81] The *Homo* line has always been mobile

---

[81] Parris GE. *Chimps descended from humans*. 2013. Available on Amazon/kindle.
I do not want to go into a defense of this hypothesis here, but briefly I see speciation as the result of major chromosomal changes (e.g., pericentric inversions) that result in families that can only breed successfully with close relatives. These families however can evolve very rapidly to take advantage of environmental conditions. Specifically, I count the number of inversions between each current species and the common ancestors as an indication of the number of

and explains the existence of *Pongo* in south east Asia as well as the world-wide distribution of humans.

Why was/is the State of Civilization in Central Africa less Developed than Europe?

The differences in physical characteristics between Europeans and sub-Saharan Africans were probably not as important to Europeans (1500-1860) as the differences in their technology and culture. When the Spanish first arrived in Mexico (1520) they realized that Native Americans (Amerindians) had a very sophisticated social structure and had independently developed technologies (e.g., pyramids, written language, organized cities, clothing, and coastal trade (Vista Alegre)) that were less than 5,000 years[82] behind Europeans. While the Europeans enslaved

---

true (extinct) species that have preceded each current species. In my model a new species arises about once every million years. Thus, I am not surprised that modern humans have interbred with Neanderthals, Denisovans, etc. over the last few hundred thousand years. [Slon et al. *Nature*. 2018 Aug 22. The genome of the offspring of a Neanderthal mother and a Denisovan father.]

[82] I arrive at this number by comparing the earliest pyramids in Egypt to the Mayan, Aztec and Inca structures and cities. I would note that the Native Americans were inhibited by the absence of horses, copper and tin, and many of the crops known in the Eurasia-Africa land mass. They worked gold and silver, but the absence of copper and tin prevented the development of a bronze age culture. For edged weapons, they imbedded obsidian into wood. On the other hand, they did not have malaria and when Europeans brought it (1500s) to

Native Americans (as they had enslaved one another), the main reaction of Europeans to Native Americans was fear. Native Americans were (as far as I can tell) never questioned as to their status as humans.

Why had black Africans not achieved the same technological status as Europeans or Amerindians? For practical purposes, when contact first became common (1600s) Central Africans were living in a stone age culture. In parts of Africa, metal work was known and even the complex operations of manufacturing iron were practiced on a small scale, but iron bars used to fabricate tools were a major import item brought by Europeans. These skills had not penetrated into the equatorial African belt. As in Central America, the absence of readily available copper and tin in Central Africa had prevented the development of a transitional bronze age society.[83] Even today, with examples of what is possible all around them, Central Africa is uniquely not a source of technological and social advancement. And it is legitimate to ask why?

America, they had the Cinchona tree and its anti-malarial products (quinine).

[83] Other than rum, the principal trading objects brought by Europeans were iron bars (which could be locally forged into tools and weapons), large knives, pewter and brass bowls, cloth, coral and cowrie shells (*Cypraea moneta*) used as coins (Dow, 1927/2002, p. 51, p. 63, p. 80). Of course, the laws of supply and demand applied in trade. (Note that cowrie is frequently written as cowpie.) The Muslims apparently introduced cowrie shells into trade in west Africa and the Portuguese who controlled the Maldive Islands, where they are plentiful, then used them extensively for trade in the early slave trade.

I have a hypothesis, which I have discussed in other places: The difference in cultural and technological development in Africa and Europe (into the 2000s) I believe, is completely explained by the fact that the human population in central Africa was (and still is) maintained by immigration from the outside into a veritable killing zone of malaria, sleeping sickness and other diseases (now including HIV/AIDS).

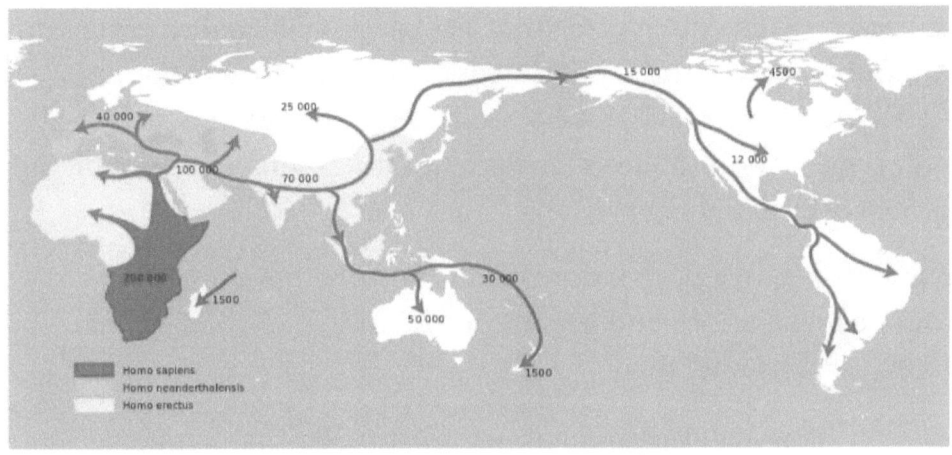

Spreading *Homo sapiens*

Source: Wikimedia Commons

Indeed, I believe that *if immigration into the major equatorial African river basins from the surrounding territories were stopped, humans would become extinct in the mosquito and fly infested regions of equatorial Africa.* I would point out that although modern humans are identified over 200,000 years ago in east Africa, DNA sequencing indicates that humans in tropical equatorial western Africa, have not been there much longer than humans in east Asia (e.g., 50,000 years). This appears to be proof that the human population in west Africa continually dies out and is replenished from the east. The fundamental problem in the past (and even today) is that people did not live long enough in the equatorial river basins (e.g., Gambia, Niger, Congo) to pass information from generation to generation and develop a complex culture built on a progression of technological achievements.

Overall, I believe the disease that primarily inhibits cultural development in equatorial Africa is malaria (which was absent in pre-Columbian Central America and controlled in Europe and Asia). Although malaria is not unique to this area, it is so prevalent that pre-pubescent mortality has routinely run as high as 50% over many generations.

For example, in a population of children who have access to routine inoculations and general health care in Gambia in the 1980s, it was stated that

> *"The infant mortality rate was 142 per 1000 live births and the child mortality rate (death in children aged 1-4 years) 43 per 1000 per year."*[84]

At 5 years of age, thus, the total mortality would be (142 + 215)/1000 = 35.7%. Even if puberty is achieved at only 12 years of age, the pre-pubescent mortality rates must approach 50%. Moreover, it has been argued that in malnourished areas, it is more important to try to suppress malaria than to attempt to grow

---

[84] Greenwood BM *et al.* 1987. Deaths in infancy and early childhood in a well-vaccinated, rural, West African population. *Ann Trop Paediatr.* 7(2):91-9.

more food because of the loss of productivity due to malaria.[85] These are only two of many papers written on the topic; many more papers could be cited regarding pre-pubescent mortality. In addition, it is estimated that *currently* nearly 200,000,000 adults are infected with malaria in central Africa. The incidence is *currently* between 30 and 40% in most countries from which African slaves were taken.

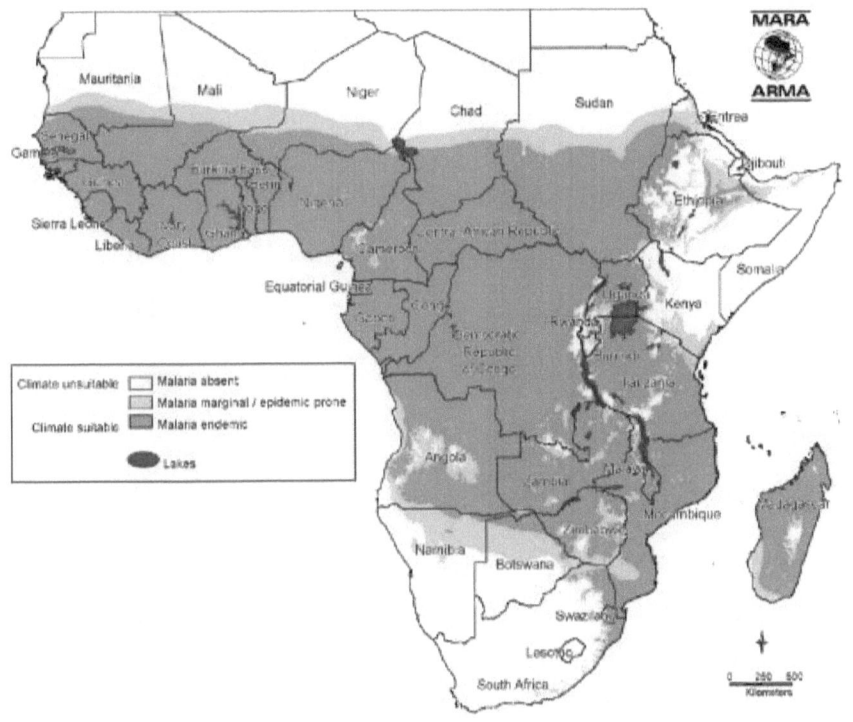

Malaria in Africa

Source: http://www.nap.edu/read/11017/chapter/3#24

---

[85] Wenlock RW. 1981. Endemic malaria, malnutrition and child deaths. *Food Policy*. 6(2):105-12.

The successful species in equatorial Africa (genus *Gorilla* and genus *Pan*) have extensive fur and typically nest well above the ground to avoid mosquitos. I hypothesize that these species (that are adapted for climbing trees to obtain fruit and defense against biting insects) likely evolved from free-ranging members of the genus *Homo* following speciation events (roughly 10 and 7 million years ago, MYA).

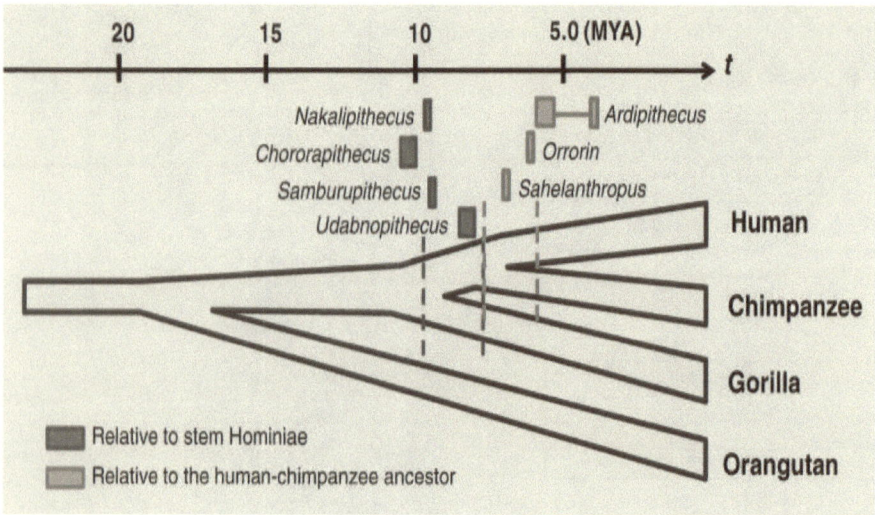

Source: Hara Y, Imanishi T, Satta Y. 2012. Reconstructing the demographic history of the human lineage using whole-genome sequences from human and three great apes. *Genome Biol Evol.* 4(11):1133-45. (Note the similarity to my chart above.)

Continued interbreeding of west central Africans with immigrants from the east has prevented speciation and limited evolution to a few (frequently adverse) mutations[86] that protect against malaria. Part of the reason for the complexity of this evolution is that it strikes hardest at pre-pubescent individuals. Thus, any mutation that increases the number of people reaching puberty will be favored *even if it causes disability or premature death in adults and prevents cultural and technological advancement.* In support of this hypothesis, it has been reported anecdotally on many occasions that Europeans and Native Americans were not as resistant to malaria as Africans and Europeans simply died out quicker under these conditions (Africa is "white man's grave").

It is also interesting to look at the principal agent of human lethality *Plasmodium falciparum.* This species of the malaria parasite apparently arose 40 to 60 thousand years ago and interestingly went through a bottleneck (greatly reduced population) 4 to 6 *thousand* years ago. Since this species is primarily a parasite of humans in west central Africa, the bottleneck suggest that it nearly killed off the entire population of humans in the region 4 to 6 *thousand* years ago.[87] The current

---

[86] Malaria Genomic Epidemiology Network. Reappraisal of known malaria resistance loci in a large multicenter study. *Nat Genet.* 2014. 46(11):1197-204.

Mangano VD, Modiano, D. An evolutionary perspective of how infection drives human genome diversity: the case of malaria. *Curr Opin Immunol.* 2014. 30:39-47.

[87] Otto TD et al. 2018. Genomes of all known members of a *Plasmodium* subgenus reveal paths to virulent human malaria. *Nat Microbiol.* 3(6):687-697.

population of humans (host for *Plasmodium falciparum*) is maintained by the adverse mutations[88] that allow the humans to survive, but inhibit human cultural advancement.

1.7 Slave and Slave Holder

North and South

Most Europeans and Americans in the north eastern and new western states had seldom seen a black African. Many in the mid-West were new immigrants straight for Ireland, Scandinavia[89] and Germany. Moreover, that experience was in a context where the African was a novelty (tiny minority of the population) and was typically the product of generations of exposure to American or European culture. Frequently, African Americans viewed by, e.g., New Englanders had been formally educated and might well be mulattoes. Even then, the European Americans and Europeans retained a very definite opinion that black Africans were a subordinate race. While, the graceful acceptance of these optimal examples of the black African race in the 1800s were in part genuine in the North, they also served as an opportunity to painlessly bury the heritage of the slave trade that had been the

---

[88]Kwiatkowski, DP. 2005. How Malaria Has Affected the Human Genome and What Human Genetics Can Teach Us about Malaria. *Am J Hum Genet*. 77(2): 171–192.

[89] 15th Regiment Wisconsin Volunteer Infantry (1862), was 90% Norwegian and not English-speaking.

foundation of much of New England's wealth. The motive of active abolitionist was, in part, an atonement for this guilt. The erasure of the slave-trade heritage from the public conscious of New England was nearly complete by the mid-1900s. I think that Anne Farrow and her co-authors summarize the situation well (Farrow et al. 2006):

> *"We have grown up, attended schools, and worked in Northern states, from Maine to Maryland. We thought we knew our home. We thought we knew our country. We were wrong."*

According to a European observer (1830s, Alexis de Tocqueville, *Democracy in America*):

> *"In that part of the Union where the Negroes are no longer slaves, have they come closer to the whites? Everyone who has lived in the United States will have noticed just the opposite. Race prejudice seems stronger in those states that have abolished slavery than in those where it still exists, and nowhere is it more intolerant than in those states where slavery was never known."*

And

> *"In the South, where slavery still exists, less trouble is taken to keep the Negro apart: they sometimes share the labors and the pleasures of the white men; people are prepared to mix with them to some extent; legislation is more harsh against them, but customs are more tolerant and gentle."*

Northern (anti-Southern) scholars sometimes claim that these quotes are "cherry-picked" and not representative. But they are very consistent with the systematic exclusion of free blacks from the American mid-West and even New England. Free blacks, were free to relocate, but did not immediately relocate into free states…why? The U.S. government was firmly involved in preventing the establishment of free blacks in western territories, where the US government's policy was to actively exterminate Native Americans (Alexis de Tocqueville, *Democracy in America*):

> *"The Americans of the United States do not let their dogs hunt the Indians as do the Spaniards in Mexico, but at bottom it is the same pitiless feeling which here, as everywhere else, animates the European race. This world here belongs to us, they tell themselves every day: the Indian race is destined for final destruction which one cannot prevent and which it is not desirable to delay. Heaven has not made them to become civilized; it is necessary that they die. Besides I do not want to get mixed up in it. I will not do anything against them: I will limit myself to providing everything that will hasten their ruin. In time I will have their lands and will be innocent of their death."*

The Cherokee are a case in point[90], by the 1830's Chief Vann owned one of the finest houses in the rural US. The Cherokee had invented a written language and many were literate. Indeed, the Cherokee were publishing a newspaper in northern Georgia printed in English and Cherokee. When issues of tribal rights arose, the tribe did not attack their neighbors but rather they took their case to the US Supreme Court. The Cherokee were every bit as civilized as the Europeans in the early 1800s.

---

[90] The Cherokee will be discussed in more detail in the context of sovereignty of the United States, below.

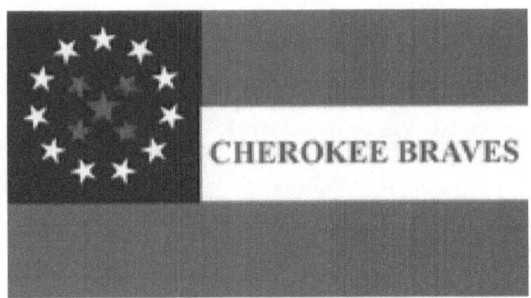

Confederate Cherokee Braves Battle Flag, Stand Watie

Yet, they were removed to Oklahoma by the Federal government to make room for Europeans. Little wonder that the Cherokee would ultimately side with the Confederacy.

Abraham Lincoln made a speech in Illinois (18 September 1858) as part of his political debates with Douglas, which accurately captures his views and the views of European Americans (especially recent immigrants):

> *"I am not, nor ever have been, in favor of bringing about in any way the social and political equality of the white and black races … I am not nor ever have been in favor of making voters or jurors of Negroes, nor of qualifying them to hold office, nor to intermarry with white people; and I will say in addition to this that there is a physical difference between the white and black races which I believe will forever forbid the two races from living together on terms of social and political equality. And inasmuch as they cannot so live, while they do remain together there must be a position of superior and inferior, and I as much as any other man am in favor of having the superior position assigned to the white race."*

https://www.snopes.com/fact-check/did-lincoln-racism-equality-oppose/

In the mid-1800s, the vast majority of northerners were content to allow slavery as long as it was confined to the old South *and free blacks were constrained to live there as well.* The rest of the country was for Europeans and this was the ugly truth behind Lincoln's First Inaugural Address:

> *"I have no purpose, directly or indirectly, to interfere with the institution of slavery in the States <u>where it exists</u>* [emphasis added]. *I believe I have no lawful right to do so, and I have no inclination to do so."*

I do not have time here to elaborate on the views of Lincoln regarding African-Americans, but I will point out that in 1862 (long after the war began), he was actively encouraging African-Americans to emigrate to Panama because he felt the races were incompatible.

Meanwhile, in the South, black Africans were viewed rather paternally. In the opinion of adult southern white males, all women, children and black Africans were generally incapable of responsible and analytical behavior. As a result, their view was that it was the *responsibility of adult white men* to make decisions for them *and take care of them.* Of course, most black Africans were slaves. This was a legal status and (from the stand point of white men) an honorable position in society; just as women had an honorable role in society. The accomplishments and behavior of slaves reflected on their owner. Slaves who earned, won or were given/bequeath their freedom were, as a matter of law, free and independent. But the owners were not generally disposed to "turn out" the old or infirm. In the South, with power, came social responsibility. Southerners were expected to care for the weak. In the case of slave labor, southerners were apt to compare the virtual agrarian *socialism* of the plantation with the brutal reality of northern (and European) mercantile *capitalism*.

Southern Socialism and Northern Capitalism

It is worth looking at the conditions of lower/working classes in Britain and the Northern States. In pre-industrial times, children had worked within the family doing simple task including tending animals, errands, and cleaning. Within the home, girls were able to learn and practice the arts of spinning and weaving. As technology advanced in spinning and weaving (which were highly repetitive and thus well suited to automation) girls were often at the forefront of learning the operations of the new technologies.   Cotton was of course the crop that was driving slavery in the period 1775-1860. With the first local textile mills (1769), labor that girls had been doing in the home shifted to a factory setting in Britain. Instead of working under the directions and discipline of mothers, the girls and young boys found themselves working in a regimented system controlled by adult men who were not interested in the personal welfare of the workers. Indeed, many of the workers were selected from orphanages and other institutions where there was no one to be responsible for their wellbeing. In the early 1800s, it is estimated that about 4% of textile workers in Britain were under the age of 10, about 15% were from 10 to 13, 20% to 50% were 13-18 and the balance were over 18.[91] The advances in lighting (gas lights) and steam power extended the workday and allowed the factory complexes to consolidate in cities independent of water power. The total number of workers was kept low because of the high productivity demanded: In 1841, approximately 45,000 boys and 60,000 girls were employed in British cotton mills.

The first factory regulations appeared in 1802, and in 1819, the Cotton Factories Regulation Act set a minimum working age at 9 years of age and limited the work day to 12 hours per day six days a week. But there was no provision for inspection and enforcement until the Regulation of Child Labor Law of 1833, and the work day was shortened to 10 hours for children and women in 1847. Not only were the work days long and provisions for worker needs (education, food, toilets) minimal, the factories were filled with unshielded power-driven pullies, belts, gears and assorted moving parts. A child who was clumsy or thoughtless could easily be torn to shreds and it was not uncommon that they were. For example, in 1818 Dr. Michael Ward working in Manchester testified to Parliament as follows: [92]

----

[91] These employment data are primarily based on *Child Labor during the British Industrial Revolution* by Carolyn Tuttle, Lake Forest College. https://eh.net/encyclopedia/child-labor-during-the-british-industrial-revolution/

[92] Dr. Ward from Manchester was interviewed about the health of textile workers on 25th March, 1819. https://spartacus-educational.com/IRaccidents.htm

"When I was a surgeon in the infirmary, accidents were very often admitted to the infirmary, through the children's hands and arms having being caught in the machinery; in many instances the muscles, and the skin is stripped down to the bone, and in some instances a finger or two might be lost. Last summer I visited Lever Street School. The number of children at that time in the school, who were employed in factories, was 106. The number of children who had received injuries from the machinery amounted to very nearly one half. There were forty-seven injured in this way."

The situation could be much worse as observed by Robert Blincoe:[93]

"A girl named Mary Richards, who was thought remarkably handsome when she left the workhouse, and, who was not quite ten years of age, attended a drawing frame, below which, and about a foot from the floor, was a horizontal shaft, by which the frames above were turned. It happened one evening, when her apron was caught by the shaft. In an instant the poor girl was drawn by an irresistible force and dashed on the floor. She uttered the most heart-rending shrieks! Blincoe ran towards her, an agonized and helpless beholder of a scene of horror. He saw her whirled round and round with the shaft - he heard the bones of her arms, legs, thighs, etc. successively snap asunder, crushed, seemingly, to atoms, as the machinery whirled her round, and drew tighter and tighter her body within the works, her blood was scattered over the frame and streamed upon the floor, her head appeared dashed to pieces - at last, her mangled body was jammed

---

[93] John Brown, *A Memoir of Robert Blincoe* (1828)

in so fast, between the shafts and the floor, that the water being low and the wheels off the gear, it stopped the main shaft. When she was extricated, every bone was found broken - her head dreadfully crushed. She was carried off quite lifeless."

The textile industry in New England began about 1821 and farm land soon became mill towns. Unlike England, the towns were new and since water powered most of the equipment, they were rather smoke- and soot-free. Following the British model, young women were initially employed because of their traditional household activities and they received reasonable pay for reasonable hours. The factories were noisy, hot and cotton lint was of course a constant irritation. Nonetheless, Charles Dickens, who famously wrote of the sad conditions in British factories, visited Lowell mills in 1842 and viewed them very favorable when compared to British factories. It is reasonable to believe that conditions in American mills were not greatly different from British mills. Harriet Hanson Robinson[94] worked in the Lowell, Massachusetts textile mills from 1834-1848. She reported that

"At the time the Lowell cotton mills were started the caste of the factory girl was the lowest among the employments of women. ... She was represented as subjected to influences that must destroy her purity and selfrespect. In the eyes of her overseer she was but a brute, a slave, to be beaten, pinched and pushed about. It was to overcome this prejudice that such high wages had been offered to

[94] Robinson, Harriet H. "Early Factory Labor in New England," in Massachusetts Bureau of Statistics of Labor, Fourteenth Annual Report (Boston: Wright & Potter, 1883), pp. 38082, 38788, 39192. https://sourcebooks.fordham.edu/mod/robinson-lowell.asp

women that they might be induced to become millgirls, in spite of the opprobrium that still clung to this degrading occupation."

The New England mill girls were as young as 10 (but most were between 16 and 25) and all worked 5 AM until 7 PM daily. Hanson's article is actually fairly upbeat because of the few opportunities that women had to earn money. Of course, there are no photographs of New England mill girls in the 1840s. Nonetheless, we do have photographs form the early 1900s that suggest that when steam power became available and factories moved to the South child labor was still very common, very hard and very dangerous.

"Textile mill workers in Newberry, South Carolina, in December of 1908"

Source: https://rarehistoricalphotos.com/child-labor-america/

"Willie, one of the young spinners in the Quidwick Co. Mill in Anthony, Rhode Island. April of 1909"

Source: https://rarehistoricalphotos.com/child-labor-america/

Bibb Mill No. 1. Macon, Georgia, 1909

Source: Lewis Hine's Photography and The End of Child Labor in the United States

https://petapixel.com/2013/09/07/lewis-hines-photography-end-child-labor-united-states/

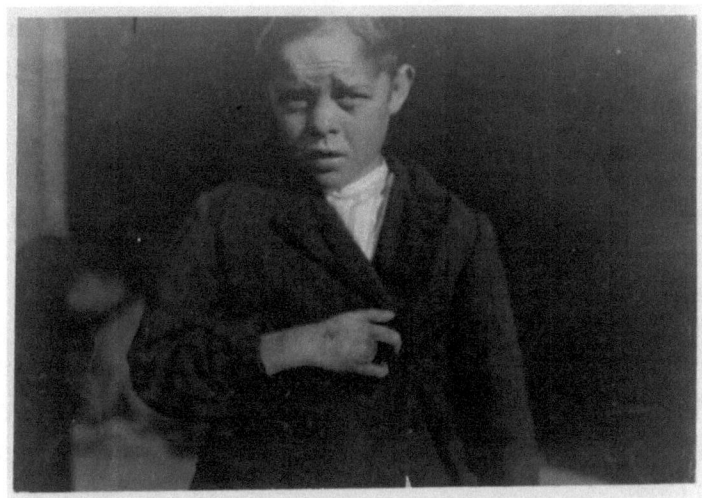

"Young cotton mill worker. A piece of the machine fell on his foot mashing his toe. This caused him to fall on to a spinning machine and his hand went into the unprotected gearing, crushing and tearing out two fingers. (Bessemer City, NC–Oct 1912)"

http://www.whizzpast.com/picture-power-the-amazing-images-taken-by-lewis-hine-that-helped-end-child-labor/

Keep in mind that these factories worked year around and were open for 12 hours or more a day even in the winter when the sun was up in new England only about 8 hours. In my opinion, and in the view of contemporary antebellum southern slave-holders, the working conditions on a cotton plantation for slaves compared favorably with the working conditions in a New England cotton mill. Agricultural work in cotton and tobacco was highly seasonal, confined to daylight hours, children were surrounded by family and owners "owned" the laborers… if the slaves were sick or injured, they were still the responsibility of the owner. In contrast, sick or injured children and other workers in cotton mills were simply replaced. According to an 1832 report by Britain's House of Commons:[95]

> *"The report added that the workers were often "abandoned from the moment that an accident occurs; their wages are stopped, no medical attendance is provided, and whatever the extent of the injury, no compensation is afforded."*

Here I have focused on the textile industry; nonetheless, the mining industry in the North East and Midwest (Pennsylvania, Ohio, Kentucky, Indiana) was also a major trap for *free (mostly European) labor.*

Although picking cotton was not an easy job, it compares favorably to the dangers and hardships of factories in the middle of the industrial revolution. Although loss of freedom created a philosophical difference between southern slavery and northern factory work, the practical differences appear to favor the agricultural life. It is worth noting that after the slaves were freed, Europeans in the South had no compunction to turning their own children to the same tasks formerly done by slaves as shown in these photographs:

---

[95] https://spartacus-educational.com/IRaccidents.htm

"Five and six-year old children pick cotton for their father to earn a wagon"

(Geronimo, OK, 1916)

Photography by Lewis Hine

https://www.dailymail.co.uk/news/article-2305630/Lewis-Hine-Harrowing-images-child-labourers-children-young-forced-breaking-work-fields-factories-mines.html

It is ironic that modern "victims of slavery" seem to believe that black African slaves were the only people ever to pick cotton. Slaves generally did not work in the fields until 10 years old.

Cotton pickers from 5 to 9 years old (Bells TX, 1913)

Source: From *Kids at Work - Lewis Hine and the Crusade Against Child Labor*

by Russell Freedman

1.8 A History of Rebellion

There was a series of newsworthy slave rebellions or plots for significant slave rebellions that weighed on the minds of slave-holders in the South in the years leading up to their secession from the United States. Of course, individual slaves rebelled virtually every day and many ran away. A rebellion is thus defined as a group of slaves not just running away, but actively trying to take over or destroy not just their owners but the European government or attempting to escape *en mass* with violent actions leading to destruction of property and especially deaths of Europeans. The histories of these episodes are almost uniformly disastrous for the slaves both in specifics and in general. In every instance in North America, the plots were either found out or quashed in execution. The slaves directly involved were either executed or shipped to the West Indies (a death sentence by another name). Indirectly, it was clear to the Europeans that educated, literate and articulate black Africans were the leaders of these rebellions; and, thus, education and uplifting of blacks was generally forbidden by law or discouraged after each episode. Freedoms that slaves had enjoyed (movement, association, ownership of property, etc.) were also typically curtailed after these episodes. And finally, these episodes demonstrated that slaves were capable of wanton murder of Europeans (without regard to slave ownership or political leanings).

Ironically, I have not found references to significant rebellion, systematic sabotage, or even settling of personnel vendettas by slaves during the War between the States. Indeed, one would have expected (and Lincoln almost assuredly intended) for the Presidential Proclamation of September 22, 1862 to have induced such activity. The latter stages of the War, saw the Confederate Armies in disarray and typically far from home. The southern men at home were either very young, very old or recovering from wounds. One might have expected a general uprising or excursion among the slaves of the entire Confederacy. Indeed,

Lincoln's proclamation… even if it was innocently proffered (with no expectation of racial strife in the South) … would have been historically judged impolitic had there been such an uprising resulting in murder or abuse of Confederate civilians in 1863. Thus, it is worth looking at some of these events that were in the minds of southerners immediately before secession.

The Stono Rebellion of 1739

The Carolina colony was begun in the mid-1600s with settlers moving from Virginia and into three locations in the Carolina grant (1663). By 1671 Charleston, South Carolina was a thriving town. In 1712 an informal boundary (not surveyed until 1771) was made between North and South Carolina. In the early days of the South Carolina colony, a number of agricultural adventures were tried and rice farming proved to be profitable. Slaves could be imported faster than European colonists could be found and soon the colony was predominately black African slaves working under European overseers.

Several factors came to a head in the late summer of 1739 around Charleston. It was not uncommon for slaves to outnumber overseers by more than 10 to 1 in the fields and it was impossible for overseers to keep track and control all of the slaves. The work was hard and the slaves were pushed to maintain thin profit margins for the rice crop. Most importantly, Spain was trying to undermine the British by promising runaway slaves that reached St. Augustine, Florida freedom and a reward.[96]

Passage of the Security Act (August 1739) was probably the event that gave slaves the opportunity to exercise their dissatisfaction. The Security Act required white males forming the militia to bring their arms with them to church on Sunday. On Sundays, slaves were also allowed to do as they pleased (e.g., work for money, which they could spend). With no armed overseers in the fields on Sunday morning, September 9, 1739, an Angolan slave named Jemmy (who may have had experience with the Portuguese) led an uprising of about 20 slaves on a plantation on the Stono River (St. Paul's Parish). They went into Hutchinson's store on Wallace Creek, killed two shopkeepers and took arms. The objective of the band is not clear, but they moved south-west (away from Charleston) attacking Europeans along the way. They killed Mr. Godfrey and his children and burned their house. The innkeeper at Wallace's Tavern was spared, but the next six families that were encountered were killed.[97] By afternoon, the band of slaves had travelled about 12 miles, encouraged about 40 additional slaves to join, killed 20 to 25 Europeans and reached the Edisto River. The militia caught up with the rebelling slaves near dusk and killed about half in a gun battle. About 30 slaves escaped and were

---

[96] This would have been a model for the likely outcome of the Presidential Proclamation of September 22, 1862.

[97] Some modern accounts claim that the slaves were marching under a banner and shouting liberty (as in an image from the French Revolution). This seems unlikely. This was not a day of a glorious march, it was a murderous rampage.

captured and executed or sold into the West Indies over the next few months.

As a result of the event, South Carolina passed the Negro Act (1740). This act is interesting for what it now forbade slaves to do (which had been previously permitted). Previously, any wages earned by the slave during time not occupied by the master (e.g., Sunday) was considered the property of the slave and could be spent as the slave pleased. This act made these earnings legally the property of the master (although the master might not take them).[98] Slaves were forbidden to assemble, travel, raise food, or learn how to write. However, they were allowed to read and schools were introduced to teach Christianity.

The French Revolution and Haitian Slave Revolts

In a pattern that became too well known, European diseases and enslavement rapidly devastated the native populations of the West Indies. Thus, African slaves were imported to the West Indies by 1518. The 1574 census recorded 1,000 Spanish and 12,000 African slaves producing sugar on the island of Hispaniola. But the short lives of slaves who died from malaria, yellow fever and abuse along with the constant encroachment of pirates in the early 1600s caused the Spanish to retrench into their most secure settlements in the east of the island. The French effectively gained

---

[98] This law was on the books until 1865 and John Belton O'Neall (1793-1863) [Chief Justice of the South Carolina Supreme Court (1859-63) and owner of approximately 150 slaves] interpreted it to mean (1848) that with the master's permission, a slave could earn money for his/her personal use and own personal property. This interpretation was accepted throughout the South.

control of the western third of the island (Saint-Domingue) by 1665 and this was formally recognized by the Spanish in 1697 (Treaty of Ryswick).

For most of the next century, France ruled the western part of the island and successfully made it the leading source of sugar in the West Indies through brutal exploitation of the African slaves. The work of harvesting and processing sugar cane was almost completely too laborious for women. Thus, female Africans that came to Haiti were typically put into domestic work and frequently ended up as wives or mistresses of the French overseers. This situation produced an entire class of mulatto/creole-speaking people who separated the Europeans from the Africans. By 1790 the island had five identifiable groups:

Population of Saint-Domingue in 1790	
European planters and shopkeepers	40,000
Mulattos and Free Africans (who frequently owned land and wealth)	30,000
African slaves	500,000
Runaway Slaves (Maroons) living beyond the law in the interior of the island	thousands

The successful American War of Independence (1775-1783), which most regarded as a revolution[99] with its stirring Declaration of Independence (e.g., ...*All men are created equal...*) inspired a revolt in France directly against the monarchy (July 14, 1789).[100] News of these events reached Saint-Domingue; and just before midnight August 22, 1791, the slaves of Saint-Domingue staged a bloody coup against the planters.[101] By 1794, the entire colony was in the hands of the Africans led by Toussaint l'Overture with 100,000 dead Africans and 24,000 dead Europeans. Obviously, slavery ended (February 4, 1794). In 1795 (Treaty of Basel) Spain relinquished the eastern two-thirds of the island to the French.[102] But this was in control of Toussaint l'Overture by 1801.

Napoleon had come to power in 1799; and in 1802; he sent 43,000 French troops to retake the island and reestablish slavery. Toussaint l'Overture was captured and taken to France where he

---

[99] It was not a revolution. The same people who were in charge before the war were in charge after the war and the principles, stated before the war, were adhered to after the war. No effort was made to topple the British monarch.

[100] This was a true revolution with a brutal destruction of the monarchy and upper classes followed by a revolutionary government that was stabilized by a dictator (Napoleon Bonaparte, 1799-1814).

[101] Many French planters with trusted slaves and free Africans from Haiti moved to US ports especially Charleston and New Orleans. The situation was concerning enough to South Carolina that its legislature blocked the international slave trade (Shugerman, 2002, p. 270).

[102] The British had unsuccessfully attempted to take over the entire island 1793-1798. Both the British and French forces suffered heavy losses from tropical diseases.

soon died in prison (1803). But the French were now again in direct combat with the British. Thus, when one of Toussaint l'Overture associates (Jean-Jacques Dessalines) stepped forward and defeated the French garrison (November 18, 1803), Napoleon did not respond, but rather recognized Haiti as an independent nation (January 1, 1804).

Unfortunately, it did not end there. Jean-Jacques Dessalines declared that all Europeans were enemies as they had supported the French, British and Spanish against the African uprising and long war of independence. There followed about four months (early January 1804 until 22 April 1804) of murder, rape, torture and abuse of all the remaining Europeans…men women and children were shown no mercy. The entire episode (1791-1804) was known to Americans who were led to fear slave/African uprisings and in particular were shocked by the fact that the 1804 murders were purely revenge killings after the political victory had been won. Naturally, this was interpreted to mean that mass emancipation of the US slaves would not be rewarded with thanks, but rather used to settle scores.

Gabriel Prosser[103] and Slave Rebellion Plot of 1800

The violence in Haiti/ Saint-Domingue certainly worried many Europeans in the southern states. In 1800, there were about equal numbers of Europeans and Africans (mostly slaves) in Charleston;

---

[103] Some people object to the use of his "slave name", i.e., he was merely owned by Thomas Prosser. Most black Africans accepted the last names of their owners prior to the Civil Rights era (1960s) in the US when Moslem and invented names (first and last) became popular.

but outside the cities in the tidewater of South Carolina and Georgia, Africans reached nearly 90% of the population (Shugerman, 2002, p. 272). Thus, the threat of a slave rebellion was real and the consequences could be very devastating at every level.

The fears of Europeans were proven to not be without merit with the plot hatched by Gabriel Prosser in Virginia. Gabriel, was a large (6'2") muscular, literate blacksmith by trade who was regarded by Africans and Europeans as well above average intelligence. For the most part, his owner rented him (i.e., "hired him out") to others to make best use of his valuable skills.

The plan was for an ideally bloodless rebellion. He wanted to take Governor James Monroe hostage and negotiate an end to slavery in Virginia. Of course, violence was a probability and he instructed his followers not to harm Methodists, Quakers and Frenchmen. Methodists and Quakers were, of course, arguing for abolition and there were apparently two white Frenchmen involved in the plot. The plot was apparently revealed to Madison who dealt with it as quietly as possible because Jefferson and Madison were politically tied to the French and the ideas of republicanism and emancipation. Gabriel attempted to escape by boat but was turned in by a hired-out slave who wanted the reward that was offered. Ultimately, Gabriel and 25 other slaves were hanged.

The 1811 Slave Revolt in Louisiana

Although it is not well known, Louisiana historians identify the revolt led by Charles Deslondes (slave from Saint-Domingo) was

the largest slave revolt in the US. Historians (and advocates) have
delved into the deeper reasons behind the revolt and the
possibility of outside (international) agitation implied by a high
level of planning among the slaves. I think that the situation is
fairly obvious, Louisiana was in many ways like Santo Domingo:
French, sugar plantations and a weak local government stressed
by outside influences (British, Spanish and French). Charles
Deslondes saw a chance and took it.

The revolt began on the evening of January 8, 1811 on the
plantation of Col. Manuel Andre. This plantation was adjacent to
the Mississippi River about 36 miles north of the limits of New
Orleans (near modern Norco). Details are sketchy and various
accounts elaborate with contemporary biases (Buman, 2012). The
facts seem to be that Col. Andre was wounded and his son was
killed. Then their slaves left the plantation walking towards New
Orleans. Col. Andre sounded the alarm and led a group of
Europeans in pursuit of the slaves. He also apparently sent
warnings down river that caused his neighbors to begin fleeing
towards New Orleans or preparing to resist. Soon, the US
military detachment under Wade Hampton and a territorial force
under Maj. Homer V. Milton were alerted. The time frame of
these events is unclear, but I would guess that after the initial
violence the slaves spend the first night organizing while the
Europeans began their response. Presumably the next day, the
organized military forces moved north from New Orleans. Most
likely on the 9th, the slaves encountered resistance by Jean-
François Trepagnier at his plantation. He became the second
European killed. On the 10th, the Europeans led by Col. Andre
caught up with the slaves at the plantation of François Bernard
Bernoudi. By now, the slaves had acquired a few weapons and

probably numbered a couple of hundred men.[104] There were likely fewer Europeans, but they were likely all armed. There was a skirmish and some of the slaves dispersed into the swamps. But the group still led by Charles Deslondes continued south to the Jean Noel Destreham[105] Plantation and Fortier Plantation, where on the morning of the 11th, they were met by the organized military forces. Trapped between these various forces, the slaves dispersed and surrendered by the evening of the 11th.

In summary, it is reported that 66 slaves were killed, and about 75 were captured and 17 were not accounted for. All but 16 of those captured were returned to their owners. Those 16 were taken to New Orleans and tried on January 13th. Many details were relayed to distant states by letter to family members or newspaper editors. These accounts agree that the convicted slaves were returned to their plantations and shot with their heads being placed on pikes along the road as a warning to other slaves.

Denmark Vesey

Slave Rebellion Plot of 1822

Denmark Vesey (a.k.a., Telemaqu) was apparently born in St. Thomas and lived in Bermuda before being brought to Charleston, SC. He was a skilled carpenter and could read and write. He literally won a lottery and was allowed to purchase his

---

[104] It is said that 3 to 5 plantations were raided and burned. This would produce about 200 male slaves.

[105] President of the Louisiana territorial legislature.

freedom. He was working to buy his family from slavery. He was also a religious leader and founder of the large African Methodist Episcopal (AME) Church in Charleston. Using his religious ties, Vesey managed to recruit a large number of free and slave black Africans in and around Charleston (which was over 50% black) into a plot to capture the local arsenal, commandeer a ship and sail to Haiti where Africans were in charge. It is impossible to keep something on this scale a secret and he was betrayed by slaves to the local authorities. In a controversial process, over 100 blacks were arrested, 67 convicted and 35 were hanged, the rest were deported to the West Indies. The history of their event is very cloudy. Although it was widely accepted that a plot existed, proof of a competent plan is lacking. The actions of the city, which carried out the trials and executions, should be held in contrast to the state led by the Governor Thomas Bennett Jr and Associate Justice of the US Supreme Court William Johnson Jr who both challenged the proceedings and argued that the trials should have conformed to normal standards. To me, the episode is reminiscent of the Salem witch trials, strongly influenced by public hysteria.

The absence of War-time Revolts

The episodes noted above all occurred before 1830 and appear to be motivated by a variety of issues. Of course, the most alarming situation was in Santo Domingo where systematic revenge killing had occurred *after* freedom had been achieved. Obviously, I have made a great distinction between the culture of sugar slavery and the situation in the American South. It is relevant that the two bloody uprisings appear to be associated with rice and sugar plantations in the southern states. The episodes in tobacco (1800) and cotton states (1822) were planned as relatively bloodless efforts and were both disclosed to authorities by slaves. It is obvious that slave owners trusted their slaves. Although slaves were, in principle, completely at the mercy of their owners; the facts of life were very different. With exception of the freedom to leave, slaves in the South by the mid-1800s had a lot of freedom and actually led the management of many plantations both as "overseers" (acting in the interest of the plantation owner) and "drivers" (i.e., immediate supervisors of daily work) (see Fogel and Engerman, 1974). This explains the continued function of plantations during the War and the willingness of southerners to join the military and leave their families surrounded by slaves.

Part 2

British Colonies of

North America

(1607 – 1790)

and

The United States

(1790-1815)

2.1 British Colonial Period in North America

New England, Barbados and the West Indies

In 1614, Thomas Hunt (a sea captain associated with John Smith) landed in Cape Cod. While bartering with the natives, he shanghaied 24 men and carried them off to Spain where they were sold into slavery (Warren, 2016, pp. 3-9). One of these Native Americans managed to win the favor of a Spanish priest and eventually made it to England, and then back to New England, where the newly arrived Pilgrims (1620) recorded the great blessing of meeting Squanto without whom they might not have survived.

The island of Barbados is at the eastern fringe of the West Indies and not on the direct routes between Europe and the major islands of the West Indies (the Greater Antilles). It was either uninhabited or stripped of Native Americans in the 1500s. The Spanish focused their energy on larger islands of the West Indies (Cuba, Hispaniola, Jamaica, Puerto Rico). Thus, when the British joined the colonization business in the 1600s, they found that Barbados could be claimed without conflict. The British, explored (1625) and began settling (1627) this overlooked island. Note that Virginia was founded much earlier (1607) and by 1625 had a going economy based on tobacco and mixed agriculture.

George E. Parris   Copyright Claimed   April 2019

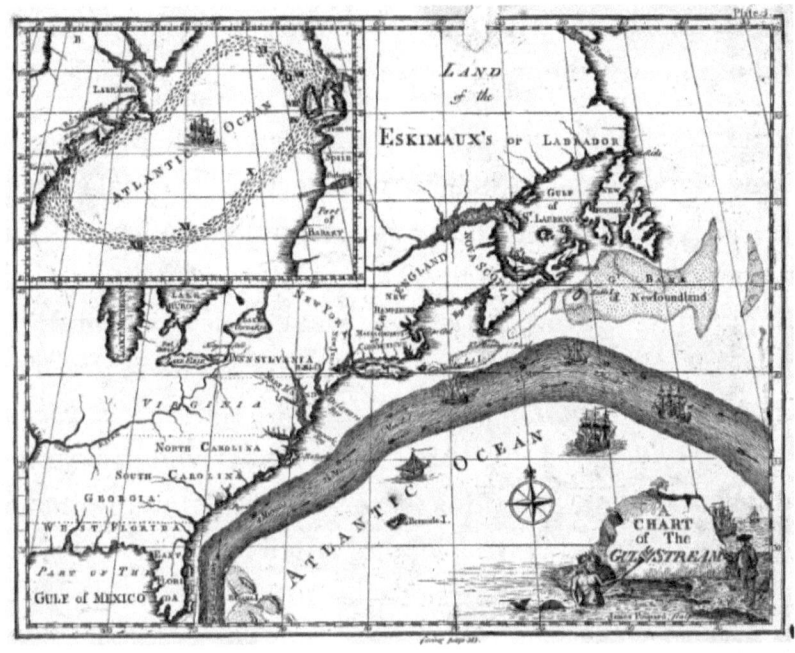

Benjamin Franklin's chart of the Gulf Stream (Philadelphia in 1786)

https://upload.wikimedia.org/wikipedia/commons/4/45/Fran klingulfstream.jpg

The settlement of Barbados, however, was concurrent with the establishment of British New England (1620-1638)[106], which helped build close ties between Barbados and the northern colonies. Indeed, the flow of the combined Antilles and the Gulf

---

[106] Approximately 20,000 colonists arrived in New England during that period (Warren, 2016, p. 2).

Stream currents made trips from Barbados to England via New England very convenient.

The influence of Barbados on the settlement of the British colonies from New York to Massachusetts was very substantial (Warren, 2016, pp. 12-14). The unhealthy climate in the tropics, induced British planters in Barbados to transfer their wives and children to New England (e.g., New York, New Haven, Newport and Boston). *You can envision, this as a plantation society in which the field slaves were kept on Barbados and the house slaves were moved to New England with the family.* African slaves arrived in Boston in 1634 and slaves from Barbados were specifically mentioned in 1638.[107] The Salem witch trials (1692) involved a slave owned by Samuel Parris (a distant relative of the author).

New England's profits from sugar produced on Barbados and other Islands in the West Indies (e.g., Antigua and Jamaica), were used to financed new businesses on the mainland.

By the late 1500s, firewood became expensive in Britain[108] and large timbers for ships' masts and spars were not readily available. Richard Hakluyt (1553–1616) had identified wood as one of the natural resources that was available in North America

---

[107] In 1638, a Bostonian shipped Native Americans as slaves to Barbados and received Africans (whom he planned to breed) in return.

[108] Coal was beginning to come into use in Britain and its smoke was causing issues: Poor people could not afford wood and were burning coal, which polluted the air used by wealthy people, and hence, wealthy people tried to legislate against burning coal.

and was one of the founders of the Virginia Company. But the proximity of hardwood trees and water power to seaports was not convenient in Virginia. Thus, the water power available near the seaports of New England was soon harnessed to drive sawmills that processed trees that were harvested in the nearby hardwood forest. Of course, removing the timber provided expanding farmable lands in New England. Soon, Barbados and other Caribbean island were stripped of trees for fuel and construction and became completely dependent upon wood products from New England. By the 1650s, New England's lumber and timber was an active commodity market.

Shipbuilding naturally followed both in Virginia and New England. For the most part Virginia shipbuilding was concentrated on moving people and materials along the rivers and bays between Maryland and North Carolina (Philadelphia, Annapolis, Jamestown, Williamsburg, New Bern, Charleston). Thus, most of these vessels were well below 100 tons.[109] In the 1680s, William Penn brought shipbuilding to Philadelphia and Quaker settlements in New England (primarily Newport, Rhode Island). With superior timber resources, water-powered sawmills and less river and bay traffic, New England tended towards larger ships. By 1700, New England shipyards were producing ocean-going ships of upwards of 300 tons. For comparison, the ships that Columbus used to cross the Atlantic were about 100 tons.

---

[109] The tidewater settlements of Maryland and Virginia were forced out of the shipbuilding business as their local hardwoods were consumed by the 1760s.

The period 1700-1717 saw an extension of credit by wealthy Boston businessmen that resulted in extensive shipbuilding for the Royal Navy[110] in New England. Building large naval ships required large logs for masts, which were harvested from British settlement in the Bay of Campeche (Belize). Access to these mast logs was ended when the Spanish successfully attacked this source of supply, but commercial shipbuilding in New England continued.

Construction of large sea-going ships brought whaling, fishing and international commerce to the ports of New England. In particular, New England became the supplier of wood, food, clothing, and other essentials of life[111] for many of the islands devoted exclusively to the production of sugar in the West Indies (Santo Domingo, Barbados, Jamaica, *et al.*).[112] The New Englanders were paid in molasses and sugar, which they converted to rum. With rum in hand, it was not long before New England was competing with Britain in the African slave trade (circa 1700). Of course, through the entire period of the 1600s ownership of slaves in New England had been common as an

---

[110] The British Navy was always requiring resources wood (especially masts and spars), tar/pitch, hemp for ropes and gun powder from foreign sources. Most of these products were imported from Europe and Scandinavia for construction in domestic British shipyards.

[111] Farrow (2014, p. 22) provides a list of commodities that were sent from Connecticut to the West Indies.

[112] It is not unusual for cash crops grown in favorable climates to become so valuable that food and other necessities are cheaper to import.

element of their business in the West Indies, but trading in slaves on the coast of African had been limited. Now, New England had the skills and resources to compete directly with the British in this very lucrative trade.

2.2 The Northern British Colonies

Massachusetts

Massachusetts was founded by people with strong Christian (Puritanical) leanings in 1628 and was soon engaged in several wars with the resident Native American tribes that resulted in capture of natives. For the most part these captives were highly likely to escape and rally more attacks and conflicts with the colonists. Thus, early in the history of the colony, it became the practice to deport these captives to Barbados or other West Indies islands. In 1636 the first black African slaves were brought to Massachusetts. In the 1641 *Massachusetts Body of Liberties*, under the section entitled "Liberties of Foreigners and Stranger" the following quote is found:

> *"There shall never be any bond slaverie, villinage or captivitie amongst us unless it be lawful captivitie captured in just wars, and such strangers as willingly sell themselves or are sold to us. And these shall have all the liberties and Christian usages which the law of*

> *god established in Iseraell concerning such persons doeth morally require. ..."*
>
> https://www.mass.gov/files/documents/2016/11/te/body-of-liberties-1641.pdf

This clause is usually presented as Massachusetts "outlawing slavery," but in truth it was carefully worded to sooth Puritan sensitivities while allowing continued participation in both the slave trade and slavery. The reference to "captives of just wars" was an *ex post facto* justification for the practice of enslaving and deporting Native Americans that were captured in various clashes with the Europeans especially the Pequot War (1636-38). One of the ships that took the Native Americans to Bermuda/Barbados (the *Desire*) returned to Boston with African slaves in 1638 (Dow, 1927, p. 267). These appear to be the first African slaves introduced into New England and they were owned/acquired by Samuel Maverick (owner of Noddle island in Boston harbor). Maverick intended to breed the slaves by forcing the males to rape the females (see Warren, 2016, p. 7). Black Africans who were presumably captured in wars and sold to European slave traders were legally enslaved in "just wars" or were "sold to" British masters. In 1643, the Plymouth Colony and New Haven Colony adopted fugitive slave laws.

Warren (2016, pp. 91-100) related an interesting series of events that reveal the view of New Englanders towards the Native

Americans and African slaves. Emmanuel Downing (related to John Winthrop by marriage) wrote to Winthrop as follows (1645):

> *"If upon a Just warre the lord should deliver* [Native American Captives] *into our hands, we might easily have me women and Children enough to exchange for Moores* [Africans], *which wilbe gayfully pilladge for us than wee conceive, for I doe not see how wee can thrive until wee get into a stock of slaves suffitient to doe our business, for our Childrens Children will hardly see this great Continent filled with people. I suppose you know verie well how we shall maynteyne 20 Moores cheaper then one English servent."*

Although there was an initial inclination to have black Africans trained in military arts (1652) by 1662 this policy was reverses in New England for fear of a slave rebellion. Indeed, such a rebellion was brewing following a Virginia ruling (1662)[113] that all children of enslaved women would be perpetually slaves and the rebellion occurred in Gloucester, Virginia in 1663. By 1670, the principle that the children of an enslaved woman were also the property of her owner was also established in Massachusetts.

By the time of King Phillip's War[114] (1765-68), the idea of deporting Native Americans as slaves was well accepted and

---

[113] Notice that the timing of this precedent-setting ruling in Virginia and Massachusetts was consistent with the first generation of births among black Africans in the North American Colonies. It had not become an issue in the West Indies because families of black Africans were very rare and not tolerated on sugar plantations.

[114] King Phillip was the name given to the Native American leader. This war was bloody and vicious with general slaughter and many Native

hundreds were shipped to the West Indies (probably in exchange for Africans). Ironically, the reputation of Native Americans as a force for resistance preceded them, and at least one ship from New England had to go all the way to Tangiers (Morocco) before discharging its cargo of Native Americans (Warren, 2016, p. 83 and 106). According to officials in Barbados (1676) *"Indians from New England, New Yorke, Roade Island, and the collonyes adjacent are known to be notorious Villanyes."*

The best-known story of the involvement of a Barbados slave in New England is found in the accounts of the Salem witch trials. One of the central figures was Samuel Parris (yes, a distant relative) who was probably typical of many of the more successful men in New England. He had been born in England and came to New England by way of Barbados where he owned a sugar plantation with slaves. When he sold his plantation in 1680 and moved to Massachusetts full time, he brought with him two slaves who supported his household. The possession of slaves did not dissuade the village from hiring him as their minister. Clearly, ownership of slaves was common and respectable.

But, the acquisition of a few slaves brought by immigrants from the West Indies was not the end of Massachusetts's participation in the slave trade; it was just the beginning. Presumably with the legal clarification provided by *Body of Liberties* (1641), Boston merchants felt free to dispatch ships to acquire slaves in Africa [*"or are sold to us"*] and deliver them to the West Indies. The

---

American captives executed or sold as slaves. It effectively broke the back of Native American resistance to British colonization in New England.

competition that these New Englanders represented to the British slave trade apparently precipitated the passage of English laws in 1672 giving the Royal African Company (RAC) a monopoly in the slave trade. Nonetheless, New England "interlopers"[115] were able to continue on a small scale until the legal monopoly was loosened in 1696. In the new system, the RAC essentially sold licenses to private companies and maintained forts/factories on the African cost from which slaves were sold by Africans to Europeans.

The familial and economic ties between Barbados and New England were such that data from Barbados in 1686 indicated that 80% of the shipping was from New England and Boston accounted for 30% all by itself (Warren, 2016, p. 77). By 1698, Massachusetts changed its tax laws to favor the slave trade and it became a major business throughout New England.

Rhode Island and Providence Plantations

In the 1600s, the large island (now called Aquidneck Island) at the mouth of Narragansett Bay (west of Massachusetts) was called Rhode Island by Roger Williams who founded plantations (i.e., a colony, 1636) at the head of the bay to escape the religious persecution that non-Puritan sects experienced in Massachusetts.

---

[115] See for example Sutton (2009). Interlopers were the equivalent of smugglers who were obviously working outside the laws of both Britain and the Dutch monopoly (West Indies Company, WIC); and were, thus, particularly targeted by pirates. By 1678, ships from Massachusetts had acquired slaves in Africa and delivered them to Virginia.

In 1638 Anne Hutchinson and other liberal-minded people settled Portsmouth on the north end of the Island and soon split the island to form Newport in the south. In 1648, these groups banded together under the leadership of Samuel Gorton to ensure their independence from Massachusetts.

With tolerant political and religious views, the colony became a haven for wide variety of people. In particular, Quakes (who were despised by the Church of England and the Puritans) flocked to the colony and constituted about 50% of its population in the late 1600s. The Quakers had been introduced to laissez-faire seafaring by the ship-captains (e.g., interlopers) who assisted their escapes from hostile English and European ports. Like most colonies, a strong economy was needed and the slave trade flourished. In the mid-1600s slaves were imported to assist in agriculture and furniture manufacture. In 1652, the Providence Plantation passed an ordinance against holding slaves for more than 10 years. There were many more African slaves than indentured servants, in part because the pool of potential European servants had different (non-Quaker) religious beliefs.

In 1688, the colony received a royal charter; and by 1698, Newport, in particular, was competing with Boston and New Haven in the triangle trade. Indeed, during the 1700s[116] over 900 voyages were sent from Rhode Island to Africa bringing about 60,000 African slaves to the British colonies and a similar number

---

[116] The US congress outlawed the international slave trade in 1807, Rhode Island defended it to the end.

(about 40,000) after the War of Independence (Rawley, 2005, p. 309). The most intense period was the mid-1700s (1750-75) when Governor Ward bragged that the colony had *"above one hundred and twenty sail of vessels"* (Rawley, 2005, p. 306). Newport alone had over 20 distilleries turning West Indies molasses into rum. Most of the rum was consumed locally, but some was used as barter for slaves in Africa. The business included shipbuilding in Bristol, Providence and Newport. Immediately after independence (1783), Rhode Island provided well over 50% of the New England slave trade. Most slaves were delivered to Barbados, Jamaica and Cuba, but about 19% went to Charleston, SC in repeat voyages and 4% went to Savanah, GA. Of course, Charleston was mainly a trans-shipment port for Georgia and Alabama.

While many Rhode Island businessmen bought shares in slaving ventures, three families became very prominent and wealthy from the trade: (1) William and Samuel Vernon of Newport financed numerous slaving expeditions; (2) meanwhile James Brown his brother Obadiah, and his sons, Nicholas, John[117], Joseph, and Moses built a large slaving operation in Providence (1736-1790); and (3) in Bristol, James De Wolf and his family became one of the largest slavers in the United States (over 80 voyages). Although Rhode Island enacted the Gradual Emancipation Act in 1784 and laws against the international trade in slaves, these laws were

---

[117] Slave traders Christopher Champlin and John Brown were elected to Congress from Rhode Island in 1800 (Rawley, 2005, p. 308). See Rawley (2005, pp. 325 and 329) for a table of major Rhode Island slave traders.

poorly enforced and business continued more or less as usual well after the Federal government passed prohibition of the international slave trade in 1807.

It is instructive to look at one of the slaving expeditions in detail. The voyage of the *Sally* from Providence (September 1764 - December 1765) has been well documented and is available on the internet.[118] The *Sally* was owned by Nicholas Brown and Company and its master was Esek Hopkins[119] who kept records showing that of the 196 Africans bought in West Africa (November 1764- August 1765), 21 were sold on the African coast and 88 died of starvation, disease and violent resistance before they could reach their destination on the West Indies island of Antigua (October 1765). This represents 50% mortality of the slaves on the ship [120] and the survivors were expected to die on the sugar plantation within a couple of years.

---

[118] *Voyage of the Sally*. John Carter Brown Library at Brown University. http://cds.library.brown.edu/projects/sally/

[119] Hopkins was a privateer, not a slaver and his inexperience led to trouble. There was a 15-man crew.

[120] Indeed, 19 Africans had died and one was dying when the ship left Africa. The source is a little obscure regarding the actual disposition of the slaves. As I understand it, 196 were bought, 21 were sold on the African coast and 20 died on the African coast before the middle passage. Apparently, a total of 88 slaves died by the time they reached Antigua. This calculation indicates that 20 died on the African coast, 68 died during the trans-Atlantic voyage and 87 (of 155) arrived in Antigua. Another 20 were reported to have died before they could be sold. Thus, only 67 of the 155 slaves were converted for profit.

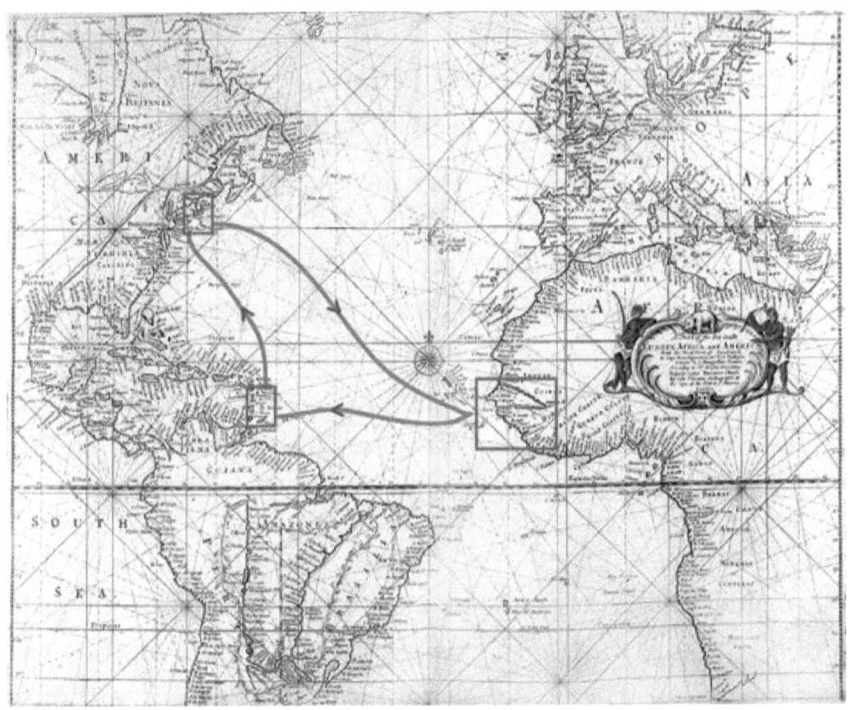

Voyage of the Sally Source: John Carter Brown Library at Brown University. http://cds.library.brown.edu/projects/sally/

Most of the Sally's slaves were in terrible condition and sold for as little as 5 pounds. The master had been instructed to bring several slaves back to Providence and one of these died between Antigua and Rhode Island.

The Brown brothers had different reactions to the voyage. Two of them gave up slaving for financial reasons. John continued and sent several financially successful voyages to Africa (1769, 1785, 1786, and 1795) and earnestly defended the business. Meanwhile, Moses who apparently was never comfortable with the slave trade (but who owned slaves) had an emotional response upon the death of his wife (1773), disposed of his slaves and joined the abolitionist movement with Reverend Samuel Hopkins, who was in Newport. Newport Gardner (a free African) established a mutual aid society of free Africans in 1780. Moses Brown lobbied for the Gradual Abolition Act of 1784 and a state law prohibiting the slave trade (1787). John Brown and Moses Brown privately disagreed until 1789 when Moses participated in the Providence Abolition Society and John published letters characterizing abolitionist as fanatics who were trying to impose their morals on others. He was particularly displeased with the idea of giving up slaves, whom he considered to be property.

Ironically, John was charged and tried for violating a Federal law (of 1793) prohibiting Americans from delivering African slaves to foreign ports (a large part of the slave trade as shown by the voyage of the *Sally*). The trial was held in Newport and, although John admitted his participation, the jury acquitted him. This outcome was a signal to New England slavers that the law would not be enforced in Rhode Island. Thus, the entire slaving business of New England moved to Newport, which was now dispatching as many as 50 ships per year to Africa until the international slave trade was outlawed by federal law in 1807. Even after that, Newport was a haven for illegal slave ships.

New Netherlands and New York

Several major European rivers including the Rhein and Muse merge and flow into the North Sea in a maze of waterways. This fertile lowland (in some ways like the Nile delta) has attracted seafarers and farmers since before Roman times. In Roman times, the land was something of a buffer between the Celts/Romans and the Germans. This political environment encouraged a Laissez-faire capitalism that proved to be very lucrative. Trade blossomed with the rivers connecting sea traffic with England and Spain and river traffic with Germany and France. With the Protestant revolution, the Netherlands (Dutch) found itself a haven for the persecuted middleclass of French and Germans sharing a religious basis with England.

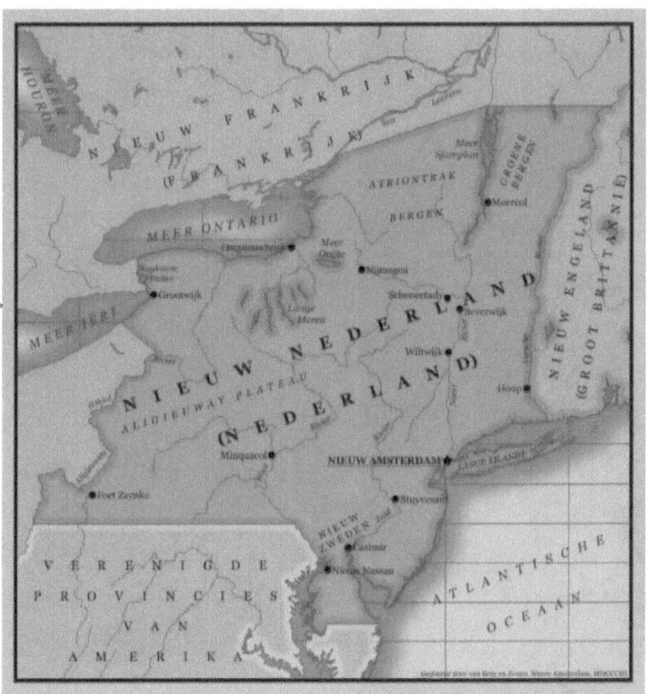

Author: rubberduck3y6

https://www.deviantart.com/rubberduck3y6/art/New-Netherlands-121465412

The country was in a nearly constant state of war (mainly against Spain, France and Britain[121]) or civil war. But the country was held together by the great profitability of its trade and business acumen. Ultimately, Dutch Protestant William of Orange (1650-1792) became the British King by deposing Catholic James II (of England and IV of Scotland).

The Dutch formed trading companies (e.g., East Indies and West Indies) and were successful in establishing control over part of the spice trade and establishing a colony in South Africa (1652).

New Netherlands[122] was established by the Dutch West India Company (WIC) in 1621. Although it was centered on Manhattan Island and the Hudson River valley, it included areas that became parts of New Jersey and Connecticut. The Dutch were active in the slave trade, but the first slaves to arrive in the colony were actually bought by the Portuguese from Angola and were taken as a prize by the WIC from a Spanish slave ship and brought to the colony in 1626. They remained the property of the WIC and were eventually given freedom. African slaves imported directly to the colony were managed differently. In 1640, a law was passed to discourage material support to run-away slaves. In 1646, a marriage among Africans was recorded. The first slave auction was held in 1655. The Dutch system generally gave rights and a path to freedom for slaves and when the change to British rule

---

[121] As a seafaring nation, the Dutch competed directly with the British and there were a number of Anglo-Dutch wars (1652-1673), if interested consult the life of the Dutch Admiral Michiel de Ruyter (1607–1676).

[122] Dutch settlement began as early as 1609.

was approaching (1664), the Dutch both freed slaves and recognized their titles to lands.

The British displaced the Dutch from North America in 1664; but in the same year, the Dutch (under Admiral De Ruyter) captured the Guinea forts of the "Company of Royal Adventurers of England for Carrying on a Trade to Africa" and a number of their ships (total value £ 200,000) (Dow, 1927, p. 4). The British imported slaves aggressively and in the early 1700s approximately 40% of the British households in New York owned slaves as servants. The Philipse family traded for east African slaves with the pirates on Madagascar. New York slave trading mainly by Dutch families peaked in the period 1750-75 when several family businesses brought slaves to the West Indies and held slave markets in New York City. Gradually during the 1700s, the Puritans and Quakers in New England discovered the conflict between their religion and their position on the slave trade (not necessarily slavery). In 1788, New York's state laws banned importation of slaves but allowed slave trading and especially welcomed ships from New England (where the trade was banned) to clear from New York harbor until the 1794 Federal law forbidding delivery of slaves to other countries (Rawley, 2005, p. 340). New York was, thus, more than happy to become the focus of the American slave trade as the importance of Newport, Rhode Island faded especially after 1807 when the trade was illegal. Ships cleared from New York for slave trading until 1862 (when the death penalty was imposed).

Connecticut

New Netherlands included portions of Connecticut and New Jersey. By 1633, the British had established settlements as far west as the Connecticut River, which roughly divided the state east and west. The New Haven settlement was established about 1638. In 1650, the colonist agreed to a boundary with the Dutch that was roughly 10 miles east of the Hudson River. When the British ousted the Dutch from New Netherlands (1664) Connecticut became a typical British colony.

Yale College was established in New Haven in 1701 partially financed by Elihu Yale. In the painting below (unknown artist) we see Elihu Yale (right) and a slave girl complete with metal collar around her neck. Elihu Yale's participation in the slave trade was actually associated with India and the East India Company in Madras (present-day Chennai). But it is a bit disingenuous for the university to lay all the blame for its tarnished name on this man; after all New Haven was one of the most important New England ports engages in the African slave trade bringing Africans to the West Indies throughout the 1700s and participating in the international slave trade even after it was outlawed in 1807 (actually 1640-1848).

Yale Center for British Art, Gift of Andrew Cavendish, eleventh Duke of Devonshire

Slavery was first mentioned in New Haven in 1644. In the last half of the 1600s, Connecticut (like the southern colonies) was a market for slaves sold by Boston or Newport slave traders, rather than a participant in the slave trade. However, when the monopoly of the West Africa Company was ended, it became attractive for all shipping ports in New England and New York to participate as slave traders. Farrow (2014, p. 1) has provided an estimate that from New London, CT alone a dozen or more ships, which were engaged in various elements of the slave trade, passed through the harbor each week. Connecticut had numerous rum distilleries in the 1700s (Farrow et al., 2005, pp. 48-52) and Connecticut became the colony with the largest number of slaves and slave owners in New England. The slaves in this colony were also managed more like in the West Indies in that owners often "turned out" slaves that were too old to work.

New England circa 1700

By the late 1600s, all the colonies (see above) now known as New England (including the urban area of New York/New Jersey) had deep involvement in the slave trade. They transported slaves from Africa to the West Indies (sugar plantations) and the southern colonies (tobacco/naval stores and rice plantations) and they routinely held domestic slaves. But these colonies had little interest in plantation agriculture except as absentee owners. As a result, they had similar issues with the expanding population of domestic black African slaves (by now they were in the third generation of American born African slaves). Thus, we see a similar set of laws coming out of most of the New England colonies around 1700. These new laws were aimed at suppressing the economic independence of slaves, the political power of slaves, the civil conduct of slaves and limiting the legal status of slaves and freed black Africans. It also addressed the growing problem of indigent black Africans (freed and "turned out" by their owners). For example, in 1703 Massachusetts passed an ordinance requiring the owners post bonds for freed slaves. About this same time, sexual relations (including marriage) between freed black Africans and Europeans was becoming an issue and Massachusetts banned it (1705).

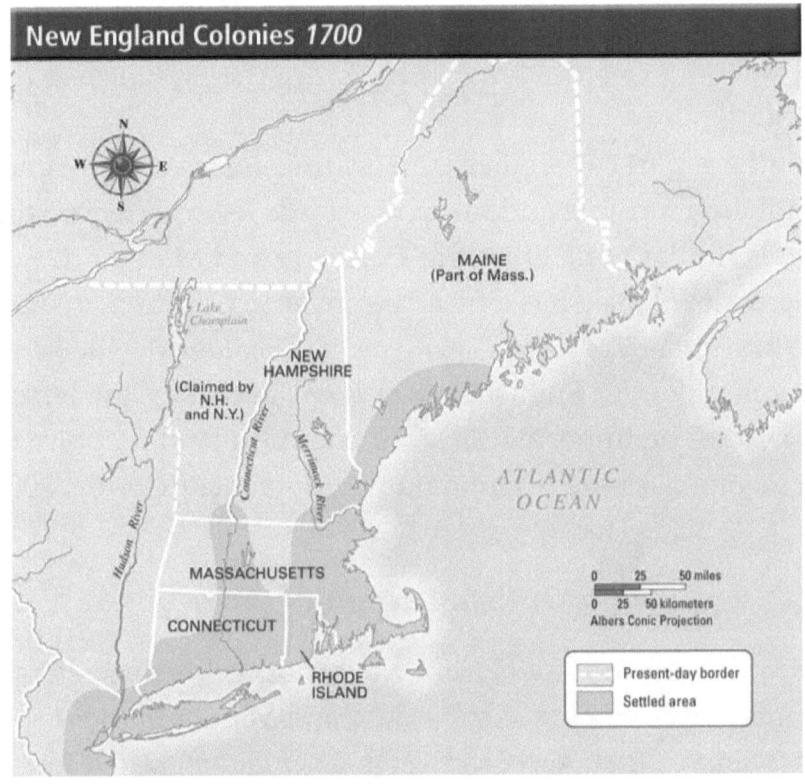

Source:
http://www.classzone.com/cz/books/north_carolina_08/resour
ces/images/chapter_maps/nc05_necolonies1700am.jpg

The region was rocked in 1712 by a slave revolt in New York City, which resulted in the deaths of Europeans and had to be put down by the militia. This event ended with the execution of 19 blacks Africans and sent New York on a path of repeated legislation against the rights of blacks, mulattos, Indians and slaves including sever punishments and a fugitive slave law.

New Jersey

The southern part of New Jersey is warm enough and flat enough for plantation farming and in some regards its experience with slavery is similar to neighboring Delaware and Maryland. Northern New Jersey has a history similar to Connecticut and New York. New York and New Jersey official legalized slavery when coming under English rule in 1663. Because New Jersey had no duties on imported slaves, it became a landing point for slaves destined for New York and Pennsylvania (Rawley, 2005, p. 336).

Pennsylvania

Dutch and Swedish settlers from New Amsterdam brought slaves to the area between New Amsterdam and Maryland (now eastern Pennsylvania). Other early settlers (e.g., Quakers) also tolerated slavery. Nonetheless, Pennsylvania is not suitable for plantation agriculture. In the late-1600s there was adequate European immigration to maintain small farms. Thus, the Quakers resolved to end slavery in 1688 and importation of slaves, blacks and Indians was banned by 1712. The Quakers of Pennsylvania were forbidden in participation in the slave trade in 1758 and in 1776 they were forbidden to own slaves. This more enlightened community passed the Gradual Abolition Act (1780) after independence from Britain was assured. The act included (i) a registry of slaves, (ii) prohibition of importation of slaves, (iii) a change in the status of children born to slave women to indentured servant (for a period of 28 years). In 1788 this was amended to prevent slave owners from carrying pregnant women out-of-state to circumvent the intent of the law and included prohibition to participation in the slave trade or providing material support to the slave trade (e.g., building or maintaining slave ships). These acts did not apply to fugitive slaves or existing slaves (before 1780). The number of slaves rapidly decreased to a thousand or so in the early 1800s. In 1826, Pennsylvania passed the Personal Freedom Act that attempted to extent the 1780 law to all slave *in or entering* (i.e., fugitive slaves) the state, but this was declared unconstitutional by the US Supreme Court in Prigg v. Pennsylvania (1842).

End of the International Slave Trade (1807)

The British and New Englanders (including New York) had largely come to dominate the international slave trade by the time of the American War of Independence. The Constitution of the United States specifically recognized slavery (1787). In Britain, the anti-slavery movement began in earnest in 1772 when a court ruled (Somerset v Stewart; 1772)[123] that English common law did

---

[123] This case involved an African slave from the West Indies. Ironically, Scottish coal miners were virtually made slaves as part of the mines they worked in 1606. This condition was first addressed with the Colliers and Salters (Scotland) Act of 1775, which recognized the situation as "a state of slavery or bondage." This act allowed for a gradual release of the colliers over a period of years, but discouraged any unified action to accomplish this. Little changed until the Colliers (Scotland) Act of 1799.

not support slavery. In the 1800s, the idea was being solidified under the guidance of William Wilberforce (1759–1833) who took up the cause of abolition in 1787 after being influenced by Thomas Clarkson (1760 – 1846).[124] The growing abolitionist movement in England faced little opposition since few slaves were owned in Britain proper.

In 1807, the British passed the Slave Trade Act, which abolished transport of slaves from Africa, but did not abolish slavery. Slavery was still legal in the British Empire (especially the West Indies and India). To enforce the law, the British passed Slave Trade Felony Act of 1811.

 In the United States, there was already a surplus of black African slaves in the Maryland, Delaware, Virginia and North Carolina so importation from Africa after 1807 was not attractive. The rising demand for slaves in the cotton fields of South Carolina, Georgia and the Mississippi Territory and Louisiana Territory provided a market for (and increased the value of) excess (unemployed) slaves. The only problem was that slave owners in the tobacco states did not like the idea of breaking up slave families or sending away loyal slaves that had served them for years, and the market in the cotton states was primarily for young (unskilled) labor. Thus, for the most part, only young adult men and women were "sold down the river" (see Fogel and Engerman, 1974, p. 48) to Mississippi, Louisiana, eastern Texas, Arkansas, and western Tennessee. Of the millions of slaves in Virginia and the Carolinas,

---

[124] Clarkson entered an essay contest in 1785 regarding the legality of slavery and won. Shortly thereafter, he was drawn by his discovery to fundamentally oppose slavery and the slave trade.

only about 100,000 were actually sold into the cotton belt. It is a myth that slaves were commercially bred for sale in the South (they bred on their own and naturally increased) although it is true that southern slave owners were concerned that importation of slaves diluted the value of their plantations.

2.3 The Southern British Colonies

Virginia

The first attempt at English colonization was at Roanoke Island (now North Carolina) in 1587. Unfortunately for the colonists, the Spanish Armada attacked England in 1588 and by the time that the British returned to resupply the colony, it had disappeared. The next attempt was farther north on the James River in 1607. The Virginia Company of London established a fort on the north shore in May 1607. This colony went through very difficult times and was nearly starved out in 1609, but at the last minute it was resupplied, reinforced and continued on as the capital of Virginia until 1699.

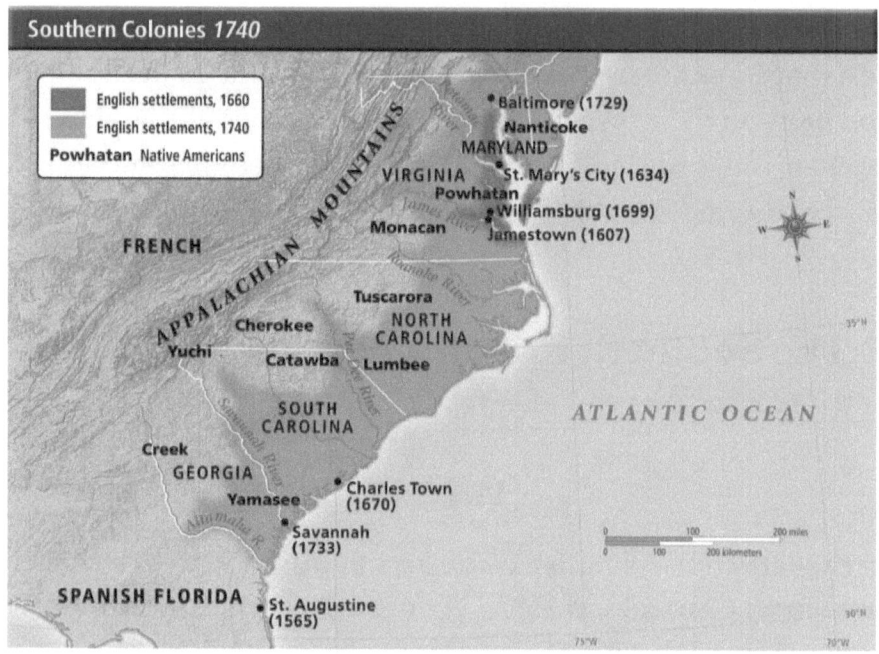

Source: http://travelsfinders.com/american-chesapeake-bay-middle-colonies.html

The interest of the Virginia Company was to develop some sort of profitable export. This goal was not achieved until tobacco seeds were acquired from the Spanish (about 1614) that produced a quality of tobacco favored in Europe. Black Africans, treated as indentured servants, were acquired from a Portuguese ship in 1619.

In a pattern that would be repeated, acquisition of more land and arrival of more settlers brought friction with the Native Americans. On March 22, 1622, the Powhatan confederacy attacked and killed about 300 settlers. Overall, of the 6,000 settlers that had been brought to the colony since its founding, only 3,200 remained in 1624 when Virginia became a crown colony. In 1654, black Africans were allowed to own slaves and in 1657 Virginia passed a fugitive slave law. In 1662, the attitude of Virginians towards slaves shifted dramatically with the legal decisions that children of enslaved mothers were the property of the mother's owner. This decision likely caused the slaves to Virginia to realize that they were not on a footing similar to European indentured servants and may have been the immediate cause of a slave revolt in Gloucester County, Virginia in 1663.

More specifically, in 1661 in York County indentured servants (presumably Europeans) became dissatisfied when it was made known that typically meat was to be provided only three times a week. Initially there was a talk of a petition to the King, but this soon turned to a decision to take up arms to force cancellation of their contracts. This plot was discovered by an overseer and the leaders were tried and one appears to have been punished for sedition. Northward, across the York River in Gloucester County, the unrest among indentured servants seemed to spread involving both Europeans and black Africans (1663). The Africans had been treated similar to the Europeans, but now they realized that neither they nor their children were ever going to be free. The stakes in Gloucester County were higher because they conspirators planned to march to the home of Governor Sir William Berkeley. This involvement with the British government turned the issue from a civil/criminal issue into a political/treason issue. When this plot unraveled, four men were tried, convicted and hanged. Some of the plotters are known to have been former Protestant soldiers (now much despised by the Court of Charles II), but the involvements of black Africans and mulattos is less certain. What is certain is that the fear in Europeans of the Native Americans and African slaves increased from 1660 to 1680. In 1667, Virginia clarified that Christian baptism did not free slaves and forbade free blacks from keeping white indentured servants. The motivation for such a law, suggests that some free back Africans had gained a significant amount to economic prosperity and stability.

A conflict with the local tribes grew into a civil war of sorts (called Bacon's Rebellion; 1676-1677) in a political power struggle to set policy regarding the Native Americans. Meanwhile, in isolated Westmorland County, many slaves had runaway and they had been replaced by slaves brought directly from Africa (not from the West Indies). These slaves were much more difficult to manage and unpredictable because they were African-born, their entire slave experience had been brutal and they spoke no English. Thus, in 1680, laws were passed to disarm and discourage communications among slaves. These laws were tightened in 1682 and 1686. Nonetheless, in 1687, Nicholas Spencer uncovered and reported a plot. The ringleaders were hastily identified, tried and executed through an extra-legal mechanism (*oyer* and *terminer* court).

It is relevant to the overall understanding of how slavery existed in Virginia in the 1600s that as a result of these trials the owners of slaves were chastised for allowing their slaves to roam freely on Saturdays and Sundays and have large gatherings for events within their community (e.g., rites-of-passage such as funerals).[125]

---

[125] Quote from https://www.encyclopediavirginia.org/Westmoreland_Slave_Plot_1687#start_entry

"Members of the Council... regretted "*the great freedome and Liberty*" masters had afforded slaves "*on Saterdays and Sundays and permitting*

Clearly, there was a black African community with autonomy and a good deal of liberty, but limited economic and political freedom (or responsibility). In 1691, Virginia passed more restrictive legislation against inter-racial marriage; and to remove the fear of free black Africans they forbade manumissions and insisted that free black Africans leave the colony. Many free blacks moved into Maryland. In 1705, Virginia enacted a fairly comprehensive slave code, which incorporated the existing restrictions and required that any imported black Africans be classified as slaves and property of their owner. With an influx of black Africans from Virginia, Maryland declared (1715) that all slaves entering the colony and their descendants were to remain slaves for life. Thus, the free black Africans leaving Virginia and runaways tended to pass though Maryland and congregate in Delaware.

William and Mary College was founded in 1693 and after Jamestown suffered a fire, it was abandoned and the legislature moved to form a capital city at Williamsburg (adjacent to the college). Richmond Virginia was established in 1742 on the fall line of the James River. It became an industrial city during colonial times and the state capital was moved there April 18, 1780.

Throughout this time, tobacco farming and related agriculture were the principal economic base of Virginia. Approximately 80,000 slaves were brought to Virginia from Africa by British ships from 1698-1775 and about 7,000 were brought from the West

---

them to meete in great Numbers and making and holding of Funeralls for Dead Negroes." Such occasions provided slaves the opportunity *"to Consult and advise for the Carrying on of the Evill & wicked purposes."'*

Indies. Virginia effective ended importation of slaves during the War of Independence and as the economy diversified after 1800, Virginia had an excess of slave labor and was in favor of abolishing the international trade to support sales of its excess slaves to the Cotton States (Rawley, 2005, p. 347). Natural expansion of the African population far out stripped labor demands in the southern states once the plantations were established. The acreages of the farms never increased, the African population did increase. The population of Virginia in 1790 was 442,000 Europeans, 293,000 African slaves and 13,000 "other free persons."

During the colonial era, Virginia had on the one hand tried to suppress the importation of slaves, which they saw as being pushed upon them by the British. At the same time, manumission (legal release of slaves) was regulated to limit the population of free Africans in Virginia particularly those who were not self-sufficient and thus would produce a drain on the resources of the colony/state and potentially contribute to an insurrection (Babcock, 1974, pp. 1-10). The potential of outside interests (first the French (1754-58) and then the British (1776-1784)) inciting insurrection as a military weapon by promising emancipation was always present.[126] Overall, the colony believed that it was safer to have Africans under the watchful eye of masters than off on their own. As a result, it was not legal to free a slave. Nonetheless, people had placed terms in their wills releasing slaves and many

---

[126] And it would be used again in the War between the States by Lincoln.

slaves (too old or too young to work) were released if they had no value on the market and were an economic burden to the owner.

Thus, in 1782 (shortly before the Treaty of Paris was signed), Virginia quietly passed a law that allowed private parties to release any slave that was under 45 years old.[127] Babcock (1974, pp. 14-25) calculates that over 15,000 slaves were thus voluntarily freed between 1782 and 1806 from a population of about 247,000 slaves in Virginia. In addition, several thousand other Africans were freed for services rendered associated with the war (e.g., soldiers, coastal pilots and laborers). Virginia's free black population also grew as a result of immigrations from North Carolina (where freed-slaves were required to leave the state within 6 months).[128]

Although some authors have argued that the spirit of the revolution had prompted a much larger rate of manumission, Babcock throws harsh light on that idea. In fact, he points out that religiously motivated petitions for emancipation created a backlash by slaveowners who strongly opposed emancipation or

----

[127] Babcock, 1974, pp. 10-14, notes that this law has no written legislative history. It just seems to have appeared. I would suggest that it was probably the work of Thomas Jefferson and George Wythe who probably could have unilaterally got it into the record without debate during the confusion at the end of the war.

[128] It is noteworthy that Delaware appears to have received freed-slaves migrating from nearby states (Virginia, Maryland and North Carolina) probably because they had no time limit. Freed-slave also moved west and north into what became West Virginia and Kentucky (southern bank of the Ohio River).

manumission. Even the politically astute supporters of emancipation were strongly of the opinion that it should not be pushed forward until there existed the means to deport freed slaves to some foreign country. The zeal of Quakers to push for emancipation legislation and use litigation based on state laws to win individual cases was regarded by those who wanted eventual emancipation and continued unencumbered manumission to be very counter-productive as it sparked backlashes from those who held religious support for slavery and fear of free Africans.

The motivations for manumission were revealed to be primarily economic. Indeed, in many cases, manumission was the product of the slave or a freed African buying the freedom of a slave (Babcock, 1974, p. 39).

Maryland and Delaware

A charter for an English colony north of the Potomac River and west of the Trent River was granted to Lord Baltimore in 1632. The western border was to be defined by the headwaters of the Potomac.[129] The original claim included a section of what is now Pennsylvania, but in practice the colony was founded on the Chesapeake Bay in 1634 (St. Mary's City) with a specific interest in ensuring religious freedom for Roman Catholics. Its population was concentrated around the Chesapeake Bay and its economy was very similar to tidewater Virginia based on tobacco and slave labor.

---

[129] This was not established until a survey was conducted to resolve the claims of Virginia and Maryland.

In the meantime, Dutch and then Swedes had laid claim to the lower Delaware River (1633-44) and were building a colony there. The British were in the process of dispossessing the Dutch from New York (Manhattan) and they also targeted this area, which was already claimed by Lord Baltimore as part of the Maryland colony. James Duke of York (who took over New York) also received a grant for the Dutch/Swedish colony west of the Delaware River (1664). Concurrent with these actions, slavery was legalized in Maryland (1663). In 1664, Maryland was among the first colonies to forbid marriage between white women and black men and validate that the children of enslaved women were property of the mother's owner. Since Lord Baltimore's colony had never actually occupied that area, he was content to have Delaware established as a new British colony (essentially a piece of the original Maryland Colony).

Things got even more complicated when William Penn obtained a charter for Pennsylvania (1681) to ensure religious freedom of Quakers. The northern boundary of Maryland would have precluded Pennsylvania access to the Chesapeake Bay. At the other extreme, the Pennsylvania claim would have included most of Maryland and some of Virginia. Ultimately, the boundary was litigated for about 100 years and was resolved with the survey line of Mason and Dixon in 1767.

It is noted that Delaware had a relatively low percentage of slaves and a high percentage of free people of color. The devotion to plantation agriculture was relatively small. The colony was never a major destination for European immigrants and was an easy refuge for slaves freed or runaway from Virginia and Maryland. Note that at in the mid-1700s, "Maryland" was primarily what we now call *southern Maryland* and the *eastern shore*, very few people lived above the falls of the Potomac River. This area was populated primarily by immigrants passing through Pennsylvania to western Virginia (e.g., Shenandoah Valley) rather than from southeastern Maryland.

In 1790 the population of Maryland and Delaware were as follows:

State	European	African Slaves	Other Free People
Maryland	209,000	103,000	8,000
Delaware	46,000	9,000	4,000

North and South Carolina

The French were the first to identify and claim what became the Carolina colonies in the 1560s. Charles I of England granted the territory to Sir Robert Heath in 1629, but he took no action. Nonetheless, an outpost of Virginia was established on the Albemarle Sound between 1640 and 1650. Adventurers from Barbados, the West Indies and Bermuda scouted the Bahama Islands and the cost of South Carolina[130] as far north as the Cape Fear and began displacing the former French settlements near modern Charleston. After the Restoration, Charles II of England in 1663 claimed title to Carolina and appointed Lord Proprietors to organize a colony.

---

[130] Judge McCrady, *History of South Carolina under the Proprietary Government, 1670-1719.*

Charleston (SC) was settled in 1670 by immigrants from Bermuda led by Captain William Sayle (c. 1590–1671). In 1671, the population was reinforced with many Dutch families who were not happy in New York after it was transferred to the English (1664). The edict of Nantes (that allowed Protestants to practice their religion in France) was reversed by Louis XIV and French Protestants (Huguenots) began arriving in Charleston in 1686. The proprietors had installed a very unpopular governor in the North Carolina colony in 1683 and when he was driven out, he moved to Charleston in 1690. From 1702 to 1706, the South Carolina colony felt strong enough to attack the long-standing Spanish colony at St. Augustine (Florida) in support of the British Queen Ann's War. They were not very successful but established a reputation for military strength.

Immigration of Protestants from France and Germany began arriving in the Albemarle colony (NC) in 1707-1710. Immigrants from Virginia (who were frequently skilled workers who had completed indentures from the vicinity of Jamestown) traversed the great dismal swamp to what is now Edenton, NC (1722). Previously, the settlers north of the Albemarle Sound and Chowan River had good relations with the Native tribes, but the influx of more Europeans south of the Albemarle caused the Tuscaroras and the Corees to plan and execute a massacre on October 2, 1711 in which about 130 European between the Pamlico Sound and the Albemarle Sound were killed. In retaliation a militia of 1000 men was raised in Charleston and they soon defeated the Tuscarora tribe in fighting over the next two years. In 1713, the Tuscarora tribe moved north to join the Iroquois Confederacy and a lasting peace was established with the Corees by 1715.

The dangerous outer banks and shoals did not attract commerce to North Carolina; but they were perfect for pirates, including Black Beard who apparently had a wife or mistress in Edenton. Governor Charles Eden (for whom Edenton is named) pardoned Black Beard in 1718.

South Carolina fought and defeated the Yamasee Tribe (1715–1717). This opened the coast south of the Savannah River for British colonization.

Both North and South Carolina had had a frustrating relationship with the proprietors. Both colonies periodically defied and banished their representatives. Thus, between 1719 and 1729 the Carolina colonies managed to have the King take back direct control over the colonies. Clearly, at this time, these colonies were mere toeholds on the North American continent.

With regard to the economy, the Native Americans grew corn and hunted deer. Deer skins were traded with the Europeans for woolen cloth, glass beads and metal objects. But this was not an economy that was going to make anyone rich. As at Jamestown (VA), a variety of crops were considered, but the one that made the most sense in the swampy, coastal low-lands was rice (1694). Many British immigrants to the Carolinas were from Barbados and the other West Indies and were encouraged to bring slaves with them. Georgetown, South Carolina (north of Charleston) was settled mainly by immigrants from Barbados. The Africans had learned the technology of rice growing in their home countries (e.g., Nigeria) and complemented this with rice species from eastern Asia. Thus, the technology of rice agriculture quickly took hold in coastal South Carolina (and on the lower Cape Fear River in North Carolina). As in Africa, rice proved to be a crop that could be produced in excess with the expertise and labor of African slaves and was the basis of the economy in South Carolina after 1670[131] but long staple cotton on the sea isles gave way to upland cotton which dominated the economy in the late 1700.

In North Carolina, the tobacco agriculture of Virginia became more important because the climate is a little too cold for rice. Nonetheless, about 1720, planters from the Goose Creek area north of Charleston, acquired lands along the lower Cape Fear and established a number of rice plantations (Wilmington, 1739). However, this area also developed a "naval stores" economy based on the abundant pine forest. These forests produced pine lumber and pine sap (which was distilled to produce tar, pitch and turpentine) all important ingredients for wooden ships. Naval stores soon replaced the rice farms of the lower Cape Fear valley. There was a major immigration of Scotts into the upper Cape Fear valley. The Argyll Colony was established in 1739 (modern Fayetteville);[132] and after the Battle of Culloden (April 16, 1746), many highlanders arrived in the 1770s.

The slave populations of the Carolinas primarily immigrated from Barbados with their masters. In 1720, the population of

---

[131] There are records of rice being brought to South Carolina in the 1680s, but it is much more likely that the slaves brought it from Barbados or other West Indies islands.

[132] Led by Duncan Campbell, Daniel McNeill, Dugald McNeill, Neill McNeill, and Coll McAlister. Neill McNeill Atkins (1837-1903) was my great grandfather. Wounded at Core Creek in the War, he lost an arm to gangrene.

immigrants to South Carolina was about 6,000 Europeans and 12,000 African slaves.

In the 1740s and 1750s, Europeans (of various nationalities including a preponderance of Scott-Irish, Northern Ireland) were arriving in ports such as Philadelphia and Baltimore and migrating to the Blue Ridge, which they followed southward into the Shenandoah Valley of western Virginia. These frontier families confronted the Native American tribes and traded with the Cherokee and Shawnee. The Cherokee of the Carolinas and Georgia highlands proved to be very friendly and reliable trading partners and allies during the French and Indian War (1754-1763). As a result, Europeans immigrated into central North Carolina (e.g., Salisbury) and western South Carolina (modern Greenville and Spartanburg). After 1763, British treaties with the Native Americans inhibited westward movement.

There was little direct import of slaves to North Carolina, they were introduced from Virginia or South Carolina. Charleston became to center of importation of British goods and British-carried African slaves (Rawley, 2005, p. 351) receiving about 110,000 from Africa and 13,000 from the West Indies before the War of Independence (mainly for cultivation of rice and indigo). Henry Laurens was the most notable slave merchant in South Carolina before 1800, but with the boom of the cotton states, New Englanders (especially Rhode Island slave traders) sent their own representative into Charleston to manage sales for them (Rawley, 2005, p. 358). After 1800, Charleston began trying to establish an African trade but ships, captains and crews were not readily available.

During the War of Independence, a civil war reigned in the up-country of South Carolina between Patriots and Loyalists. The Scotts staged an initial show of support for the British in the Cape Fear valley, but the tidewater of the Carolinas was firmly in support of the Patriot cause. When the South Carolina Loyalist militia was destroyed at Kings Mountain (1780) through the inept leadership of Patrick Ferguson and the resolute determination of the "Over-Mountain Men" from western North Carolina, the fate of the South and all the American colonies was determined. Subsequently, Cornwallis led his army blindly across North Carolina into an indefensible *cul de sac* at Yorktown and was forced to surrender by the French.

The piedmont and uplands of Virginia, Maryland, the Carolinas and Georgia were not suitable for plantation farming, and as a result, in the 1790 census, the population of South Carolina had grown to about 140,000 Europeans and 107,000 Africans slaves and 1,800 "other free persons." In North Carolina, slaves were being used on tobacco farms, which were often large, but which were generally not describable as "plantations." The population was 288,000 European, 101,000 African slaves and 5,000 "other free persons."

Georgia

In 1704, the British destroyed Spanish missions north of Saint Augustine and the war between South Carolina and the Yamasee Tribe (1717) opened the area south of the Savannah River for British settlement.

At this time, it was common for debtors to be imprisoned for their debts in Britain. Of course, it was nearly impossible to pay off debts while confined. James Edward Oglethorpe (1696–1785) was a British nobleman who decided to solve the problem of debtors by transporting them to a colony in North America. He received permission to establish a colony (known as Georgia) and carried the first shipload of colonists to North America in late 1732. The so-called Oglethorpe Plan involved a system in which each household acquired 50 acres of land but could not increase the size of their personal holding. If indentured servants were acquired, they were also allowed similar 50-acre plots, which they initially worked for their manager, but which they owned outright when the indenture ended. Minimal urbanization was allowed by forming small villages with plots of 5 acres (of the allowed 50 acres) in a central location surrounded by the farms (45-acres). The farms were to be based on the cash crop cotton[133] because rice would restrict development to marshy regions. It was also known that rice farms tended to evolve into larger plantations with slaves. Under the Oglethorpe Plan, slavery was not anticipated. The original settlement was on the south side of the Savannah River.

Francis Moore (born ~1708, died ~ 1756) had become a clerk and agent for the Royal African Company and was sent to the mouth of the Gambia River July 1730. He was one of the first and few Europeans to travel far into the interior of sub-Saharan Africa. He made his way up the Gambia River for over a hundred miles and wrote a classical account, *Travels into the Interior Parts of Africa.*

---

[133] The cotton seeds were probably of the Egyptian variety (long staple) obtained from the Chelsea Medicinal Garden in London.

Along the way he made acquaintance with local leaders including the slaver/slave-trader Ayuba Suleiman Diallo[134] (1701 – 1773). Diallo was an intelligent man of native stock (i.e., black African) who had been raised in Islam for generations. He was engaged in providing natives into the Islamic slave network that mainly transported slaves north to Morocco and the Mediterranean coast.

Ironically, after Moore departed, Diallo and his interpreter were kidnapped by Mandingos (also Muslims) who claimed him as a prisoner of war and sold him to the Royal African Company who transported him to Maryland where he was held until 1733 on Kent Island in the Chesapeake Bay (working in tobacco and then herding cattle). He obviously was a knowledgeable person and it was discovered that he was able to read and write Arabic. Thus, he was allowed to send a letter to his father in Africa. This letter made its way to James Oglethorpe (a director of the Royal African Company) who purchased Diallo and had him delivered to England in 1733 in the care of the RAC. There he learned to speak and write English and performed important services in translation before returning to Gambia in 1734. His translator was returned to Gambia in 1738. Obviously, Ayuba Suleiman Diallo was now assisting the British Royal African Company to acquire slaves.

In the meantime, Francis Moore had become the secretary to Oglethorpe and sailed to Georgia with him in 1735. Augusta was founded in 1736. Moore became the commissary at Fort Frederica until 1743. The colony was invaded by the Spanish from Florida in 1742 and became a crown colony in 1752, which permitted

---

[134] A.k.a., Job ben Solomon. If you are conquered by the Muslims, you must convert to their religion. This story is usually presented as an example of a slave returning home. It is probably better presented as a slaver establishing a good relationship with the British slave traders.

slavery. Back in Africa, Diallo was captured and imprisoned by the French, who were in competition with the British in expanding the slave trade.

Although cotton was raised on the sea isles of Georgia, the first major export was corn. Silk was exported by 1735 and reached about 1 ton in 1767. Georgia established an agricultural experiment station in 1740 to identify crops that would be successful in its climate and soil. After slavery was allowed (1752), rice and indigo soon displaced silk in importance. Cotton would not be the major crop until a variety that would grow on uplands was available.

Overall, before the War of Independence, Georgia was little more than a strip of land along the Savannah River adjacent to South Carolina. In 1790, the population was 53,000 Europeans and 29,000 African slaves.

2.4 The French Colonization of North America

Explorers vs Families

The Catholic nations of Europe (Spain, Portugal, France and Italy) had originally (1492-1600) dominated international explorations and conquest. Their view of and approach to these new lands was that they were to serve the parent country. Domestically these countries were relatively wealthy with firmly established monarchies that were in complete control with the religious blessing of the Pope. Thus, their view of the new world was very much that outpost were merely subservient provinces that were to be exploited for glorification and enrichment of the home country. Although males from the countries went overseas to conquer, exploit and trade with the natives, there was very little inclination to send women from the Catholic European countries overseas. The result was that French, Spanish and Portuguese men in the new world, typically took Native American or African (slave) concubines some of who were effectively wives. The product of these unions were mulattoes, creoles and mixed-race natives (who were often not readily distinguishable from Europeans).

Britain and the Netherlands, in contrast, were struggling to maintain a Protestant religious base and were relatively late to the conquest of the new world. The mainland European conflicts between Catholic and Protestant factions always were dominated by the Catholic majority. As a result, Britain and the Netherlands were constantly receiving immigrant *families* from mainland Europe. There were also splinter Protestant groups in Britain who were not appreciated by the Church of England and finally, as the British conquered Ireland (1690), they gained control over a population of Catholic *families*. It thus became British and Dutch policy to encourage the emigration and deportations of males *and females* to the new world as colonists. The unintended consequence of this was to transplant European culture, values and customs to the new world in the North American Colonies.

The impact of British colonization was much more threatening to the Native Americans than explorers and soldiers from France and Spain. The British were there to take the land and displace the natives that did not assimilate with them. On the other hand, the French and Spanish were more or less assimilated into the native culture. The British unintentionally were introducing a system that would lead to the virtual genocide of the Native Americans of North America.

The Sugar Plantations

We have already described the style of operation of West Indies sugar plantations, the most notorious example being Hispaniola (modern Haiti). Slaves were fed into this machine starting in 1501 and consumed like a raw material; but it made France rich. The first slave revolt in Hispaniola was in 1522. In 1562, John Hawkins became the first British slave trader bringing slaves to Hispaniola.

Canada and Louisiana

The French interest in the far northern part of North America is traced to 1534 when Jacques Cartier (1491-1557) explored the Gulf of St. Lawrence (modern Gaspé, Quebec). But it was not until 1603 that Samuel de Champlain (1567-1635) managed to start permanent settlements and outpost at Port-Royal (1605), Quebec City (1608) and Trois-Rivières (1634). Montreal (1642) was settled after his death. In 1682 (Mr. de la Salle), the French claimed the Mississippi and Ohio watersheds as Louisiana. The lower Mississippi River was explored and mapped 1698-99 by Mr. le Chevallier d'Iberville. The map he created (1701) shows a number of native settlements west of Mobile Bay especially on the Pearl River and a fort at New Orleans. Baton Rouge was literally a red pole marking the boundary between the hunting grounds to two tribes. The French settlement of Baton Rouge began in 1721. The

French established sugar plantations in western and southern Louisiana. The French held this are until 1763 and imported about 6,000 black African slaves between 1712 and 1763 (when the British occupied the east bank of the Mississippi and the Spanish were ceded the west bank after the Seven Years War/ French and Indian War).

Except for modern Louisiana, the lands that the French had claimed in North America were not suitable for cash crops (at that time, grains could not be shipped from the American mid-west to Europe without spoilage) and the French did not have enough Europeans in place to farm. For the most part, French trade with the native tribes was limited to fur trapping especially beaver. Concurrently, the British were developing a deer skin trade with the Cherokee (located in north Georgia, northeast Alabama and western Carolina, which included eastern Tennessee). This trade was primarily via Charleston, but enterprising Virginians from the Shenandoah Valley followed the trail south (roughly modern I-81 and I-26) to the Cherokee villages along the Little Tennessee River (east and west of the highlands). The Cherokee had established their dominance over the Creek tribes to the south and west, but had a long-standing rivalry with the Shawnee who were mainly north of the Ohio River and into western Pennsylvania. The French mainly traded with the Shawnee in this area. Thus, the French-Shawnee and the British-Cherokee alliances were about to be tested.

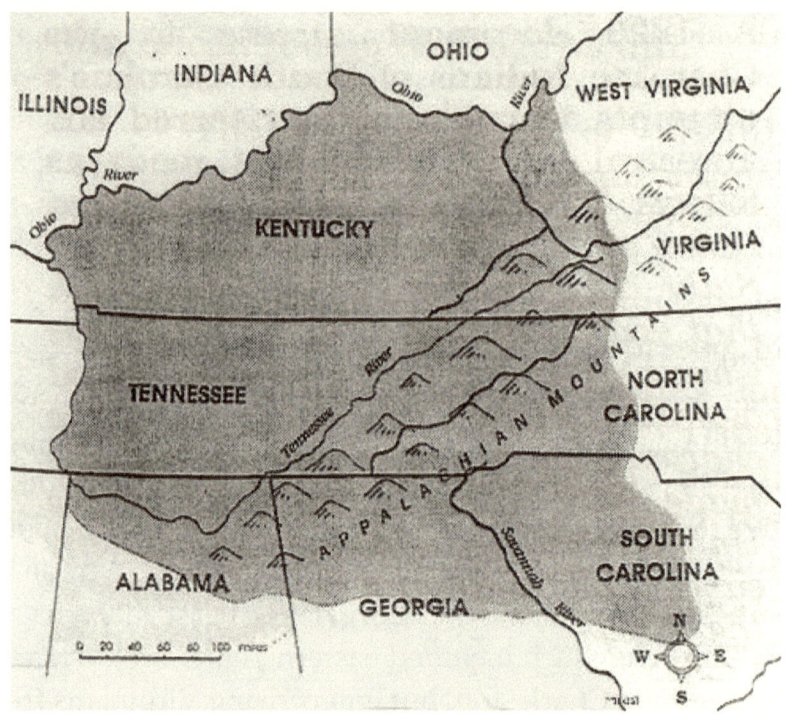

Cherokee Homeland 1700

Source: Clipart Library

https://www.knowitall.org/sites/default/files/cherokeeterritor
y_L_0.jpg

The French claim to New France included territories that the British colonies claimed. The British and French had been fighting over this land since 1605 with significant battles in 1613, 1689 and 1710. These wars took on a distinct Catholic vs Protestant tone, frequently associated with Catholic priest. In 1754, the entire French population in North America was approximately 60,000 compared to the British colonies with over

2,000,000 Europeans. But the French had good relations with the native tribes (e.g., Shawnee) while in the Northeast, the British had few native friends. The war took on a new dimension when the French built a fort (Fort Duquesne) at the forks of the Ohio River (now Pittsburg, PA) to enforce their claim to the Ohio River valley.

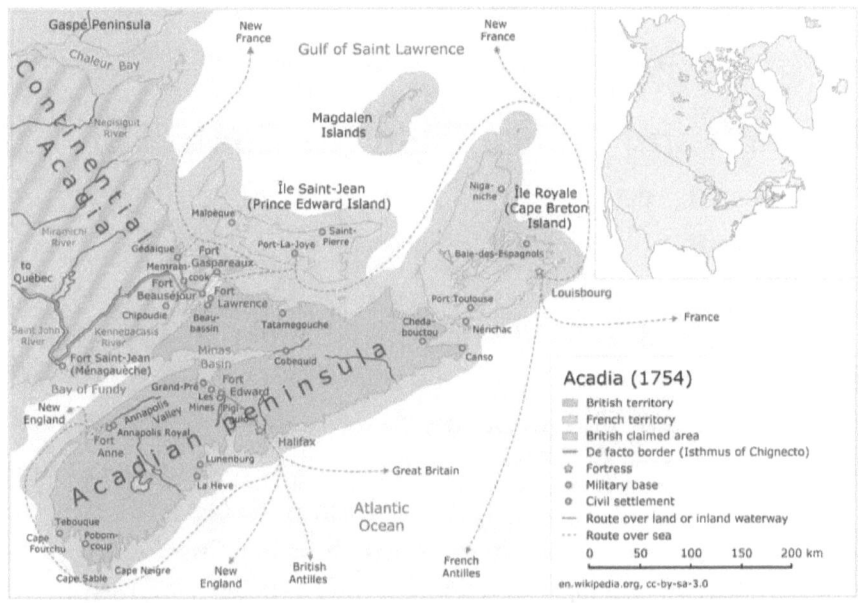

Arcadia with overlapping French and British Claims

Author: Mikmaq; Source: Wikimedia Commons

It was clear that the French now intended to block westward expansion of the British colonies, many of which had claims at least to the Mississippi River, if not all the way to the west coast. In addition, the Shawnee were terrorizing western British settlements (Virginia, Maryland and Pennsylvania) with the encouragement of the French. Even Lord Fairfax who had an estate just east of the Blue Ridge was threatened.

In 1754, a contingent of Virginia militia defending against Shawnee attacks, was ambushed by a French patrol at the Battle of Jumonville Glen. The British took a variety of actions against the French. In particular, in the northern colonies, the British captured Fort Beauséjour (1755) and William Shirley, British Commander-in-Chief, North America ordered all French Arcadians deported to Louisiana (now known as Cajuns).

2.5 Britain and France Fight for Control of North America

In 1755, the most directly affected (mi-Atlantic) colonial governors met with British General Braddock and a plan was formulated to attack the French at Ft. Duquesne. George Washington who was working as a surveyor out of Winchester, VA (west of the Blue Ridge) led a contingent of Virginia militia with General Braddock's British regulars into Pennsylvania. They were ambushed and Braddock (1695-1755) was killed. Washington then retreated with the survivors.

The war that unfolded pitted the militias of the British colonies and regular British troops allied with the Cherokee and a few New England tribes against the French and their Native American (mainly Shawnee) allies. From the British point of view, they were expending substantial resources to defend the colonies as an element in a war that was fought in a number of theaters around the world. The conduct of the war is only peripheral to the objectives of this book. It was more or less decided in major battles including capture of Ft. Duquesne (September 1758) and

Québec (September 1759). The latter battle, essentially won
Canada (which was not at that time colonized by the British) for
the British. Ultimately, in the Treaty of Paris (1763), the French
gave up lands east of the Mississippi to the British and west of the
Mississippi to the Spanish.

Of course, although Britain was victorious, the victory was
expensive and the prevailing view in Britain was that the colonies
and the Cherokee had been axillaries. Indeed, the Cherokee were
viewed as a foreign ally and the Shawnee were also protected by
the peace treaty as a defeated foe. To ensure no farther trouble
with the Native Americans, the British Proclamation of 1763
stated that the colonists should not move farther west than the
Blue Ridge mountains. The remainder of the British territories
were dedicated as a preserve for the Native Americans with
representatives in various British forts. This, of course, infuriated
the British colonists, who were already settling in Kentucky and
Ohio and had ambitions that reached all the way to the Pacific
Ocean. And, of course, the British though it was quite fair that the
colonists should be taxed to reimburse Britain for its support and
ongoing protection. The French and British were destined to fight
off and on for the next 50 years.

2.6 Dissatisfaction with British Rule (1760-1775)

Suffice it to say that the egos of many (mainly upper class)
European colonists were hurt by the recognition that Native
Americans were treated by the British as co-equal allies while
they were treated as provincial bumkins. The Cherokee

representatives were afforded state honors in the British court while the colonists were under the supervision of unpopular British governors appointed from London.

At the request of Barbados, Jamaica and Antigua, in 1733, the British had imposed a tax (i.e., protective tariff) on molasses imports to New England from non-British sources in the West Indies (e.g., Spanish, French and Dutch). This tax was not aggressively enforced by Britain[135] and was easily circumvented by New England rum distillers. The first aggressively enforced, direct *revenue tax* placed on the colonies by Britain came after the French and Indian War in 1764 with the Sugar Act, which attempted to place a tax on sugar and a number of other products imported to the colonies from the West Indies. Because, New England imported sugar and molasses not just for human consumption, but as a raw material for the manufacture of rum as part of their slave trading activities, the act primarily impacted New England (Rawley, 2005, p. 269).

However, in 1765 the British introduced a requirement that the colonists provide shelter for British soldiers stationed in North America. In practice, this meant that British soldiers would be quartered in the homes of colonists.[136] The homes of Americans

---

[135] It was essentially "a wash" as far as the British government was concerned, the tax mainly determined whether New England or the West Indies would become rich. In some cases, New England families had a hand in each business.

[136] It should be noted that in WWII some American soldiers were quartered with British families. This was undoubtedly doubly galling as in many cases the sons of British families were fighting in North Africa or the Far East in 1942-43. But the early 1940s was war-time in

on the frontier were frequently small, offering minimal privacy. Many of the British soldiers were mercenaries and not necessarily people you would want to introduce to your children. In the eastern cities (far from hostile natives), the higher-ranking British soldiers were viewed as potential spies and the British officers frequently carried the contempt of British nobility towards the colonials. All in all, what may have seemed to be a reasonable war-time expedient in Britain was an incredible invasion of privacy and financial burden for the colonists. Also, in 1765, the colonists were made subject to the Stamp Act, which essentially placed a small burden on most paper good. Although the actual burden was not great, it was clear that the tax was to raise revenue to support the British soldiers (about 10,000) that were now being quartered in American homes.

The intensions of these moves by Britain may have been a simple benign attempt to secure the Empire from *outside enemies*; but, in the absence of manifest outside threats, the colonists tended to interpret the British action as an attempt to ensure that they (British subjects) remained loyal to the King. The British experience during the French and Indian War showed that the Americans were developing independent military and economic strength (beyond any other element of the British empire) and that there was a growing unity among the colonies. But rather than attempt to increase the affection between England and America, the British felt that a strong hand was the best way to

---

Britain and the presence of Americans assured Britain that they would not be facing the Nazis alone. In contrast, by 1765, the American colonists viewed the British soldiers as unnecessary outsiders.

ensure colonial allegiance. In Virginia, Patrick Henry managed to get some resolutions repudiating the British approach through the colony's House of Burgesses, but these were dismissed by the British Royal Governor.

Doubling down on the Stamp Act and Sugar Act, Britain imposed the Townsend Acts in 1767. These acts included tariffs on certain goods imported to the colonies, which raised money for the British treasurer. But the acts went far beyond collecting money; they imposed a sanction on colonial governments and imposed British inspectors/regulators in a heavy-handed attempt to stop circumvention of the British taxing acts by trading with other countries (e.g., smuggling sugar from the West Indies and smuggling tea by the Dutch, which reduced profits of the India Company). The position of the British government was to encourage British imports especially slaves (a very high profit merchandise).

The Townsend Acts definitely provoked resistance in the colonies. The primary method of resistance was boycott of British goods (including slaves). In the Carolinas, a revolt and civil war was brewing.[137] In the western part of the Carolinas, an anti-British movement called the "Regulators" was actively defying British officials (e.g., sheriffs and judges). In May 1771, several thousand regulators marched against Governor Tryon of (New Bern) North Carolina who called out the colonial militia. The two forces met at Alamance Court House in central North Carolina and the militia held the ground (with 9 dead and 61 wounded). Casualties among the Regulators are not known, buy the leaders

---

[137] This history is little known in a typical example for bias towards New England history.

were tried and 7 were hanged. The remainder of the regulators (about 6000) were forced to swear an oath of allegiance. Although this temporarily settled the situation, this division would be replayed in the southern colonies when the general War of Independence broke out.

John Hancock (1737-1793)

John Hancock III is the most remembered member of a Massachusetts family described as "clergy, soldier, planter" from as early as 1671. Although history does not reveal any particular activities related to the slave-trade, Hancock III owned several ships and was very likely a sophisticated smuggler. Thus, it is hard to imagine that the family was not familiar with the slave-trade and likely had connections to the West Indies. Hancock III inherited the family businesses (1764) and likely expanded his profits by smuggling sugar/molasses and other commodities to avoid British taxation in the mid-1700s. By 1768, he was one of the wealthiest men in the colonies.

Hancock III opposed British policies because they hurt his businesses, but he had entered local politics and was mentored by Samuel Adams who was pushing a separatist political agenda with the Whig party; i.e., without representation in Parliament, only the colonies should be able to tax the colonies. This conflict in viewpoint arose from the fact that the colonies had originally been the property of the King, not separate geographic districts as represented in Parliament. The so-called "*Liberty* affair" (1768) has been debated as either an example of smuggling by one of Hancock's ships or a complicated conspiracy by Royal officials to enrich themselves and punish him for his political affiliation.

Adams particularly inflamed the British by sending out a Circular Letter (1768) encouraging other colonies to follow the lead of Massachusetts in opposing the British.

A change in the Royal Governor created a brief improvement in relations to the British, but the British philosophy was still to deal very firmly with the colony and this soon led to a situation where British troops fired on a Boston mob (March 1770). Handcock's popularity grew as he threatened to lead attacks on the British that caused them to withdraw some men to more secure locations. The next act of defiance came to a head with the Tea Act of 1773, which precipitated the Boston Tea Party in December 1773.

The British responded by declaring that Massachusetts was in rebellion, closing Boston Harbor and replacing their civilian governor with General Thomas Gage (May 1774).

A Continental Congress of the British colonies was called in September-October of 1774 and met in Philadelphia, PA (Georgia did not attend). The British had blundered into bringing the colonies together in resistance to British domination. There was a general boycott against British imports including slaves. Many colonies already had an excess of slave labor and had incurred significant debt to British merchants in buying slaves (Rawley, 2005 p. 271).

Payton Randolph (VA) and Henry Middleton (SC) were leaders of the meeting. The meeting split into two general groups: (i) those who merely wished to ask the British for relief and reconciliation and (ii) those who wished to affirmatively set out rights of the colonies. Overall, the results were conservative with a call for general boycott of British goods (which was effective). It also planned for a second congress which included invitations to the

British in Quebec, Nova Scotia, east and west Florida, and others to be held in 1775. This put the British on notice that the 13 colonies had designs on all British possessions in North America.

In May 1775 Hancock was elected President of the Massachusetts colonial congress and was chosen to represented them at the Second Continental Congress in Philadelphia (April 1775). The rhetoric coming from these meetings was becoming more and more rebellious. In April of 1775, British in Boston became very concerned that colonial militia in nearby towns were hording weapons and set out to take the weapons. They met and routed small bands of militia in Lexington and Concord, but they sustained casualties during their retreat. Gage apparently did not directly order the arrest of Hancock and Adams, but instead focused on the military equipment being accumulated. Regardless, the colonists' assumption was that he intended to arrest Handcock and Adams.

Handcock and Adams escaped and Handcock made his way to the 2nd Continental Congress where he was elected president (May 1775). From there he was able to influence the other colonies who had various grievances against British rule. According to text books written in the North, this was the official beginning of the War of Independence.

At the Second Continental Congress (beginning May, 1775), the mood began with efforts to achieve relief and achieve reconciliation. Little was accomplished and the meetings continued into 1776. Finally, it was decided that there was no turning back and that independence from Britain was the only answer. Thomas Jefferson was given the task of writing a *Declaration of Independence*, which he delivered.

Its title clearly recognized the independent status of the 13 sovereign states (claiming independence from their colonial status) and it began with a stirring assertion of natural rights of political liberty and unambiguous equality of all men/women regardless of birth station.

In CONGRESS
July 4, 1776.

The unanimous Declaration of the thirteen United States of America

When in the Course of human events, it becomes necessary for one people to dissolve the political bands which have connected them with another, and to assume among the powers of the earth, the separate and equal station to which the Laws of Nature and of Nature's God entitle them, a decent respect to the opinions of mankind requires that they should declare the causes which impel them to the separation.

We hold these truths to be self-evident, that all men are created equal, that they are endowed by their Creator with certain unalienable Rights, that among these are Life, Liberty and the pursuit of Happiness.
"That to secure these rights, Governments are instituted among Men, deriving their just powers from the consent of the governed, That whenever any Form of Government becomes destructive of these ends, it is the Right of the People to alter or to abolish it, and to institute new Government, laying its foundation on such principles and organizing its powers in such form, as to them shall seem most likely to effect their Safety and Happiness. Prudence, indeed, will dictate that Governments long established should not be changed for light and transient causes; and accordingly all experience hath shewn, that mankind are more disposed to suffer, while evils are sufferable, than to right themselves by abolishing the forms to which they are

---

> *accustomed. But when a long train of abuses and usurpations,*
> *pursuing invariably the same Object evinces a design to reduce them*
> *under absolute Despotism, it is their right, it is their duty, to throw off*
> *such Government, and to provide new Guards for their future*
> *security. …*

The declaration then innumerate the abuses to the colonies by the British King. Among these abuses Jefferson included the following:[138]

> *"He has waged cruel war against human nature itself, violating*
> *its most sacred rights of life and liberty in the persons of a distant*
> *people who never offended him, captivating & carrying them into*
> *slavery in another hemisphere or to incur miserable death in their*
> *transportation thither. This piratical warfare, the opprobrium of*
> *infidel powers, is the warfare of the Christian King of Great*
> *Britain. Determined to keep open a market where Men should be*
> *bought & sold, he has prostituted his negative for suppressing*
> *every legislative attempt to prohibit or restrain this execrable*
> *commerce. And that this assemblage of horrors might want no*
> *fact of distinguished die, he is now exciting those very people to*
> *rise in arms among us, and to purchase that liberty of which he*
> *has deprived them, by murdering the people on whom he has*
> *obtruded them: thus paying off former crimes committed again*

---

[138] Thomas Jefferson, The Writings of Thomas Jefferson: Being His Autobiography, Correspondence, Reports, Messages, Addresses, and other Writings, Official and Private (Washington, D.C.: Taylor & Maury, 1853-1854).
https://blackpast.org/primary/declaration-independence-and-debate-over-slavery

the Liberties of one people, with crimes which he urges them to commit against the lives of another."

This, specific abuse was strongly objected to by the slave-traders of New England and New York, because they had also participated in the slave trade (Rawley, 2005, p. 274). If the "Christian King of Great Britain" was guilty of the crime of the slave trade, so were they. As a result, this was the only serious objection raised to the declaration as Jefferson (a southern slave-owner) drafted it. The fact that it does not condemn *slave ownership*, I think, reflects the general opinion that black Africans were better off in America than in Africa and the implicit notion that they would eventually be free in an independent United States. The passage was replaced in the approved document by a simple note that the British incited *"domestic insurrections among us,"* which could include both slave revolts and attacks by Native Americans.

After declaring independence, it was clear that a continental army was required and George Washington of Virginia was put in charge. The Second Continental Congress was to stay in cession until 1889.

2.7 The British Colonies become Independent States (1775-1783)

It was not a Revolution

From the stand point of this book, the most important thing to remember is that the American War of Independence was not a "revolution." There was no change in the *internal* moral character or power structure of the American colonies associated with the war. The same people were in charge before and after the war. The Congenital Congress was the collective governing body before, during and after the war.

The War of Independence gained independence of the respective colonies from the British government and established a Confederation of independent, sovereign states (not unlike the German states in central Europe). The British colonies in Canada were not included and the 1763 line limiting the westward claims of the colonies became moot. The colonies now reached as far to the west as they could enforce their will on the Native Americans and European claimants (France and Spain).

North Carolina declares its Independence

The war itself was fought in three main theaters New England, the Mid-Atlantic and the South (primarily Virginia and the Carolinas). Our histories generally only focus on New England. It is hard to find references to the Battle of Alamance Court House (NC, May 1771) and the pattern that it set for the war in the South.

Following the encounters at Lexington and Concord (April 1775), the 2nd Continental Congress convened in Philadelphia, PA. George Washington was appointed commander of the Continental Army (June 1775) essentially concurrent with the defeat of New England militias on Breed's Hill outside Boston. It is important that in 1775, the British were essentially trying to suppress anti-British rebellion in Massachusetts. But there were obvious signs of unrest throughout the colonies.

In early 1776, Patriots in North Carolina once again took up arms against the Royal Governor at Moore's Creek Bridge. This battle was set into motion when Loyalist Scotts from the upper Cape Fear River (Cross Creek, now Fayetteville, NC) attempted to join Loyalists and Redcoat soldiers at Brunswick near the coast. The Patriot militia, however, intercepted them at Moore's Creek and the Loyalists ran headlong into an ambush and were readily defeated (February 27, 1776). This battle effectively ended British rule in North Carolina as the governor was isolated on the coast with minimal military support. North Carolina was actually the first colony to vote for independence on April 12, 1776.

The Articles of Confederation (1777-1786)

It is important to appreciate the courage and commitment of all the signatories of the Declaration of Independence (July 1776), who risks their lives and fortunes in a war against the largest military power in the world.

The colonies claimed the status of independent states and banded together under a confederation primarily for the purpose of pursuing the war against the British. Washington's army was forced to retreat from New York and across New Jersey in 1776. He finally stopped the British at the Delaware River and brought new life to his army with an audacious raid across the river into Trenton, NJ (December 25–26, 1776) and was able to re-enter New Jersey in the spring of 1777.

Articles of Confederation, which gave very limited power to the Continental Congress, were agreed by the Congress of the states (November 17, 1777). This document was not fully ratified until relatively late in the war (1 March 1781) when Maryland finally agreed.

ARTICLES OF CONFEDERATION AND PERPETUAL UNION, between the States of New Hampshire, Massachusetts Bay, Rhode Island and Providence Plantations, Connecticut, New York, New Jersey, Pennsylvania, Delaware, Maryland, Virginia, North Carolina, South Carolina, and Georgia.

ARTICLE 1. The style of this confederacy shall be, "THE UNITED STATES OF AMERICA."

ART. 2. Each State retains its sovereignty, freedom, and independence, and every power, jurisdiction, and right, which is not by this confederation, expressly delegated to the United States, in Congress assembled.

ART. 3. The said States hereby severally enter into a firm league of friendship with each other, for their common defence, the security of their liberties, and their mutual and general welfare, binding themselves to assist each other against all force offered to, or attacks made upon them, or any of them, on account of religion, sovereignty, trade, or any other pretence whatever.

Source: https://memory.loc.gov/cgi-bin/ampage?collId=llsl&fileName=001/llsl001.db&recNum=127

The British captured Philadelphia in the fall of 1777 and Washington's army spend a miserable winter at Valley Forge, PA (December 1777-spring 1778). The British could hold the cities, but were not able to control the country side. In particular, after suffering a defeat at Saratoga, NY (September-October 1777), the French began supporting the Colonists and the British were forced to reinforce New York and abandon Philadelphia (June 1778). The year 1779 was mainly a stalemate throughout the states. The British decide to focus on the South in 1780 where there is active Loyalist support in the rural areas.

In the Carolinas and Georgia, the population was divided between Loyalists and Patriots and there was something of a civil war in the South Carolina up-country. In May 1780, the British recaptured Charleston and were attempting to break the stalemate in the North by attacking from the South. After routing Patriot militia and Continental army units in South Carolina, the British appeared to be poised to break out into North Carolina. But their commander Lord Cornwallis fell ill and the Patrick Ferguson who had been placed in charge of the Loyalist South Carolina militia foolishly challenged and threatened the North Carolinians. Some of the most determined anti-British Patriots and most proficient soldiers were the "over-mountain" men who were in what is now eastern Tennessee (they had been directly affected by the 1763 proclamation line). They were roused by Ferguson's threats and moved to attack him when he foolishly encamped his forces on the table top-hill known as King's Mountain. He must have thought that the Americans would politely line up and volley back and forth on the field; instead they climbed the sides of the hill and fired from the woods on the edges of the field at the helpless South Carolina Loyalists standing in lines in the open.

This engagement (October 7, 1780) seemed to set Cornwallis off on a blind charge across North Carolina (Guilford Court House, March 15, 1781) and south eastern Virginia placing himself in an indefensible and unescapable position at Yorktown. With massive French support surrounding the British and the imposition of the French fleet preventing evacuation, Cornwallis surrendered his command (October 19, 1781) and the British essentially decided that further combat was not worth the effort. American independence was won by French intervention although the British continued to occupy New York pending a formal peace treaty. Hint, the war was won in the South.

The Treaty of Paris (September 3, 1783)

After the surrender of Lord Cornwallis at Yorktown, the British (*i.e.*, King George III) who still controlled important territory in America decided to negotiate a conditional peace treaty with the colonies. The negotiations were held in Paris (France) and went through a series of drafts and a final document that was produced on September 3, 1783 and ratified in 1784 by the U.S. and Britain. *Each colony was granted individual sovereignty and independence.*

The Definitive Treaty of Peace 1783

In the name of the most holy and undivided Trinity.

It having pleased the Divine Providence to dispose the hearts of the most serene and most potent Prince George the Third, by the grace of God, king of Great Britain, France, and Ireland, defender of the faith, duke of Brunswick and Lunebourg, arch-treasurer and prince elector of the Holy Roman Empire etc., and of the United States of America, to forget all past misunderstandings and differences that have

---

unhappily interrupted the good correspondence and friendship which they mutually wish to restore, and to establish such a beneficial and satisfactory intercourse , between the two countries upon the ground of reciprocal advantages and mutual convenience as may promote and secure to both perpetual peace and harmony; ....

... agreed upon and confirmed the following articles.

Article 1:

His Brittanic Majesty acknowledges the said United States, viz., New Hampshire, Massachusetts Bay, Rhode Island and Providence Plantations, Connecticut, New York, New Jersey, Pennsylvania[139], Maryland, Virginia, North Carolina, South Carolina and Georgia, to be free sovereign and independent states, that he treats with them as such, and for himself, his heirs, and successors, relinquishes all claims to the government, propriety, and territorial rights of the same and every part thereof.

...

Article 7:

There shall be a firm and perpetual peace between his Brittanic Majesty and the said states, and between the subjects of the one and the citizens of the other, wherefore all hostilities both by sea and land shall from henceforth cease. All prisoners on both sides shall be set at liberty, and his Brittanic Majesty shall with all convenient speed, and without causing any destruction, or carrying away any Negroes or other property of the American inhabitants, withdraw all his armies,

---

[139] The original copy listed Delaware but some copies left Delaware out.

garrisons, and fleets from the said United States, and from every post, place, and harbor within the same; leaving in all fortifications, the American artillery that may be therein; and shall also order and cause all archives, records, deeds, and papers belonging to any of the said states, or their citizens, which in the course of the war may have fallen into the hands of his officers, to be forthwith restored and delivered to the proper states and persons to whom they belong.

....

Done at Paris, this third day of September in the year of our Lord, one thousand seven hundred and eighty-three.

D. HARTLEY (SEAL)

JOHN ADAMS (SEAL)

B. FRANKLIN (SEAL)

JOHN JAY (SEAL)

Aftermath of the War of Independence

The colonies and the Continental Congress each amassed debt during the War of Independence. When the war ended in 1783, each state was independently identified as sovereign by the British government in the Treaty of Paris. Thus, from 1783-1789 each State managed its own affairs. The Continental Congress actually had no mechanism for addressing its debts. The money had been loaned primarily out of patriotism with little expectation of ever being paid back (e.g., the British might well have won the war).

The issue of forming a stronger union came up spontaneously at a routine meeting of the committee on trade issues at Annapolis in 1786. It was recommended to the Congress of the Confederation that a constitution should be developed and a convention was called in 1787 at Philadelphia. Rhode Island realized that it was such a unique and small state that any change in the Confederation would likely work against it. Thus, Rhode Island did not participate in the convention.

Shay's Rebellion (1786-87)

Even in New England, there was a political division between rural and urban areas. The inland farmers were basically engaged at the level of subsistence farming while along the sea coast, the triangle trade (slaves to cotton/sugar to rum/clothing) created a wealthy merchant class. At the end of the war, absent British backing, European lenders wanted hard cash (backed by some reliable government) for payment of debts. Without cash, the interior farmers found themselves unable to pay taxes that the merchants were demanding be paid in cash. The states (in the North) were also demanding taxes in cash. The results were that the farmers were being crushed financially and having the only thing they owned (their land) taken from them. In the middle of this situation, a farmer (known derisively as a "plough jogger") made this widely cited statement:[140]

> *"I have been greatly abused, have been obliged to do more than*
> *my part in the war, been loaded with class rates, town rates,*
> *province rates, Continental rates and all rates ... been pulled and*

---

[140] SOURCE: https://en.wikipedia.org/wiki/Shays%27_Rebellion

*hauled by sheriffs, constables and collectors, and had my cattle
sold for less than they were worth ... The great men are going to
get all we have and I think it is time for us to rise and put a stop
to it, and have no more courts, nor sheriffs, nor collectors nor
lawyers."*

Daniel Shays (1747–1825) had joined the Continental Army;
fought in several important battles; left that army unpaid to
return to his farm and immediately found himself defending
himself in court for non-payment of taxes. Petitions to the state of
Massachusetts were ignored. John Hancock resigned as governor
(1785) and was replaced by one of the principal antagonists of the
farmers (James Bowdoin, another wealthy Boston merchant).
Predictably, the situation for the farmers got worse and local
protest soon turned to serious action.   In August and September
1886, Shays led disturbances that shut down local courts and the
local militias refused to respond to the governor's call. When the
supreme court of Massachusetts attempted to arrest the leaders,
opposing forces (1200 of Shays' supporters and 800 men hired by
the governor) faced off at the Springfield Armory in November.
This episode (November 1786) was deescalated, but when leaders
in the eastern part of the state were apprehended with violence in
December, Shays and his followers rose up in the west with a plan
to capture the Springfield Armory. Unfortunately, the governor
had already taken the armory and used it to arm 1200 men. The
proposed attack on the armory (January 25th) was thwarted by
overwhelming firepower (cannon firing grape shot) and poor
coordination of the attacking forces. The blooded rebels hastily
retreated to the north and west with several thousand organized
soldiers in pursuit. On the night of February 3-4, the governor's
troops surprised and scattered the rebels. The leaders mainly

escaped into New Hampshire and Vermont. Amnesty was offered to the others who admitted participation. This drew out about 4,000 signatures (who wished to avoid and potential punishment). Eighteen leaders were identified, tried, convicted, and sentenced to hang. With Shays hiding in Vermont, two men were in fact hanged and the rest either were released on appeal or eventually pardoned (including Shays).

2.8 Political Fusion of the States (1787-1790)

To reiterate: The Confederation of States continued under the Continental Congress but many people recognized its weakness and the potential for piece-meal destruction of the states by outside powers (e.g., Spain in Florida and just west of the Mississippi River and Britain in Canada) and the desirability to eliminate friction among the States that could interrupt trade and economic development. The States had differences in size, resources, industries, population and laws (particularly with respect to the institution of slavery) that presented substantial problems in their coalescence. Nonetheless, a convention was called in Philadelphia to see if common ground could be found.

The international slave trade was not needed because the numbers of black Africans was expanding faster than agricultural land. Thus, New Englanders were getting out of the slaving business. Domestic slavery was becoming unprofitable in Virginia and North Carolina and even South Carolina was losing interest as its tenable lands became less productive through loss of nutrients (especially nitrate).[141] The thought that all slaves would eventually be free was in the air. Georgia was, however, growing rapidly and there was the Mississippi territory to the west where cotton might be grown. However, much of this land was occupied by Native American tribes (Cherokee, Creek, Choctaw). In addition, there was still a major technological problem in growing cotton economically…the cotton gin was not invented until 1793 and did not become widely applied until 1800.

The Constitutional Convention (1787)

The Constitutional Convention among the sovereign States proceeded between May 25 and September 17, 1787. The state delegates authorized to negotiate for the sovereign States created a system of committees, which debated in secret to allow free expression of opinions without impact on the political or personal careers of members especially if no agreement was reached. Thomas Jefferson, who was in France at the time, condemned the secrecy, but I think he was naïve about the influence that public debate would have had. Because of the secrecy, our insight into the debates is primarily dependent upon notes taken by Madison and released much later.[142] These notes are generally description

---

[141] Nitrate is a limiting nutrient in most soil. Cotton "wears out" soil very quickly because the mass of the plant is much greater than the mass of the cotton bolls themselves… a tremendous amount of biomass has to be produced for a small amount of product.

[142] See the Avalon Project, Yale Law School.
http://avalon.law.yale.edu/subject_menus/debcont.asp

by the note-taker of what was said/meant, with occasional paraphrases and frequent abbreviations (and misspellings). In some places, the notes appear to have been supplemented with comments that were not obvious at the time of the actual debates. The most relevant notes will be shown below.

The convention began with several proposals regarding its goals and some specific proposals regarding form.[143] Very early, the idea of three independent elements of government: The Legislature, The Executive and the Judiciary was proposed and generally agreed (May 30th -31st). Most of the early debated then centered around how these bodies should be organized and staffed. With regard to the legislature, it was quickly decided that there should be two bodies one very responsive to the people of each State and one more representative of the States. The easy consensus was that the executive should never approach being a monarch. The issue was how to make the executive independent and equal to the legislature without giving him too much power. Suggestions that there should be several people acting as the executive was eventually cast aside and it was proposed that the executive should have ability to unilaterally negate legislation. However, the flaw in this proposal was revealed by state experience with such a system that evolved into the executive essentially holding all legislation hostage until some perk was

---

[143] See May 29, 1787, "The Virginia Plan" speech by Edmund Jennings Randolph (1753-1813). He identified defects in the Articles of Confederation and offered specific resolutions to form elements of a new government. Mr. Pinckney also offered ideas, which were not formally debated but appear to have addressed some details that were eventually incorporated into the general plan. See also June 13th for decisions on resolutions.

conceded to him by the legislature. This this flaw was eventually overcome by giving the executive a veto that could be overridden by a super-majority of the legislature.

A problem that repeatedly came up was how the positions should be filled, how often they would be elected/appointed (i.e., how long they would serve), and especially how would the interests of small states like Rhode Island and Delaware (and Georgia which was small, but obviously growing rapidly) would be protected. On June 11th 1787 (Madison Debates) this issue began to come to a head and the issue of the slaves came to the center:

> *"It was then moved by Mr. RUTLIDGE[144] 2ded. by Mr. BUTLER to add to the words "equitable ratio of representation" at the end of the motion Just agreed to, the words "according to the quotas of contribution." On motion of Mr. WILSON seconded by Mr. C. PINCKNEY, this was postponed; in order to add, after, after the words "equitable ratio of representation" the words following "in proportion to the whole number of white & other free Citizens & inhabitants of every age sex[145] & condition including those bound to*

------

[144] John Rutledge of South Carolina, (1739-1800). Pierce Butler of South Carolina (1744-1822), James Wilson of North Carolina (1742-1798) and Charles Pinckney of South Carolina (1757-1824).

[145] Interestingly, the issue of women voting was not considered. It was generally assumed that any respectable women would eventually be married and that her interest were represented by her husband. Although men tended to die in accidents and war, many men married a succession of women who frequently died in child birth or related diseases. While the standards for voting rights within States was left to the states, it was clear that the total number of land-owning voters would be limited in agricultural states.

servitude for a term of years and three fifths of all other persons not comprehended in the foregoing description, except Indians not paying taxes, in each State," this being the rule in the Act of Congress agreed to by eleven States, for apportioning quotas of revenue[146] on the States, and requiring a Census only every 5-7, or 10 years."

---

[146] Under the Articles of Confederation, *taxation* had originally been based on wealth, which was originally computed by the value of real estate. It was soon realized that counting people was easier than appraising real estate.   In transitioning from wealth (real estate) to population, slave-free states argued that the full number of slaves would be the correct element to account for their contribution to each state's wealth. This was not any sort of ideal of equality of slaves and free men, it was an attempt to maximize the taxes paid by slave-owning states. Taking into consideration the cost associated with slave ownership, the slave states argued for less valuation (representing the slaves productive years, e.g., 30 out of 50). This valuation was ultimately accepted in 1783. In the Constitutional Convention, the question of *representation* became more important than taxation because Federal taxes were to be paid by tariffs on goods imported (e.g., see debates of July 11-15, 1787). Thus, the slave holding states wanted to maximize their representation and political power by maximizing the way that slaves were counted. This disagreement was ultimately resolved by accepting the precedent previously accepted that for representation, the slave population would be counted at three-fifths of the free population. Again, this was not a value judgement on the moral value of slaves, but rather a compromise among the States to balance political power within the Federal government.

*"**Mr. GERRY**[147] thought property not the rule of representation. Why then shd. the blacks, who were property in the South, be in the rule of representation more than the Cattle & horses of the North."*

It should be clear that the issue was political power (i.e., representation in congress) not considerations of the morality of slavery or the equality of black Africans. While modern critics of the South point to the 3/5th rule (i.e., five slaves would be counted as three free whites for purposes of representation in the lower chamber [House of Representatives] of congress), by striking this deal, the slave-owning states were not degrading the moral value of slaves; they were actually acknowledging an opinion that was widely assumed at the time: *The slaves would eventually be free and should be represented.* It should be noted that, by freeing the slaves, a State's representation in Congress would potentially be increased. Moreover, at the time in *all the states* black Africans (free or slave) were expected to have limited political power (e.g., voting, holding office or sitting on juries).

In the early debates, the issue of the discussion included consideration of the relationship of the new government to the existing States. The terms "Federal" and "National" were considered with the possibility of dissolving the State government in favor of a single national government. Obviously, the idea of a national government was gradually abandoned. Within the discussion of a central government and its relationship to the States, an early resolution included the idea that the central government might "force" a State to comply with a

---

[147] Elbridge Gerry of Massachusetts (1744-1814).

policy/law/rule of the central government. With respect to that idea…

> **On May 31st:** *"Mr. MADISON, observed that the more he reflected on the use of force, the more he doubted the practicability, the justice and the efficacy of it when applied to people collectively and not individually. -A union of the States containing such an ingredient seemed to provide for its own destruction. The use of force agst. a State, would look more like a declaration of war, than an infliction of punishment, and would probably be considered by the party attacked as a dissolution of all previous compacts by which it might be bound. He hoped that such a system would be framed as might render this recourse unnecessary, and moved that the clause be postponed. This motion was agreed to nem. con."*

Clearly, the States were motivated to maintain their sovereignty, economic status and culture while angling to maximize their individual and sectional political power in the new Federal entity. On June 15th 1787, after much progress had been made on the Virginia Plan, there was a serious retrenchment by delegates from Connecticut, New York, New Jersey, Delaware and Maryland (known as the Patterson[148] Plan). The Patterson Plan essentially reverted to the position that, rather than producing a new form of general government, minor fixes to the Articles of Confederation (of the sovereign States) was all that were needed. Indeed, in the discussions of June 16th, Mr. Lansing[149] argued that anything

---

[148] William Paterson (1745-1806) of New Jersey.

[149] John Lansing, Jr. (1754-1829) of New York.

beyond a Federal government (of sovereign States) was never authorized by the States and would never be approved. This alleged conflict was skillfully resolved by Mr. Wilson, who pointed out that the recommendations of the convention must be ratified by the people of the States and *"With regard to the power of the Convention, he [Wilson] conceived himself authorized to conclude nothing, but to be at liberty to propose any thing."*

On June 18th Mr. Hamilton made a long speech criticizing both plans and proposing a system that had some features of a monarchy. It apparently received no serious debate. On the 19th of June, Madison challenged one of Mr. Patterson's key arguments as follows:

> *"It had been alleged [by Mr. Patterson], that the Confederation having been formed by unanimous consent, could be dissolved by unanimous Consent only. … A breach of the fundamental principles of the compact by a part of the Society would certainly absolve the other part from their obligations to it. … Clearly, according to the Expositors of the law of Nations, that a breach of any one article, by any one party, leaves all the other parties at liberty, to consider the whole convention as dissolved, unless they choose rather to compel the delinquent party to repair the breach. … So far from it that there is not even an express stipulation that force shall be used to compell an offending member of the Union to discharge its duty. He observed that the violations of the federal articles had been numerous & notorious. Among the most notorious was an act of N. Jersey herself… ."*

The debate of the Patterson Plan soon ended and the convention returned to discussions of the Virginia Plan with the benefit of ideas and concerns that had been raised over the previous three days. In particular, the sensitivity to (and rejection of) the idea of a unified "national" government (as opposed to a federal government of the States) was now so strong that the convention deleted the word "national" from previously accepted resolutions (June 20th). The discussion on the 21st turned to how federal and state governments could co-exist and what the consequences would be of one overbearing the other would be.

The details of selection and compensation of representatives, terms of service and restrictions on service returned to the forefront over the next few days. It was largely a battle to protect the smaller states especially those that were obviously limited geographically and could never expand. On the 27th and 28th of June, Mr. Luther Martin (1748-1826) of New Jersey defended the position of the smaller states by delivering a very long speech insisting that the "general government" should only represent the states (not individuals).[150] By this time the big-state/small-state debate had become so intense that the much-respected Benjamin Frankland (1706-1790) earnestly admonished that the convention return to the practice of beginning each session with an invocation to God (June 28th).

On the 29th it was voted that the 1st branch of the legislative body would be determined by population. This might have caused the convention to dissolve except for immediate action by Oliver Ellsworth (1745-1807) of Connecticut:

> *"**Mr. Elseworth** moved that the rule of suffrage in the 2d. branch be the same with that established by the articles of confederation." He was not sorry on the whole he said that the vote just passed, had determined against this rule in the first*

---

[150] L. Martin ultimately refused to sign the Constitution because he believed it violated states' rights.

branch. He hoped it would become a ground of compromise with regard to the 2d. branch. We were partly national; partly federal. The proportional representation in the first branch was conformable to the national principle & would secure the large States agst. the small. An equality of voices was conformable to the federal principle and was necessary to secure the Small States agst. the large. He trusted that on this middle ground a compromise would take place. He did not see that it could on any other. And if no compromise should take place, our meeting would not only be in vain but worse than in vain."

Nonetheless, on the 30th, efforts were made to have representatives of New Hampshire and perhaps Rhode Island join the convention to provide more votes against proportional representation. This idea was quashed and the convention began debate of the Elseworth proposal. In this debate Mr. Elseworth effectively defended his position.   On July 5th a committee reported to the Convention:

" That the subsequent propositions be recommended to the Convention on condition that both shall be generally adopted. 1. That in the 1st. branch[151] of the Legislature each of the States now in the Union shall be allowed 1 member for every 40,000 inhabitants of the description reported in the 7th. Resolution of the Come. of the whole House: that each State not containing that number shall be allowed 1 member: that all bills for raising or appropriating money, and for fixing the Salaries of the officers of the Governt. of the U. States shall originate in the 1st. branch of the Legislature, and shall not be altered or amended by the 2d. branch: and that no money shall be drawn from the public

---

[151] Here it should be obvious that the two "branches" are what we now (2019) call the two "chambers" of the legislative branch.

Treasury. but in pursuance of appropriations to be orginated in the 1st. branch" II. That in the 2d. branch each State shall have an equal vote."

The proposal gradually moved to details of how many members there should be in each of the two parts of the Legislature; and this question raised the issue of a periodic census and issues related to the likely addition of western states. Again, the issue of State sovereignty became a topic of periodic discussion:

On July 11th: *"Mr. MASON ... Strong objections had been drawn from the danger to the Atlantic interests from new Western States. Ought we to sacrifice what we know to be right in itself, lest it should prove favorable to States which are not yet in existence. If the Western States are to be admitted into the Union, as they arise, they must, he wd. repeat, be treated as equals, and subjected to no degrading discriminations. They will have the same pride & other passions which we have, and will either not unite with or will speedily revolt from the Union, if they are not in all respects placed on an equal footing with their brethren. ..."*

Notice that no one questioned the option of a state to "revolt from the union."

On July 14th: *"Mr. L. MARTIN ... The States that please to call themselves large, are the weekest in the Union. Look at Masts. Look at Virga. Are they efficient States? He was for letting a separation take place if they desired it. He had rather there should be two Confederacies, than one founded on any other principle than an equality of votes in the 2d. branch at least."*

The large states believed that they had acquired the concession of some of the small states and brought a vote on the issue on July

16th, which surprisingly revealed the continued split. The large states held an informal caucus on the morning of July 17th that accomplished nothing.

The discussion moved to the definition of powers of the Executive (e.g., appointment of judges, impeachment, veto, term limits, mode of election) for a few days. This bled into the discussion of the judges and judiciary. And, by July 23th, they were discussing how the Constitution could be ratified. On that date, the convention also took up the number of senators to be included from each state. Finally, the issue of a committee to draft the constitution was opened.

> *Genl. Pinkney reminded the Convention that if the Committee should fail to insert some security to the Southern States agst. an emancipation of slaves, and taxes on exports, he shd. be bound by duty to his State to vote agst. their Report-*

The convention debated the election of the Executive until July 26th and on that day, a series of resolutions (summarizing the decisions of the convention over the previous weeks) was placed before the "committee of detail" tasked with assembling the Constitution:

> *"The proceedings since Monday last were referred unanimously to the Come. of detail, and the Convention then unanimously Adjourned till Monday, Augst. 6. that the Come. of detail might have time to prepare & report the Constitution."*

On Monday, August 6th 1897 the draft Constitution was presented to all the members of the convention in printed form:

> *"We the people of the States of New Hampshire, Massachussetts, Rhode-Island and Providence Plantations, Connecticut, New-*

York, New-Jersey, Pennsylvania, Delaware, Maryland, Virginia, North-Carolina, South-Carolina, and Georgia, do ordain, declare, and establish the following Constitution for the Government of Ourselves and our Posterity."

The name of the government was to be *"The United States of America."*

The last article of the draft constitution was as follows:

"XXIII To introduce this government, it is the opinion of this Convention, that each assenting Convention should notify its assent and ratification to the United States in Congress assembled; that Congress, after receiving the assent and ratification of the Conventions of ----- States, should appoint and publish a day, as early as may be, and appoint a place for commencing proceedings under this Constitution; that after such publication, the Legislatures of the several States should elect members of the Senate, and direct the election of members of the House of Representatives; and that the members of the Legislature should meet at the time and place assigned by Congress, and should, as soon as may be, after their meeting, choose the President of the United States, and proceed to execute this Constitution."

Obviously, this is a government created by the States that may or may not choose to join. On August 7th the convention began debating the document article-by-article. One issue that came up was the right to vote, in particular restriction of voting to "freeholders" (i.e., people who own land). Mr. Madison argued that people without property in cities would be easy targets for manipulation by rich officials. The following day (August 8th) Mr. Ghorum countered that the landholders (being fewer in number) were an easier target for corruption.[152] In the end, the impracticality of withdrawing the vote from people who were already voting dictated that voting rights were ultimately decided by the individual states.

Immigration was also discussed regarding residency, voting and holding office:

> *"**Col. MASON** was for opening a wide door for emigrants; but did not chuse to let foreigners and adventurers make laws for us & govern us. Citizenship for three years was not enough for ensuring that local knowledge which ought to be possessed by the Representative. This was the principal ground of his objection to so short a term. It might also happen that a rich foreign Nation, for example Great Britain, might send over her tools who might bribe their way into the Legislature for insidious purposes. He moved that "seven" years instead of "three," be inserted."*

> *"**Mr. MASON** thought 7 years too long, but would never agree to part with the principle. It is a valuable principle. He thought it a defect in the plan that the Representatives would be too few to bring with them all the local knowledge necessary. If residence be not required, Rich men of neighbouring States, may employ with success the means of corruption in some particular district and thereby get into the public Councils after having failed in their own State. This is the practice in the boroughs of England."*

In this context (the 3/5th rule having already been accepted), the issue of the slave trade and slavery came up on August 8th. Mr.

---

[152] I would point out, however, that the cities have many more voters and are more available for mass manipulation. Corruption of a small percentage of urban votes can override the entire vote of the freeholders. Of course, I was not there!

Rufus King (1755–1827) of Massachusetts observed that *"The importation of slaves could not be prohibited-exports could not be taxed."* And he concluded that *"At all events, either slaves should not be represented, or exports should be taxable."* This opened the door for a wider debate. Gouverneur Morris (1752-1816)[153] of Pennsylvania displayed his naivete, bias and abolitionist views (please pay attention to my footnotes):

> *"Mr. Govr. MORRIS moved to insert "free" before the word inhabitants. Much he said would depend on this point. He never would concur in upholding domestic slavery. It was a nefarious institution. It was the curse of heaven on the States where it prevailed. Compare the free regions of the Middle States, where a rich & noble cultivation marks the prosperity & happiness of the people, with the misery & poverty which overspread the barren wastes of Va. Maryd. & the other States having slaves. Travel thro' ye. whole Continent & you behold the prospect continually varying with the appearance & disappearance of slavery. The moment you leave ye. E. Sts.[154] & enter N. York, the effects of the institution become visible, passing thro' the Jerseys & entering Pa. every criterion of superior improvement witnesses the change. Proceed south wdly & every step you take thro' ye. great region of slaves presents a desert increasing, with ye. increasing*

---

[153] He was born in New York. According to his biography in the National Archives, *"A strong advocate of nationalism and aristocratic rule, he served on many committees, including those on postponed matters and style, and stood in the thick of the decision-making process. Above all, it was apparently he who actually drafted the Constitution."*

[154] "Ye. E. Sts" referred to New England where the *slave trade* was still making the population rich.

proportion of these wretched beings.[155] *Upon what principle is it that the slaves shall be computed in the representation? Are they men? Then make them Citizens and let them vote. Are they property? Why then is no other property included? The Houses in this city [Philada.] are worth more than all the wretched slaves which cover the rice swamps of South Carolina. The admission of slaves into the Representation when fairly explained comes to this: that the inhabitant of Georgia and S. C. who goes to the Coast of Africa*[156]*, and in defiance of the most sacred laws of humanity tears away his fellow creatures from their dearest connections & damns them to the most cruel bondages, shall have more votes in a Govt. instituted for protection of the rights of mankind, than the Citizen of Pa. or N. Jersey who views with a laudable horror, so nefarious a practice. He would add that Domestic slavery is the most prominent feature in the aristocratic countenance of the proposed Constitution. The vassalage of the poor has ever been the favorite offspring of Aristocracy. And What is the proposed compensation to the Northern States for a*

---

[155] "Wretched beings" does not sound endearing to black Africans. "Wretched" has several meanings. Some readers will conclude that Morris was alluding to the Africans' displeasure with slavery; but he might also be describing them as ugly. In particular the later statement *"The Houses in this city [Philada.] are worth more than all the wretched slaves which cover the rice swamps of South Carolina."* sounds more like a slander against Africans than a rejection of slavery.

[156] Here Morris displays complete and willful ignorance of the *slave trade*. The middle passage was entirely within the hands of the New Englanders, who he lauds. Either through gross ignorance or malice, he laid the foundation of anti-southern bias that became the trademark of abolitionists.

*sacrifice of every principle of right, of every impulse of humanity.
They are to bind themselves to march their militia for the defence
of the S. States; for their defence agst. those very slaves of whom
they complain. They must supply vessels & seamen in case of
foreign Attack. The Legislature will have indefinite power to tax
them by excises, and duties on imports: both of which will fall
heavier on them than on the Southern inhabitants; for the bohea
tea used by a Northern freeman, will pay more tax than the whole
consumption of the miserable slave, which consists of nothing
more than his physical subsistence and the rag that covers his
nakedness. On the other side the Southern States are not to be
restrained from importing fresh supplies of wretched Africans[157],
at once to increase the danger of attack, and the difficulty of
defence; nay they are to be encouraged to it by an assurance of
having their votes in the Natl. Govt. increased in proportion, and
are at the same time to have their exports & their slaves exempt
from all contributions for the public service. Let it not be said
that direct taxation is to be proportioned to representation. It is
idle to suppose that the Genl. Govt. can stretch its hand directly
into the pockets of the people scattered over so vast a Country.
They can only do it through the medium of exports imports &
excises. For what then are all these sacrifices to be made? He
would sooner submit himself to a tax for paying for all the
negroes in the U. States, than saddle posterity with such a
Constitution."*

It is fairly obvious that Mr. Morris regards the southern states
with great contempt and denies any role of northern states in
slavery. (i) His liberal use of the word "wretched" to describe not

---

[157] Apparently, the condition of being "African" also makes a person "wretched."

only "slaves" but also "Africans;" (ii) his appraisal of "wretched slaves" less than the value of houses in northern cities and (iii) his concerns that the major reason for defending the south would be in the event of a slave revolt all suggest to me that he also harbors extensive racial bias. This speech is not a condemnation of *slavery*; it is a condemnation of *black Africans* and *southerners*. Interestingly, Morris's outburst did not prompt much dignifying response. In a short comment,

> *"Mr. Pinkney, considered the fisheries & the Western frontier as more burdensome to the U. S.[158] than the slaves. He thought this could be demonstrated if the occasion were a proper one."*

Pinkney (South Carolina) did not take the bait and enter into a debate about slavery. He merely pointed out that New England fisheries were causing conflicts with Canada and European countries that could lead to war; and the entire western frontier of the United States was facing both Native tribes and the European claims to this territory that could also produce hostilities.

The "origin of money bills" became a subject of discussion that was tied to the decision of having all money bills originate in the house (determined by proportion) rather than in the Senate (where all states were equally represented).

On August 9th, the discussion returned to representation and qualifications for office and Pierce Butler (1744-1822) who was born in Ireland and immigrated to South Carolina in 1771 had some interesting comments:

---

[158] With respect to provoking a need for military action, fishing on the Grand Banks and the western frontier were likely to involve international conflict.

"Mr. BUTLER was decidedly opposed to the admission of foreigners without a long residence in the Country. They bring with them, not only attachments to other Countries; but ideas of Govt. so distinct from ours that in every point of view they are dangerous. He acknowledged that if he himself had been called into public life within a short time after his coming to America, his foreign habits opinions & attachments would have rendered him an improper agent in public affairs. He mentioned the great strictness observed in Great Britain on this subject."

On August 10th the main topic was what should constitute a quorum of the legislative bodies. On the 11th, they considered the need for records and the possibility that the legislature might fail to meet or otherwise obstruct actions. On the 14th the responsibilities of the legislature regarding "money bills" came up again and again the questions of eligibility for Federal office came up in the context of existing State legislators.

By August 16th, the issue of taxation of exports was under discussion. By the 18th, Madison asked that topics related to patents and copyrights be considered in the power of the congress. And Mason raised the issue of regulating the militia.

"Mr. MASON introduced the subject of regulating the militia. He thought such a power necessary to be given to the Genl. Government. He hoped there would be no standing army in time of peace, unless it might be for a few garrisons. The Militia ought therefore to be the more effectually prepared for the public defence. Thirteen States will never concur in any one system, if the displining of the Militia be left in their hands. If they will not give up the power over the whole, they probably will over a part as a select militia. He moved as an addition to the propositions

just referred to the Committee of detail, & to be referred in like manner, 'a power to regulate the militia.'"

Thus, it is clear that the term "well regulated" in the 2nd Amendment (i.e., item 2 of the Bill of Rights) is intended to *encourage ownership and proficiency* with arms by the civilian population (i.e., a *well-regulated* militia is an *effective* militia; *[t]he Militia ought therefore to be the more effectually prepared for the public defence*; not a militia that is deprived of weapons). There followed a discussion of how best to regulate the militia, i.e., under the States, the general government or both. Regardless of the organization of regulation, it was essential that it was essential for the population to be armed (i.e., their rights to keep and bear arms must not be infringed).

On August 20th, the convention moved to a consideration of advisors to the Executive addressing various topics (now called the cabinet).

On August 22nd, the convention took up Article VII, section 4. Dealing with the slave trade and slavery. It was an issue that aroused diverse opinions. George Mason (1725-1792) of Virginia agreed with Thomas Jefferson's opinions that had been deleted from the Declaration of Independence:

"Mr. Mason: This infernal trafic originated in the avarice of British Merchants. The British Govt. constantly checked the attempts of Virginia to put a stop to it. The present question concerns not the importing States alone but the whole Union. The evil of having slaves was experienced during the late war. Had slaves been treated as they might have been by the Enemy, they would have proved dangerous instruments in their hands. But their folly dealt by the slaves, as it did by the Tories. He

mentioned the dangerous insurrections of the slaves in Greece and Sicily; and the instructions given by Cromwell to the Commissioners sent to Virginia, to arm the servants & slaves, in case other means of obtaining its submission should fail. Maryland & Virginia he said had already prohibited the importation of slaves expressly. N. Carolina had done the same in substance. All this would be in vain if S. Carolina & Georgia be at liberty to import.[159] The Western people are already calling out for slaves for their new lands, and will fill that Country with slaves if they can be got thro' S. Carolina & Georgia. Slavery discourages arts & manufactures. The poor despise labor when performed by slaves. They prevent the immigration of Whites, who really enrich & strengthen a Country. They produce the most pernicious effect on manners. Every master of slaves is born a petty tyrant. They bring the judgment of heaven on a Country. As nations can not be rewarded or punished in the next world they must be in this. By an inevitable chain of causes & effects providence punishes national sins, by national calamities. He lamented that some of our Eastern brethren had from a lust of gain embarked in this nefarious traffic.[160] As to the States being in possession of the Right to import, this was the case with many other rights, now to be properly given up. He held it essential in every point of view that the Genl. Govt. should have power to prevent the increase of slavery."

---

[159] As mentioned elsewhere, by 1790, slavery was not profitable in the tobacco states (VA, MD, NC) and even the ports of SC and GA and their tidewater (rice) areas were mainly viewed as ports of entry for demand in western areas.

[160] As noted elsewhere, the New England slave trade.

Further relevant comments followed:

Mr. ELSWORTH. As he had never owned a slave could not judge of the effects of slavery on character: He said however that if it was to be considered in a moral light we ought to go farther and free those already in the Country. -As slaves also multiply so fast in Virginia & & Maryland that it is cheaper to raise than import them, whilst in the sickly rice swamps foreign supplies are necessary, if we go no farther than is urged, we shall be unjust towards S. Carolina & Georgia. Let us not intermeddle. As population increases poor laborers will be so plenty as to render slaves useless. Slavery in time will not be a speck in our Country. Provision is already made in Connecticut for abolishing it. And the abolition has already taken place in Massachusetts. As to the danger of insurrections from foreign influence, that will become a motive to kind treatment of the slaves.

Mr. PINKNEY. If slavery be wrong, it is justified by the example of all the world. He cited the case of Greece Rome & other antient States; the sanction given by France England, Holland & other modern States. In all ages one half of mankind have been slaves. If the S. States were let alone they will probably of themselves stop importations. He wd. himself as a Citizen of S. Carolina vote for it. An attempt to take away the right as proposed will produce serious objections to the Constitution which he wished to see adopted.

General PINKNEY declared it to be his firm opinion that if himself & all his colleagues were to sign the Constitution & use their personal influence, it would be of no avail towards obtaining the assent of their Constituents. S. Carolina & Georgia cannot do without slaves. As to Virginia she will gain by stopping the importations. Her slaves will rise in value, & she has more than she wants. It would be unequal to require S. C. & Georgia to confederate on such unequal terms. He said the Royal assent before the

Revolution had never been refused to S. Carolina as to Virginia. He contended that the importation of slaves would be for the interest of the whole Union. The more slaves, the more produce to employ the carrying trade; The more consumption also, and the more of this, the more of revenue for the common treasury. He admitted it to be reasonable that slaves should be dutied like other imports, but should consider a rejection of the clause as an exclusion of S. Carola. from the Union.

Mr. BALDWIN had conceived national objects alone to be before the Convention, not such as like the present were of a local nature. Georgia was decided on this point. That State has always hitherto supposed a Genl. Governmt. to be the pursuit of the central States who wished to have a vortex for every thing- that her distance would preclude her from equal advantage-& that she could not prudently purchase it by yielding national powers. From this it might be understood in what light she would view an attempt to abridge one of her favorite prerogatives. If left to herself, she may probably put a stop to the evil. As one ground for this conjecture, he took notice of the sect of -------- which he said was a respectable class of people, who carried their ethics beyond the mere equality of men, extending their humanity to the claims of the whole animal creation.

Mr. WILSON observed that if S. C. & Georgia were themselves disposed to get rid of the importation of slaves in a short time as had been suggested, they would never refuse to Unite because the importation might be prohibited. As the Section now stands all articles imported are to be taxed. Slaves alone are exempt. This is in fact a bounty on that article.

Mr. GERRY thought we had nothing to do with the conduct of the States as to Slaves, but ought to be careful not to give any sanction to it.

Mr. DICKENSON *considered it as inadmissible on every principle of honor & safety that the importation of slaves should be authorised to the States by the Constitution. The true question was whether the national happiness would be promoted or impeded by the importation, and this question ought to be left to the National Govt. not to the States particularly interested. If Engd. & France permit slavery, slaves are at the same time excluded from both those Kingdoms. Greece and Rome were made unhappy by their slaves. He could not believe that the Southn. States would refuse to confederate on the account apprehended; especially as the power was not likely to be immediately exercised by the Genl. Government.*

Mr. WILLIAMSON *stated the law of N. Carolina on the subject, to wit that it did not directly prohibit the importation of slaves. It imposed a duty of 5. on each slave imported from Africa. 10 on each from elsewhere, & 50 on each from a State licensing manumission. He thought the S. States could not be members of the Union if the clause shd. be rejected, and that it was wrong to force any thing down, not absolutely necessary, and which any State must disagree to.*

Mr. KING *thought the subject should be considered in a political light only. If two States will not agree to the Constitution as stated on one side, he could affirm with equal belief on the other, that great & equal opposition would be experienced from the other States. He remarked on the exemption of slaves from duty whilst every other import was subjected to it, as an inequality that could not fail to strike the commercial sagacity of the Northn. & middle States.*

Mr. LANGDON *was strenuous for giving the power to the Genl. Govt. He cd. not with a good conscience leave it with the States who could then go on with the traffic, without being restrained by the opinions here given that they will themselves cease to import slaves.*

Genl. PINKNEY thought himself bound to declare candidly that he did not think S. Carolina would stop her importations of slaves in any short time, but only stop them occasionally as she now does. He moved to commit the clause that slaves might be made liable to an equal tax with other imports which he thought right & wch. wd. remove one difficulty that had been started.

Mr. RUTLIDGE. If the Convention thinks that N. C. S. C. & Georgia will ever agree to the plan, unless their right to import slaves be untouched, the expectation is vain. The people of those States will never be such fools as to give up so important an interest. He was strenuous agst. striking out the Section, and seconded the motion of Genl. Pinkney for a commitment.

Mr. Govr. MORRIS wished the whole subject to be committed including the clauses relating to taxes on exports & to a navigation act. These things may form a bargain among the Northern & Southern States.

Mr. BUTLER declared that he never would agree to the power of taxing exports.

Mr. SHERMAN said it was better to let the S. States import slaves than to part with them, if they made that a sine qua non. He was opposed to a tax on slaves imported as making the matter worse, because it implied they were property. He acknowledged that if the power of prohibiting the importation should be given to the Genl. Government that it would be exercised. He thought it would be its duty to exercise the power.

The issue of slavery was clearly tied up in the issues of taxation and representation. The moral dilemma was as likely to be in the minds of southerners (e.g., Mason) as northerners (e.g., Morris). The role of New England and New York in being the suppliers of imported slaves to South Carolina and Georgia and the beneficiaries of taxes and commerce related to the agricultural productivity of the slaves was rarely hinted at.

 On August 25th, in the context of taxing imports, the topic of the slave trade was rejoined as the draft Constitution targeted 1800 as the date the *international* slave trade would be banned.

> **Genl. PINKNEY** *moved to strike out the words "the year eighteen hundred" as the year limiting the importation of slaves, and to insert the words "the year eighteen hundred and eight"*

> **Mr. MADISON.** *Twenty years will produce all the mischief that can be apprehended from the liberty to import slaves. So long a term will be more dishonorable to the National character than to say nothing about it in the Constitution.*

> *On the motion; which passed in the affirmative.*

> *"New Hampshire, Massachusetts, Connecticut, Maryland, North Carolina, South Carolina, Georgia, aye-7; New Jersey, Pennsylvania, Delaware, Virginia, no-4."*

It is relevant that the slave-trading states (NH, MA, CT[161]) sided with the slave-holding states where the demand for slaves continued (MD, NC, SC, GA) to pass this extension to the international slave trade. Gouverneur Morris (born in NY, but representing PA), of course, took the opportunity to once more attempt to slander the southern states:

---

[161] Rhode Island was not at the convention and no vote is recorded for New York.

Mr. Govr. MORRIS was for making the clause read at once, "importation of slaves into N. Carolina, S. Carolina & Georgia shall not be prohibited &c." This he said would be most fair and would avoid the ambiguity by which, under the power with regard to naturalization, the liberty reserved to the States might be defeated. He wished it to be known also that this part of the Constitution was a compliance with those States. If the change of language however should be objected to by the members from those States, he should not urge it.

Col: MASON was not against using the term "slaves" but agst. naming N.C. S.C. & Georgia, lest it should give offence to the people of those States.

Morris was merely trying to embarrass the southern states while obscuring the role of the New England states. Thus, he withdrew his motion.

The discussion then turned again to the taxation of imports:

Mr. BALDWIN in order to restrain & more explicitly define "the average duty" moved to strike out of the 2d. part the words "average of the duties laid on imports" and insert "common impost on articles not enumerated" which was agreed to nem: cont:

Mr. SHERMAN was agst. this 2d. part, as acknowledging men to be property, by taxing them as such under the character of slaves.

Mr. KING & Mr. LANGDON considered this as the price of the 1st. part.

Genl. PINKNEY admitted that it was so.

Col: MASON. Not to tax, will be equivalent to a bounty on the importation of slaves.

Mr. GHORUM thought that Mr. Sherman should consider the duty, not as implying that slaves are property, but as a discouragement to the importation of them.

Mr. Govr. MORRIS remarked that as the clause now stands it implies that the Legislature may tax freemen imported.

Mr. SHERMAN in answer to Mr. Ghorum observed that the smallness of the duty shewed revenue to be the object, not the discouragement of the importation.

Mr. MADISON thought it wrong to admit in the Constitution the idea that there could be property in men. The reason of duties did not hold, as slaves are not like merchandize, consumed, &c

Col. MASON (in answr. to Govr. Morris) the provision as it stands was necessary for the case of Convicts in order to prevent the introduction of them.

It was finally agreed nem: contrad: to make the clause read "but a tax or duty may be imposed on such importation not exceeding ten dollars for each person," and then the 2d. part as amended was agreed to.

Thus, although most found it awkward to tax imported slaves as property, the issue was set aside by rationalizing that it nominally discouraged importation of slaves and would cover certain classes of non-slaves.

Moving ahead to August 29th, the issues of trade and commerce were under debate. It is relevant to note some of the discussion where we see opposing sectional interests:

Mr. PINKNEY moved to postpone the Report in favor of the following proposition-"That no act of the Legislature for the purpose of regulating the commerce of the U- S. with foreign powers, or among the several States, shall be passed without the assent of two thirds of the members of each House." He remarked that there were five distinct commercial interests. 1. the fisheries & W. India trade, which belonged to the N. England States. 2. the interest of N. York lay in a free trade. 3. Wheat & flour the Staples of the two Middle States (N. J. & Penna.). 4 Tobo. the staple of Maryd. & Virginia & partly of N. Carolina. 5. Rice & Indigo, the staples of S. Carolina & Georgia. These different interests would be a source of oppressive regulations if no check to a bare majority should be provided. States pursue their interests with less scruple than individuals. The power of regulating commerce was a pure concession on the part of the S. States. They did not need the protection of the N. States at present.

Mr. MARTIN 2ded. the motion

Genl. PINKNEY said it was the true interest of the S. States to have no regulation of commerce; but considering the loss brought on the commerce of the Eastern States[162] by the revolution, their liberal conduct towards the views of South Carolina, and the interest the weak Southn. States had in being united with the strong Eastern States, he thought it proper that no fetters should be imposed on the power of making commercial regulations; and that his constituents though prejudiced against the Eastern States, would be reconciled to this liberality. He had himself, he said, prejudices agst. the Eastern States before he came here, but

---

[162] References to "Eastern States" mean New England.

would acknowledge that he had found them as liberal and candid as any men whatever.

Mr. CLYMER. The diversity of commercial interests of necessity creates difficulties, which ought not to be increased by unnecessary restrictions. The Northern & middle States will be ruined, if not enabled to defend themselves against foreign regulations.

Mr. SHERMAN, alluding to Mr. Pinkney's enumeration of particular interests, as requiring a security agst. abuse of the power; observed that the diversity was of itself a security, adding that to require more than a majority to decide a question was always embarrassing as had been experienced in cases requiring the votes of nine States in Congress.

Mr. PINKNEY replied that his enumeration meant the five minute interests. It still left the two great divisions of Northern & Southern Interests.

Mr. Govr. MORRIS, opposed the object of the motion as highly injurious. Preferences to American ships will multiply them, till they can carry the Southern produce cheaper than it is now carried. -A navy was essential to security, particularly of the S. States, and can only be had by a navigation act encouraging American bottoms & seamen. In those points of view then alone, it is the interest of the S. States that navigation acts should be facilitated. Shipping he said was the worst & most precarious kind of property, and stood in need of public patronage.

Mr. WILLIAMSON was in favor of making two thirds instead of a majority requisite, as more satisfactory to the Southern people. No useful measure he believed had been lost in Congress for want of nine votes. As to the weakness of the Southern States, he was not alarmed on that account. The sickliness of their climate for invaders would prevent their being made an object. He acknowledged that he did not think the motion requiring 2/3 necessary in itself, because if a majority of Northern States should push their regulations too far, the S. States would build ships for themselves: but he knew the Southern people were apprehensive on this subject and would be pleased with the precaution.

Mr. SPAIGHT was against the motion. The Southern States could at any time save themselves from oppression, by building ships for their own use.

In the context of the slave-trade, it is obvious that the southern states (lacking ships) were only involved in receiving slaves that had been bought in Africa and imported to North America. It should be noted that investment in the Navy was an investment in the Federal government (i.e., not building up southern industry since the shipyards were in the North) and this oversight on part of the southern states was to make them forever the vassal[163] of the Federal government. Some people realized this issue:

Mr. BUTLER differed from those who considered the rejection of the motion as no concession on the part of the S. States. He considered the interests of these and of the Eastern States, to be as different as the interests of Russia and Turkey. Being notwith-standing desirous of conciliating the affections of the East: States. he should vote agst. requiring 2/3 instead of a majority.

---

[163] Definition: "a holder of land by feudal tenure on conditions of homage and allegiance." The southern states could hold the land, but without a Navy they would never be independent of the Federal government.

> *Col. MASON. If the Govt. is to be lasting, it must be founded in the confidence & affections of the people, and must be so constructed as to obtain these. The Majority will be governed by their interests. The Southern States are the minority in both Houses. Is it to be expected that they will deliver themselves bound hand & foot to the Eastern States, and enable them to exclaim, in the words of Cromwell on a certain occasion-"the lord hath delivered them into our hands."*

Mason's words were to be prophetic.

Butler introduced an uncontroversial article that would develop into a large issue over the next 60 years:

> *Mr. BUTLER moved to insert after art: XV. "If any person bound to service or labor in any of the U. States shall escape into another State, he or she shall not be discharged from such service or labor, in consequence of any regulations subsisting in the State to which they escape, but shall be delivered up to the person justly claiming their service or labor," which was agreed to nem: con:*

On August 30th, the convention took up the issue of formation of new states in lands claimed by existing states (e.g., Virginia and North Carolina).

In September 1787, the convention began considering the draft Constitution in its whole; not just its parts. Issues came up, were discussed and generally resolved. Much of this had to do with the powers of the Executive and the Senate and whether these would tend towards an aristocracy.[164] In particular, the election,

---

[164] We have seen some tendencies in that direction with families such as the Roosevelts, Kennedys, and Bushes rising into power in these offices. But none have been so bold as to defy the Constitution.

term of service, term-limits, veto power, over-ride of vetoes, appointments and confirmation, mode of impeachment and trial were all discussed and refined.

On September 8th 1787, the Convention created the *Committee on Style and Arrangement* made up of Alexander Hamilton (NY), William Johnson (CT), Rufus King (MA), James Madison (VA) and Gouverneur Morris (PA). In a mere four days, this committee created the final draft of the Constitution. It is widely agreed that Gouverneur Morris essentially singlehandedly assembled the final draft. This is interesting because Morris was no friend of the South.

On September 12th a new draft of the Constitution was printed and circulated. After review and debate regarding the fraction of legislature needed to override a veto (2/3 or 3/4) the conference came to the question of implementation of the constitution. At this point, 9 of 13 states was proposed to implement the Constitution *among those states*. It was anticipated that some states (e.g., Rhode Island) might never join.

On the 17th September, Benjamin Franklin (old and frail) offered a written statement that was read on his behalf. It is rather long and not directly related to the current book, but I recommend that it be read. He with his humor and perspective encouraged all the members of the convention to sign the Constitution and encourage its passage by the Continental Congress and States…not because it was perfect, but because it was as close to perfect as human's could expect.

Ultimately some members of the convention refused to sign for mostly procedural reasons. For example, Randolph was concerned that agreement of nine states could not be assured; and thus, failure of the measure would create confusion among the people.

The members then proceeded to sign the instrument.

Whilst the last members were signing it Doctr. FRANKLIN looking towards the Presidents Chair, at the back of which a rising sun happened to be painted, observed to a few members near him, that Painters had found it difficult to distinguish in their art a rising from a setting sun. I have said he, often and often in the course of the Session, and the vicisitudes of my hopes and fears as to its issue, looked at that behind the President without being able to tell whether it was rising or setting: But now at length I have the happiness to know that it is a rising and not a setting Sun.

The Constitution being signed by all the members except Mr. Randolph, Mr. Mason, and Mr. Gerry who declined giving it the sanction of their names, the Convention dissolved itself by an Adjournment sine die-

Ratification

When the Constitution reached the States, many of the same reservations voiced in the convention resurfaced and were analyzed in the context of each state's particular gains and losses. I will not go into great detail here.

In the fall of 1787, Delaware, Pennsylvania, New Jersey, Georgia and Connecticut ratified the Constitution. The document was more controversial in the more populous states (Pennsylvania and Connecticut). Massachusetts (the 2nd most populous state) initially voted against the Constitution, but by in February 1788 accepted it by a slim margin (187–168). In April and May,

Maryland and South Carolina similarly amassed a majority for the Constitution. This added to a total of 8 states supporting the Constitution. In June, New Hampshire and Virginia each narrowly approved the Constitution, but each proposed numerous amendments to the Constitution. Importantly, in addition to modifications of the processes of the government described in the Constitution, Virginia proposed a *Bill of Rights* to guarantee specific personal rights to all citizens:

> *Mr. WYTHE reported, from the committee appointed, such amendments to the proposed Constitution of government for the United States as were by them deemed necessary to be recommended to the consideration of the Congress which shall first assemble under the said Constitution, to be acted upon according to the mode prescribed in the 5th article thereof; and he read the same in his place, and afterwards delivered them in at the clerk's table, where the same were again read, and are as follows:*
>
> *"That there be a declaration or bill of rights asserting, and securing from encroachment, the essential and unalienable rights of the people, in some such manner as the following:*[165]

Notice that Wythe's view was that the Bill of Rights were *secure from encroachment, essential* and *unalienable*. The point is that unlike other amendments to the Constitution, they cannot be changed by any government.

---

[165] Elliot's Debates: Volume 3. In Convention, Richmond, Friday, June 27, 1788
(http://teachingamericanhistory.org/ratification/elliot/vol3/june27/)

In July, New York also ratified the Constitution and submitted numerous amendments including a *Bill of Rights*.

North Carolina (the 4th most populous state) firmly rejected the Constitution (193 no, 74 yes) in August 1788. The Constitution was not approved until November 1789 with numerous proposed amendments and a *Bill of Rights*. Rhode Island, which had not participated in the drafting of the Constitution resisted considering the documents and only ratified it in May 1790 with recommended amendments and Bill of Rights.

The chief objections to the Constitution was not associated with the Nationalist *versus* Federalist divide. The idea of a *single nation* without sovereign States had long since been abandoned. The main issue was that the Federalists did not go far enough to ensure individual liberties. These sentiments were generally presented under the banner of "Anti-Federalists" who felt that the proposed Federal government did not guarantee the rights that they expected within their States. In retrospect, it seems obvious that the convention focused on the "nuts and bolts" of *government organization, legislative process* and *State versus Federal* power. The debates noted above and in Madison's notes, clearly indicated a desire to protect the people's liberty from anarchy and aristocracy and the absence of a Bill of Rights was an important oversight. In the final analysis, it is probably good that the Bill of Rights arose directly from the people who were to be governed and not presumed by their representatives that organized the form of government.

The Bill of Rights

The *Bill of Rights* needs to be placed into proper perspective. The colonists set out on the War of Independence with this view of humanity in mind:

> *...We hold these truths to be self-evident, that all men are created equal, that they are endowed by their Creator with certain unalienable Rights, that among these are Life, Liberty and the pursuit of Happiness. — That to secure these rights, Governments are instituted among Men, deriving their just powers from the consent of the governed,... IN CONGRESS, JULY 4, 1776*

After winning their independence, they were tasked to actually implement a government. The Constitution begins with the stirring words of the *Preamble*:

> **We the people** *of the United States, in Order to form a more perfect Union, establish Justice, insure domestic Tranquility, provide for the common defense, promote the general Welfare, and secure the Blessings of Liberty to ourselves and our Posterity, do ordain and establish this Constitution for the United States of America.*

The body of the Constitution is primarily a structure of government intended to secure the "self-evident" rights given by God. But it was also a manmade set of rules that did not get specific about what were considered to be the natural rights of humans. Thus, rather than allow anyone to question what they considered to be self-evident they proposed and enacted a list of specific rights (the *Bill of Rights*).

I personally believe that their process became a little sloppy here. The Constitution provided for a mechanism of amendments (i.e., changes) to the constitution. Although the Bill of Rights (in my view and that of George Wythe, 1726-1806) should stand alone as a statement of God-given rights (not subject to debate or change), the simple way to incorporate them into the Constitution was to call them amendments. I believe it is a mis-characterization to describe the *Bill of Rights* as "amendments to the Constitution," because they are *not changes*; rather *they are an integral part of the Constitution*.[166] Indeed, as enumerations of God-given rights, they are beyond review, whereas the body of the Constitution and actual amendments to the Constitution are not beyond review and change. The practice of calling the ten items of the *Bill of Rights* "amendments," I believe, lessens their status. *Specifically, I do not believe that the "Bill of Rights" can be legitimately changed by amendment. They are the heart of our freedoms* **given by God, _not by any government_**.

These *enumerated rights* include the following concepts:

> **(1) Ultimate Empowerment of *the People* to protect their rights against foreign or domestic authorities.**

---

[166] James Madison proposed them on June 8, 1789 with the idea that they would be incorporated into the existing articles. However, the fight to get the Constitution ratified had been long and hard so that to avoid collapsing the entire Constitution over quarrels that might arise, they were submitted to the states as individual line items that could be voted up or down individually without destroying the Constitution.

*"A well regulated Militia[167], being necessary to the security of a free State, the right of **the people** to keep and bear Arms, shall not be infringed."*

Notice that these are the same "people" mentioned in the *Preamble* (*i.e.*, all the citizens). This statement has been much debated. The essential element is that the individual people should be as well armed as the police or the army. In practice, this means that the people should be able to carry on a guerilla war, if necessary, against an oppressive government. No other principle ensures that democracy will prevail.[168]

(2) Freedom of the Communication and Thought

The principle is that all ideas are allowed and may be freely transmitted as long as they are not threats to individuals (intimidation) or orders to carry out illegal acts.

---

[167]I believe that the militia is cited here because many states did not allow slaves or free black Africans to join the militia. *The militia* was made up of free citizens.

[168] Unfortunately, the death toll from modern weapons in the hands of criminals or incompetents or the merely distressed has become alarming. It is therefore within the spirit of the Constitution to "infringe" on this right, so long as that the general population stays well-armed with combat-ready weapons (suitable for an insurgent war against the government); although, some classes of weapons may be forbidden.

"Congress shall make no law respecting an establishment of religion, or prohibiting the free exercise thereof; or abridging the freedom of speech, or of the press; or the right of the people peaceably to assemble, and to petition the Government for a redress of grievances."

In the afterglow of the war, the framers of the Constitution realized that peacefully assembly was an essential element in communication. In this modern time, peaceful assembly would include cyberspace (the internet).

(3) Privacy and Protection of the Rights to Private Property

The principle of privacy and ownership of private property is that people can keep their lives and business private from the government (except as allowed by law) and the general public.

"The right of the people to be secure in their persons, houses, papers, and effects, against unreasonable searches and seizures, shall not be violated, and no Warrants shall issue, but upon probable cause, supported by Oath or affirmation, and particularly describing the place to be searched, and the persons or things to be seized."

"No person… shall be compelled in any criminal case to be a witness against himself, nor be deprived of life, liberty, or property, without due process of law; nor shall private property be taken for public use, without just compensation."

(4) Limitations on the Federal Government

The 10th element of the Bill of Rights makes it clear that the *People and the States* empower the Federal government; not the other way around. The Federal government can only have the power that the People and the States explicitly and conditionally give it:

The powers not delegated to the United States by the Constitution, nor prohibited by it to the States, are reserved to the States respectively, or to the people.

Although some statesmen believed the 10th item (and last item) in the original list was redundant[169], it is very important to the interpretation of the Constitution and it played an enormous roll in the thinking of statesmen before the War between the States.

This statement makes it crystal clear that the original *contract* among the sovereign States (individually given independence from Britain in the Treaty of Paris (1783))

---

[169] United States v. Darby Lumber Co., 312 U.S. 100 (1941): *"The amendment states but a truism that all is retained which has not been surrendered. There is nothing in the history of its adoption to suggest that it was more than declaratory of the relationship between the national and state governments as it had been established by the Constitution before the amendment or that its purpose was other than to allay fears that the new national government might seek to exercise powers not granted, and that the states might not be able to exercise fully their reserved powers."* I would say that the fears of the States were well justified, with the key turning point being the War between the States.

involved the understanding that the Federal government is the creation of the *sovereign independent states* and *people* and only derives power from the States or People...who retain all authority not specifically assigned to the Federal government.[170]

The *Bill of Rights* was ratified 15 December 1791

The Sovereignty of States

versus

the Federal Government

Creation of the United States from a collection of independent and sovereign states was a tricky business. The Constitution had been carefully crafted (for the most part) by the States such that certain joint interest (primarily national defense) could be provided and trade/immigration barriers among the states would be minimized. However, the document as ratified with the Bill of Rights, both implicitly and explicitly limited the powers of the "General Government" (i.e., Federal Government) to those enumerated in the Constitution and allotted to the States everything else. But *in purely practical terms, once provided with a source of revenue and control of the organized military, the General Government has the power to do great good or great harm.*

---

[170] Implicitly, the States or People should adjudicate any ambiguous situations and decide the issues. This, of course, is the root of "nullification theory" and States' Rights.

In particular, the Constitution optimistically envisions growth and expansion and is thus mute on the possibility of retrenchment (e.g., disunion or secession). The States naturally assumed that that was one of the options left to the States. Time would soon tell (as soon as the generation of the War of Independence had died off) that many viewed the General Government as the most important to their wellbeing. Moreover, the carefully constructed compromises that had been worked out to facilitate unification of the States in the first place, were thrown into imbalance by expansion of the union and largely forgotten by many in the ensuing generations or never known by immigrants.

For the most part, the divisions of opinions broke down over sectional (regional) lines in the 1830s and beyond. Culminating in the War between the States 1861-65. Thus, please focus on the original understanding of the relationships of the States and the General Government. The best sources for this are the documents of ratification of the constitution by Virginia (1788), New York (1788) and Rhode Island (1790) in which each of these states specifically anticipates secession, for example:

> *...DO in the name and in behalf of the people of Virginia, declare and make known that the powers granted under the Constitution, being derived from the people of the United States may be resumed by them whensoever the same shall be perverted to their injury or oppression, and that every power not granted thereby remains with them and at their will...*

Other documents produced in Virginia before 1800 by the man considered the father of the U.S. Constitution (James Madison).

VIRGINIA RESOLUTIONS OF 1798,

PRONOUNCING THE ALIEN AND SEDITION LAWS TO BE UNCONSTITUTIONAL, AND DEFINING THE RIGHTS OF THE STATES.

DRAWN BY MR. MADISON.

IN THE VIRGINIA HOUSE OF DELEGATES,
FRIDAY, December 21, 1798.

Resolved, That the General Assembly of Virginia, doth unequivocally express a firm resolution to maintain and defend the Constitution of the United States, and the Constitution of this state, against every aggression, either foreign or domestic; and that they will support the government of the United States in all measures warranted by the former.

That this Assembly most solemnly declares a warm attachment to the union of the states, to maintain which it pledges its powers; and that, for this end, it is their duty to watch over and oppose every infraction of those principles which constitute the only basis of that Union, because a faithful observance of them can alone secure its existence and the public happiness.

That this Assembly doth explicitly and peremptorily declare, that it views the powers of the federal government as resulting from the compact to which the states are parties, as limited by the plain sense and intention of the instrument constituting that compact, as no further valid than they are authorized by the grants enumerated in that compact; and that, in case of a deliberate, palpable, and dangerous exercise of other powers,

not granted by the said compact, the states, who are parties thereto, have the right, and are in duty bound, to interpose, for arresting the progress of the evil, and for maintaining, within their respective limits, the authorities, rights and liberties, appertaining to them.

That the General Assembly doth also express its deep regret, that a spirit has, in sundry instances, been manifested by the federal government to enlarge its powers by forced constructions of the constitutional charter which defines them; and that indications have appeared of a design to expound certain general phrases (which, having been copied from the very limited grant of power in the former Articles of Confederation, were the less liable to be misconstrued) so as to destroy the meaning and effect of the particular enumeration which necessarily explains and limits the general phrases, and so as to consolidate the states, by degrees, into one sovereignty, the obvious tendency and inevitable result of which would be, to transform the present republican system of the United States, into an absolute, or, at best, a mixed monarchy.

That the General Assembly doth particularly PROTEST against the palpable and alarming infractions of the Constitution, in the two late cases of the "Alien and Sedition Acts," passed at the last session of Congress; the first of which exercises a power no where delegated to the federal government, and which by uniting legislative and judicial powers to those of executive, subverts the general principles of free government; as well as the particular organization and positive provisions of the Federal Constitution; and the other of which acts exercises, in like manner, a power not delegated by the Constitution, but, on the contrary, expressly and positively forbidden by one of the amendments thereto, – a power which more than any other, ought to produce universal alarm, because it is levelled against that right of freely examining public characters and measures, and of free communication among the people thereon, which has ever been justly deemed the only effectual guardian of every other right.

That this state having, by its Convention, which ratified the Federal Constitution, expressly declared that, among other essential rights, "the liberty of conscience and the press cannot be cancelled, abridged, restrained, or modified, by any authority of the United States," and from its extreme anxiety to guard these rights from every possible attack of sophistry and ambition, having, with other states, recommended an amendment for that purpose, which amendment was, in due time, annexed to the Constitution, – it would mark a reproachable inconsistency, and criminal degeneracy, if an indifference were now shown to the most palpable violation of one of the rights thus declared and secured, and to the establishment of a precedent which may be fatal to the other.

That the good people of this commonwealth, having ever felt, and continuing to feel, the most sincere affection for their brethren of the other states; the truest anxiety for establishing and perpetuating the union of all; and the most scrupulous fidelity to that Constitution, which is the pledge of mutual friendship, and the instrument of mutual happiness, – the General Assembly doth solemnly appeal to the like dispositions in the other states, in confidence that they will concur with this commonwealth in declaring, as it does hereby declare, that the acts aforesaid are unconstitutional; and that the necessary and proper measures will be taken by each, for coöperating with this state,

> *in maintaining unimpaired the authorities, rights, and liberties, reserved to the states respectively, or to the people.*
>
> *That the Governor be desired, to transmit a copy of the foregoing resolutions to the executive authority of each of the other states, with a request that the same may be communicated to the legislature thereof, and that a copy be furnished to each of the senators and representatives representing this state in the Congress of the United States.*
>
> *Attst,   JOHN STEWART*
>
> *1798, December 24. Agreed to by the Senate.*
>
> H. BROOKE.
>
> *A true copy from the original deposited in the office of the General Assembly.*
>
> JOHN STEWART, Keeper of Rolls

Kentucky offered a similar rebuke of the General Government in 1799:

> ## Excerpt from the Kentucky Resolution of 1799
>
> ...
>
> *Resolved, That this commonwealth considers the federal Union, upon the terms and for the purposes specified in the late compact, conducive to the liberty and happiness of the several states: That it does now unequivocally declare its attachment to the Union, and to that compact, agreeably to its obvious and real intention, and will be*

*among the last to seek its dissolution: **That, if those who administer the general government be permitted to transgress the limits fixed by that compact, by a total disregard to the special delegations of power therein contained, an annihilation of the state governments, and the creation, upon their ruins, of a general consolidated government, will be the inevitable consequence: That the principle and construction, contended for by sundry of the state legislatures, that the general government is the exclusive judge of the extent of the powers delegated to it, stop nothing short of despotism — since the discretion of those who administer the government, and not the Constitution, would be the measure of their powers: That the several states who formed that instrument, being sovereign and independent, have the unquestionable right to judge of its infraction; and, That a nullification, by those sovereignties, of all unauthorized acts done under color of that instrument, is the rightful remedy:** That this commonwealth does, under the most deliberate reconsideration, declare, that the said Alien and Sedition Laws are, in their opinion, palpable violations of the said Constitution; and however cheerfully it may be disposed to surrender its opinion to a majority of its sister states, in matters of ordinary or doubtful policy, yet, in momentous regulations like the present, which so vitally wound the best rights of the citizen, it would consider a silent acquiescence as highly criminal: That although this commonwealth, as a party to the federal compact, will bow to the laws of the Union, yet it does, at the same time, declare, that it will not now, nor ever hereafter, cease to oppose, in a constitutional manner, every attempt, from what quarter soever offered, to violate that compact: And finally, in order that no pretexts or arguments may be drawn from a supposed acquiescence, on the part of this commonwealth, in the constitutionality of those laws, and be thereby used as precedents for*

> *similar future violations of the federal compact; this commonwealth does now enter against them, its solemn PROTEST.*
>
> *Extract, &c.   Attest,   THOMAS TODD, C. H. R.*
>
> *In Senate, Nov. 22, 1799. – Read and concurred in.*
>
> *Attest,   B. THURSTON, C. S.*

It is clear, that within 20 years of the founding of the United States, the General Government was already on its way to exercising powers not delegated by the States and essentially relying on the fear of dissolution as a tool to obtain acquiescence in laws and policies antithetical to the words and spirit of the Constitution and Bill of Rights.

2.8 The Origins of American Economic Policy 1783 – 1790

After the U.S. Constitution was accepted (March 4, 1789) there were still many practical issues that had not been settled (i.e., things that were not mentioned in the Constitution such as (i) where the national capital would be located and (ii) exactly how the taxes collected by the Federal government were to be managed). These issues were left to the first presidential administration of George Washington to work out.

Alexander Hamilton (1790)

In Article 1. Section 8 of the Constitution the powers of the Congress are spelled out. The first three items are the main focus of interest here.

> *To lay and collect Taxes, Duties, Imposts and Excises, to pay the Debts and provide for the common defense and general Welfare of the United States; but all Duties, Imposts and Excises shall be uniform throughout the United States;*
>
> *To borrow Money on the credit of the United States;*
>
> *To regulate Commerce with foreign Nations, and among the several States, and with the Indian Tribes;*

The three people who had the most influence over the interpretation of these items in the antebellum period were Alexander Hamilton, James Madison and Thomas Jefferson.

Hamilton (1755 or 1757–1804, killed in a duel) was born in the West Indies and did not come to the mainland colonies (New York and New England) until 1772. He became a war-time confidant of George Washington and played a role drafting the Constitution (1787). His view was that the Congress had only one concern when taxing and spending and that was that the burden and benefit of the taxes should be uniform (e.g., taxes should be apportioned by population and no tariffs should be applied on trade among the States). Otherwise, he saw no limits on taxing or spending by the Federal government. Meanwhile, native-born Virginians, Jefferson (1743-1826) who was overseas and Madison (1751-1836) a participant in the Constitutional convention, had a more restrictive view of Federal power (embodied in the Congress). In particular, they took the position that

Congressional authority (and hence the Federal power to tax and spend) was limited to those things specifically enumerated in the Constitution. We see here a basic regional difference of opinion regarding the interpretation of the Constitution (i.e., the agreement that bound the States together). This difference persisted and will become progressively more important in the 1800s.

Hamilton became Washington's Secretary of the Treasury (1789-95); and was, thus, very influential in setting up the Federal *economic infrastructure*. Washington tasked Hamilton with the question about how to manage the national debt and to report to the House of Representatives in 1890. The combined debts of the States and Continental Congress added to about $80-million and the revenue of the Federal government was only about $4.4-million a year. In his report, Hamilton proposed consolidating the State debts into the Federal debt and paying them off with a tax on alcohol and sale of western lands owned by the Federal government. This was a very controversial issue, which again broke down along regional lines. While the northern states had a cumulative debt of over $20-million, the southern states had actively paid off almost all of their debts. Thus, assumption of state debts by the federal government made southerners jointly responsible for settling northern debts (from before, during and after the War of Independence). The House accepted this proposal by the summer of 1790. Hamilton's only bargaining point was the location of the U.S. Capitol, which was thus located in a federal district created on the border of Maryland and Virginia in order to obtain their support for the assumption of State debts.

But, once you have a consolidated Federal debt, you need to have some organization to administer the revenue and pay the debts. So, Hamilton then proposed a national bank. This proposal was strongly contested by Jefferson and Madison who found no basis for a national bank in the Constitution and feared that the Federal control of these moneys would greatly increase the power of the Federal government. Again, the issue divided the nation north and south. Nonetheless, Washington signed the legislation based on Hamilton's argument that the bank was required implicitly to execute the powers defined in the Constitution.

This *economic infrastructure* became a powerful economic tool capable of accumulating large amounts of money and potentially capable of financing very large projects (e.g., national defense[171]). However, Hamilton's influence over *economic (tax and spend) policy* was strongly limited in the *antebellum* period.[172]

The projects proposed in Congress generally applied the *economic policy* derived from the Constitutional interpretation of Madison and Jefferson. For example, support to a glass manufacturer, restoring Savannah after a fire and dredging the Savannah River

---

[171] The major military expenditure was for six 44-gun frigates (including the *Constitution* and the *Constellation*) for about $700 thousand between 1794 and 1800. These were well designed and (except when poorly handled) accounted for themselves very well in the War of 1812. It is relevant that, in order to win the favor of this expenditure, each ship was built in a different state, but the only southern state that was prepared to build large ships was Virginia and one ship was built at Gosport (Portsmouth, VA).

[172] However, after the War between the States, his (minority) economic views were cited as precedent for modern economic policy.

were projects rejected by the Federal government (we do not know the specific reasons, but they can be argued to be local projects for local benefit); on the other hand, a lighthouse at the mouth of the Chesapeake Bay (of direct interest to Maryland and Virginia and indirect interest to all that traded with these states, i.e., interstate commerce) was approved and a road through the Cumberland Gap to strategically link the original colonies to western territories (a project that George Washington had championed) was approved.

The French Revolution

France, under the control of the monarch, was decisive in the success of the American War of Independence. Thus, most liberal-minded Americans were strongly pro-France (most British Loyalists had left the country voluntarily or involuntarily to Canada or the West Indies). However, especially in New England, the similarity in the economy and customs of the Americans and British generally led to a rapid post-war reconciliation. For years, the term "republican" was anti-monarchist in Britain and in the States of North America, anti-government views tended to be viewed as republican.

In 1793, the anti-monarchists in France deposed their monarchy and guillotined the king and queen. Thousands of nobles and government officials (including tax collectors such as Lavoisier) were imprisoned and after a perfunctory trial scheduled to die as well. The Federal government entered into the Jay Treaty (1794–1795) trying to restore good relations with Britain. The new French ambassador (Citizen Genêt) worked to develop anti-British feeling in the US by focusing on the Democratic-

Republicans (anti-Federalists).   While the anti-Federalist in the United States initially identified with the spirit of liberty of the French revolutionaries, the sentiments progressively turned as the magnitude of the killing in France became apparent. Nonetheless, in the South, the normally pro-British, conservative Federalists generally either lost power or switched sides to oppose the broad reconciliation with the British.

The Whiskey Rebellion

Hamilton shepherded the first major federal tax bill through congress in 1791. It was an excise tax on distilled spirits (e.g., whiskey), which was an important commodity in the upland agriculture practiced in the western piedmont and mountainous regions that bounded the original colonies. Not only was alcohol a universally barterable commodity, it was an efficient value-added and easily storable/transportable product obtained from locally grown corn. In these times, it was very difficult to store or ship grains because of the difficulties of keeping it from rotting. The resistance to the tax was most acute in western Pennsylvania and in 1794, about 500 farmers took up arms against the local tax collector.

Washington gathered the militia from adjacent states and led 13,000 men to negotiate and combat, if necessary, the revolt. The local farmers wisely dispersed before Washington arrived and a small number of leaders were charged, but not punished. The distillers in Kentucky and many places in the Appalachian Mountains circumvented the law beginning the traditional practice later known as "bootlegging."

On the one hand, Washington's actions had demonstrated the resolve of the Federal government to enforce its laws. On the other hand, the practice of enforcing the laws on a free and armed population was institutionalized.

The Federalist Party

The Whiskey Rebellion forced a clear distinction between the politics of Hamilton and Jefferson. Hamilton and the supporters of the central government coalesced into what became formally known as the Federalist Party. Washington personally avoided a party affiliation but saw himself duty-bound to enforce the Constitution. The political landscape divided between those who supported the current administration (dominated by Hamilton's views) and those who saw a much more limited role of the Federal government (anti-federalist...states' rights). Washington was followed by John Adams (of Massachusetts) and the Federalists tended to favor and be favored by banking and business interest of the northeastern states. In 1801, Thomas Jefferson and the Democratic-Republicans displaced the Federalists and pursued a policy that did not support Hamilton's ideas of *implied powers* of the Federal government. However, the importance of presidential appointments weighed on the government as John Marshall (1755-1835) who had been the Secretary of State under Adams (1800-1801) was appointed to the Supreme Court by Adams and became the Chief Justice of the Supreme Court 1801-1835. Thus, through a very important period of the nation's evolution, Federalist's policies were generally favored by the Judiciary when enforced by the Executive.

2.9 The Politics of Federal Taxation and Spending 1790-1820

Hamilton vs Jefferson and Madison

The national debt stayed in the range of 70 to 85 million dollars from 1790 until 1807 (the last years of Jefferson's presidency). After that, (under Madison) progress was made in paying it off and the debt declined to 45 million dollars in 1812.

Internationally, Hamilton had patched up political relations and economic cooperation with the British, which led to a reversal in alliances regarding post-revolutionary France. While Washington maintained official neutrality, by the time that John Adams was in office (1797-1801), France was attacking American shipping. But Adams steered clear of war recognizing that war would greatly increase the national debt. In his first inaugural address to the House of Representatives (November 22, 1797), Adams summarized his concerns as follows:

> " ... no nation can raise within the year by taxes sufficient sums for its defense and military operations in time of war. [punctuation added] The sums loaned and debts contracted have necessarily become the subjects of what have been called funding systems. The consequences arising from the continual accumulation of public debts in other countries ought to admonish us to be careful to prevent their growth in our own. The national defense must be provided for as well as the support

of Government; but both should be accomplished as much as
possible by immediate taxes, and as little as possible by loans."

Adams was followed as President by Jefferson (1801-1809). We
have already seen his views on spending power. It is noteworthy
that Jefferson immediately entered into a war with the Barbary
pirates (1801) in the interest of free trade and aggressively
pursued the acquisition of the Louisiana Territory from France in
1803 for $15-million mainly borrowed in Europe.[173] He then
supported the explorations of Lewis and Clark, Pike and others
throughout his presidency. Legal, international slave trade ended
in 1807.

During the last two years of his presidency (1807-09), Britain
(which was in a world-wide conflict with Napoleonic France)
resorted to the desperate measures of impressing US sailors by
stopping ships on the high seas with the pretense of recovering
British deserters (and there undoubtedly were some). Several US
warships were also fired upon. This prompted a build-up of US
costal defenses, but the US stopped short of getting involved with
the Napoleonic Wars (which ended at Waterloo in 1814). Indeed,
the US had been trading extensively with France; and to avoid
conflict with the British, Jefferson supported the passage of the
Embargo Act (1807) and the Non-Intercourse Act (1808). These

---

[173] It is fair to say that without the economic structure created by
Hamilton, borrowing this money would probably have been impossible.
It is interesting to speculate what would have happened had the
individual states bough the Louisiana Territory in shares and
subdivided it among themselves without the involvement of the Federal
government.

acts were generally opposed by northeastern banking, shipping and trading interests (identified as Federalists) although it increased the expansion of domestic manufacturing in the northeastern states, which had access to water power and anthracite coal from northeastern Pennsylvania. Southern states had neither water power nor coal reserves that were located anywhere near seaports or navigable rivers.

Water Power and Economic Development in the United States Early 1800s

There are many designs of water wheels but economically efficient water wheels of the "overshot" design require a vertical drop of water. This is only available in large volume at the fall line (i.e., the line between the piedmont and coastal plain).[174]

The fall line follows approximately the 150-meter elevation. In New England it is very near the coast and can provide power to industries well positioned to receive raw materials and ship finished products by ocean-going vessels. The line has determined the location of many cities since most rivers are navigable until they fall line is reached. The fall line passes

---

[174] Small local mills can be constructed on dammed creeks in the piedmont or mountains and most places you travel in the eastern states will yield a number of rural roads named after the grist mill that they served (e.g., Manchester's Mill Road, Vier's Mill Road). These local mills, served the community and were not situated on large waterways that developed high power or were supportive of long-distant trade or international export.

through Boston (MA), Providence (RI), New Haven (CT), New York (NY), Trenton (NJ), Philadelphia (PA), Baltimore (MD), Washington (DC), Richmond (VA), Petersburg (VA), Raleigh (NC), Columbia (SC), Savannah (GA), Macon (GA) and Columbus (GA).

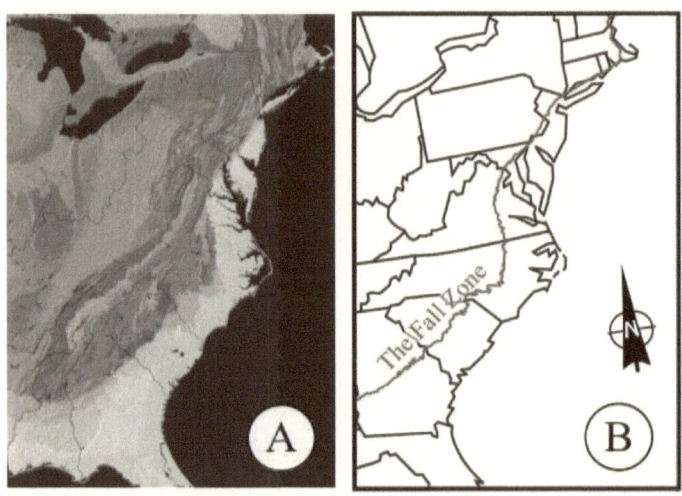

Source: http://enb105-2012s-drs.blogspot.com/2012/04/lab-8-fall-line.html

Not only is the fall line close to seaports in the northern states, the elevation drop is very steep (e.g., from 150 meters to sea level in a few miles in New England), but in the south the fall line represents a drop of 10 meters or less and the decline is over a longer distance. Thus, south of Richmond, Virginia large water-powered industrial mills were seldom feasible.

According to Taussig (1888, p.3), the colonial period of American economics persisted until about 1808. But by then, the advantages of borrowing large sums of money to finance expansion of the nation across the North American continent became apparent. In addition, the idea of applying protectionist tariffs, not just to raise money (most of which went towards paying off the national debt) but also to favor the growth of domestic industries relative to European industries became a political option. It is probably not completely coincidental that while leading science still flowed from Europe, eastern Pennsylvania's clean-burning anthracite coal became available for northeastern industries in 1808.

The War of 1812 and its Aftermath

Jefferson was followed by Madison (1809 to 1817) who shared Jefferson's views on spending (shown by significant reduction of national debt from 1807-1812), but he was unfortunate in that the conflicts with Britain came to a head in 1812. The war with Britain (1812-14) caused the national debt to grow rapidly due to cost of the military and repair of damage to Federal property (e.g., Washington, DC was looted and burned by the British). A number of Federal forts were also built or improved to protect major harbors.[175] These were financed by a tariff on importation of manufactured goods enacted in 1816. The focus on manufactured goods was, at least in part, because the war showed that the US needed to build a strong manufacturing capability in order to have a strong military. The national debt shot up from

---

[175] Between 1807 and 1814 the defenses of New York City went from 164 guns to about 900 guns in forts protecting every sea approach to the city. Except for Ft. McHenry (Baltimore, MD) the British never seriously attacked these forts by sea.

$45-million in 1812, leveled off in 1816 and topped at $123-million in 1817. But with the tariffs in place and peace, the national debt was soon beginning to decline. Congress recognized the potential for ending the national debt and passed the Redemption Act of 1817 to control spending and ensure that surpluses went towards the debt. Tariffs on imports tended to favor the northeastern states because the southern (agricultural) states manufactured very little and could otherwise import manufactured goods as cheaply from Britain/Europe as from New England (…recall that travel by ship was much faster and cheaper than travel by land).

Hartford Convention and Demise of the Federalist Party

The banking, shipping and trading businesses of New England had been adversely impacted by the policies of Jefferson and Madison and although they had created a golden opportunity for expansion of manufacturing in New England, those developments had just begun and had not produced tangible politically important economic benefits. Thus, the Federalists of the northeast were not happy with the fact that their economic interests were in decline and "Federalism" was declining in the southern states. It looked as though southern agricultural interests would continue to dominate the national political landscape. In 1814, Madison had just been re-elected (1812), imposed even more restrictive trade acts, and would serve until 1817. James Monroe (Virginia) was looking like a successor that could keep the Federalists out of power indefinitely. Ironically, John Marshall who while ensuring the power of the Federal government, was not helping the interests of the northeast. Finally, in the summer of 1814, Britain had (temporarily) ended its war with France (Napoleon was exiled to Elba, April 11, 1814), which allowed them to focus on the US with invasions of Maine (northern Massachusetts) and sack of Washington, DC (August 1814). Not only did it look like the Democratic Republicans had ruined the economy of the northeast, it looked as though the United States might be re-conquered by the British. The New England states were already denying support of their militias to the Federal government.

Thus, in a time of war with Britain, the Federalists of New England began a series of meetings at Harford, Connecticut (December 15, 1814 – January 5, 1815). The documentation for these meeting is obscure. The intent and conclusions of the convention are also not provided in a record comparable to the either the US (see above) or Confederate (see below) constitutional conventions. The general conclusion immediately after the fact was that the convention was secretive because it was treasonous (occurring in wartime in the face of the enemy), however, there are credible historians that argue that this conclusion is a politically inspired overstatement.

http://projects.leadr.msu.edu/uniontodisunion/files/original/b
cc872b4457b362d74babc9bb0e6ff56.jpg

The cartoon lampoons the indecisiveness of the New Englanders who are represented as a range of traitors and want-to-be traitors who are being tempted by the British who hold out the things that the New Englanders value. The British king says:

"O'tis my Yankey boys! Jump in my fine fellows, plenty of molasses[176] and codfish, plenty of goods to smuggle, Honors, Titles, and Nobility into the bargain.

---

[176] Molasses is the third leg of the slave trade from the West Indies sugar plantations to New England whisky distilleries.

It is not clear what courses of action were discussed or how strongly and widely the opinions for these proposes were held. But the following facts seem well supported:

(1) In October 1814, the Governor of Massachusetts (Caleb Strong) called the state legislature into session; and in November 1814, he made private suggestions of a separate peace (of New England) with Britain and an alliance (against the US) to General Sir John Sherbrooke, the British Governor of Nova Scotia. Such a plan would obviously need concurrence with the other states and a call was made for a convention of the relevant states to convene December 15, 1814 in Harford, CT.

(2) According to the man assigned to organize the convention (Harrison Gray Otis), the purpose of the convention was to discuss sectional defense against the British and modifications of the US Constitution to promote New England interests. Given the view of state sovereignty that was accepted at the time, this was certainly not a violation of the US Constitution and can be viewed as prudent given the inability of the Federal government to defend the capitol.

(3) There was a conscious effort in selecting the delegates to the convention and composing the committees that explored its issues to avoid radical (pro-British/anti-American) views and voices.

(4) At the close of the convention, Otis prepared a summary
(dated January 3, 1815) that was to be delivered to the US
Congress. The report began with the official purposes of
the convention as stated above. But, it went to lengths to
express the objections of the more extreme elements of the
delegations and suggested that disunion was a real
possibility unless Madison changed Republican policies
that New Englander's objected to. Finally, it introduced
seven proposed amendments to the Constitution that were
clearly intended create a permanent imbalance in the
control of the Federal government putting New England in
charge and placing the South in a position of vassalage.
The primary tool used by New England was to effectively
declare slaves to be property, not people, and thus not
count them in the allocation of congress or the electoral
college. Of course, that is not the way that history books
published in New England addresses the topic, they simply
say that the convention wanted to end the 3/5th rule, which
can be *misrepresented* to be an anti-slavery move, when in
fact it was a raw political effort to assert New England
dominance. The theme of New England dominance was
continued in making it more difficult to introduce new
states and prevention of naturalized citizens (who were
moving into western territories) from having any role in
the Federal government. The contemporary cartoon above
summarizes the view of the New England States from the
other States.

By the time the representatives of the Harford Convention arrived
in Washington to deliver their ultimatum, "instant karma" struck

them down. News had arrived that a treaty had been signed with the British (Treaty of Ghent, December 24, 1814), which restored *status quo ante bellum,* and Andrew Jackson had soundly defeated the British at the Battle of New Orleans (January 8, 1815). The end result was that the Federalist party was embarrassed and discredited. It had a poor showing in the 1816 elections and effectively disbanded by 1820.

With the extinction of the Federalist Party, the republicans (Democratic Republicans) ushered in a period of political harmony and prosperity. But within the ranks of the republicans (particularly younger and northern members) the economic philosophy of Jefferson and Madison was becoming lost. Several leading southerners (John Randolph and John Taylor of Virginia and Nathaniel Macon of North Carolina) vigorously defended Jefferson ideals in the Congress. Although infrastructure bills arose in Congress, Jefferson's views were honored by vetoes from Virginia-born Presidents (Madison and Monroe). The only remarkable spending legislation that got by Monroe was a mere $30,000 for unspecified surveys of desirable routes for roads and canals by the Corps of Engineers.

www.ingramcontent.com/pod-product-compliance
Lightning Source LLC
Chambersburg PA
CBHW032045280526
45784CB00011B/2779